LETTERS HOME

LETTERS HOME

A REFLECTION OF A MAN'S SURVIVAL

MAXWELL M ANDLER, JR., M.D.

EDITED BY
Valeda Andler

Letters Home: A Reflection of a Man's Survival by Maxwell M Andler Jr. M.D.,
edited by Valeda Andler.

Published by:
The Center Press P.O. 6936 Thousand Oaks, CA 91360-6936

Library of Congress Cataloging-In-Publication Data
Andler, Maxwell M, 1914–1996
Letters home : a reflection of a man's survival /
by Maxwell M Andler, Jr. ; edited by Valeda Andler.
p. cm.
ISBN 1-889198-11-0
1. Andler, Maxwell M, 1914–1996—Correspondence. 2. World War, 1939–1945—Prisoners and Prisons, Japanese. 3. World War, 1939–1945—Personal narratives, American. 4. Concentration camps—Philippines. 5. Concentration camps—Japan. 6. Prisoners of war—Japan—Correspondence. 7. Prisoners of war—United States—Correspondence. 8. Neurosurgeons—United States—Correspondence.
I. Andler, Valeda, 1927- II. Title
D805.P6A53 2005
940.54'7252'092—dc22
2005020799

Written material is taken from original letters and therefore any inconsistencies, spelling errors or errors in names are artifacts from the original handwritten manuscript and are intentional.

Use of ADBC logo courtesy of American Defenders of Bataan and Corregidor
Cover and interior design: Tanya Maiboroda
Cover photo: Max Andler released from Prison Camp, 1945
Printed by Trade Printing Services, LLC

10 9 8 7 6 5 4 3 2 1

~

I would like to dedicate this book
to Max's dearest friends who were with him
at the County Hospital before the War, in the Philippines,
Japan, and afterward until his death, January 8, 1996.

Left to right: Dr. Nathan Bashop, Dr. Marvin Pizer, Max,
Dr. Dan Golenternek and Dr. Harry Levitt.

MY GRATEFUL THANKS

Lily Brown, for her typing and help in editing of this manuscript.

Harry Levitt, for help with names, dates, times,
and for being Max's good friend.

To Max's many friends and patients
who encouraged me to publish his letters.

To my family, Jolie, Max, and Steven,
who have given me their love and support in this endeavor.

CONTENTS

EDITOR'S NOTE

I met Dr. Maxwell Andler, Jr. at the Los Angeles County, USC General Hospital in May 1946 when I was a student in the Cadet Nurse Corps. There was a severe shortage of nurses then, and as a first year student, I was assigned to staff the Neurosurgical admitting room. It was my first time in that position and I was to be alone on the 3 PM to 11:30 PM shift. As a Sophomore Class fundraising project, I was selling donuts in the main hall that noon, when Dr. Andler passed by, I asked him to buy some of my donuts so I could get ready to go on duty for my first time in Neurosurgical-admitting at 3 PM. He bought all of the donuts.

After I was on duty, trying to figure out what I was supposed to do, Dr. Andler arrived and started showing me how things were done. We got very busy and he stayed all evening helping me assist the interns and residents, from other services, who were caring for all of the new admissions. As he was the chief neurosurgical resident and not on call that night, it was quite a surprise to those present. We were kept busy until after 12 midnight so Dr. Andler called the nurse's residence to tell the Matron that we were very busy and I would be late. Students were not allowed to be out after midnight, nor to walk from the hospital to the residence after midnight without a guard, so he said he would walk me to the residence when I could be replaced.

After all of the patients were sent to the wards and my replacement took over, Dr. Andler said that he did not date student nurses but as he was hungry after all that work, he would allow me to buy him a hamburger at the local all night restaurant. To go there he borrowed the car of Dr. Pete

Valeda Andler, 1946.

Lindstrom's wife, who was in New York doing a play. This happened several times, even when I was transferred to a different assignment.

One night, two months later, when he walked me to the residence, I asked what I should call him, as some of his friends called him Max and a few people called him Buster (that is what he called his child patients). He answered that I could call him Dr. Andler and he kissed me goodnight and left. I learned that that was Max, serious, proper and had an unbelievable sense of humor (and he always called me Miss Johnson).

Max continued to maintain that he did not date student nurses, but he did make an exception for me. I worked on many different services at the hospital, sometimes with Max and with his friends. All of that time I received humorous letters from him on stationery from the morgue, meetings, dining room, dull lectures, and even on my test sheets from the class he was teaching student nurses on Neurosurgery.

I chose as my specialty, the operating room, and after I graduated in 1948, I continued to work at the County Hospital because that is where Max was, and I could not imagine returning to my home in Redlands where I would not see him again. We were married in 1950 in the Hollywood home of Stanley Freeman, his School chum from Brookline, Mass.

Over the years we kept close friendships with the Doctors from the County Hospital. Their conversations and stories over dinners recalled many of their exploits with the Japanese and they laughed a lot. Some of the stories are here in this book but some are not. Max never let anyone read this collection of letters except one or two dear friends, who he let look at them when they were in the hospital with serious illnesses. After his death I started reading them but it took a long time, and a lot of encouraging before I was able to think of publishing. I do this out of love and as a tribute to him.

PREQUEL

Maxwell M Andler, Jr. was born in Mauldin, MA, July 2, 1914. He was named after his father, who died before Max was born. He was loved by his mother Jenny and his older sisters, Sonia and Katherine, and later by his half brother Albert Rosen. As you will see from his correspondence, Max's Mother was the light of his life. She was a woman who put great importance in family, charity and good deeds.

This book is a compilation of letters Max composed to his mother, brother and college friend Bud while he was in the Philippines and Japan. Some of the letters were mailed and some of these were kept by the recipients and given to Max when he returned. After the war began he continued to write, hoping to be able to send the letters later. Many times these letters were lost but he recomposed them. After the start of hostilities, Max's family tried to find out where he was. On May 1942 he was listed as missing in action, so the letters they had received were treasured. It was not until May 1943 he was listed as a prisoner of war in the Philippines.

Max, like many other doctors at that time, signed up for the reserves. He was one of the early ones to be called up to report to Fort Ord for basic training. Dr Sidney Garfield, another good friend from the County Hospital, drove him up and stayed at a nearby resort while Max was in training. I was told that on the weekends he had leave, they partied as men do on their way to war. Max shipped out from there to the Philippines, May 1941.

FOREWORD BY HARRY LEVITT

Maxwell Andler was an unusual man who could get things done even in difficult situations. I was fortunate to know him for over sixty years: first at Los Angeles County General Hospital. Later I knew him when he was a flight surgeon at Nichols Field near Manila, and as a prisoner of the Japanese in a number of prison camps. We were on the same ship, the **Kenwa Maru**, when we were sent to camps in Northern Japan, After the war, we continued our friendship.

Dr. Andler was a man who knew his own worth. Just to be with him made you feel important. He was able to get things from the Japanese captors without being a collaborator. One of our friends, who was about to die, owes his survival to what Dr. Andler was able to get for his needs. On several occasions, Max Andler was able to get extra food from the Japanese. He did not benefit from this for himself, but distributed it to the group.

Looking back, if I ever had to face the same difficult situation as when I was a prisoner of war, the man I would want to be with is Maxwell Andler.

Harry Levitt

LETTERS HOME

A REFLECTION OF A MAN'S SURVIVAL

LETTERS FROM PHILIPPINES

1941

FORT MCKINLEY ***Aug. 30, 1941, Saturday afternoon***

Dear Mom,

I have just finished a swim in the pool at the Army Navy Club and as the Clipper Mail leaves in bout an hour I will write a few lines. I sent 3 messages thru and amateur radio station here on the Islands. Please let me know if you received them. They only cost 20 centavos.

We landed here Thursday morning and were given a royal welcome. Then we were taken to our new posts. I am not sure yet what I am going to do, but I probably won't be in the hospital.

This is quite a strange place. The humidity is so high, that one is quite wet through in a short time. I have already been measured for my tropical uniforms, but they aren't ready yet. I am living in a house at Fort McKinley with 3 other officers. We have two servants and 3 *lavenderas*—making 5 in all. A *lavendera* is a laundress and she washes for me every day. Her pay is 10 pesos a month, or 5 dollars and she washes our uniforms every day and irons them. We have a cook and a number one boy who does all the shopping. But I will tell you more later, when I get a typewriter.

FORT MCKINLEY ***Sept. 18, 1941***

Dear Mom,

I was going to wait until we returned from tonight's maneuvers before writing, but I see the Clipper is going to leave a day earlier which means tomorrow at dawn. Here everyone knows exactly when every Clipper arrives and leaves, and the newspaper publishes the schedule every day. It comes in from San Francisco then goes to Shanghai and leaves here for the states 4 days after arriving. The last plane came here on the 16th, 4 days late because of a typhoon. It left the States on the 6th and it brought me your letter which you mailed from Boston on the 3rd of Sept. with Sonia's letter enclosed. GOSH it feels good to get a letter out here. When the Clipper mail comes in, they have a special delivery to our headquarters at 9 at night, and all the officers are waiting to hear from home. You see until 3 months ago, all the officers here had their families with them, but in June they were all ordered back to the States. That increased the Clipper mail from a hundred to 300 pounds each trip.

Mom, Sonia told me to register a cable address, which I will do, and let you know what it is, but if I want to, I can send a message just about as fast by our Ft McKinley Amateur Station here. All we have to do is send it off from here and pay the Western Union fee from San Francisco to Boston which is $.50 for a night letter, and $1.50 for a straight telegram. So if I sent you a message that way tonight, Thursday. You would get it some time this morning, as we are about 12 hours later that you. If you want to send me an urgent message, you could either send a message by Western Union to the Amateur Station in San Francisco or you could contact the Army Wireless station right there in Boston. Call the Corps Headquarters in Boston. It would be faster.

Momsie. Each time I write I cannot believe I am here. It just doesn't seem possible, 10,000 miles away. It really is nicer here at Ft McKinley than at Fort Ord. When we are not on maneuvers, I have been playing tennis and taking a dip in the pool at the Officers Club. I am going to attend a special Red White and Blue Ball for the Officers in the Army and Navy. Only 60 Girls and 75 Officers were invited and I really did not get an invitation. But, an older officer said to come along with him in my dress uniform and it would be alright. So I decked myself out in my formal mess jacket with gold braid and gold buttons and left for the Manila Polo Club, and exclusive English Club where the dance was being held. It was a lovely affair and the first time I had been out. They had all kinds of people here, 20 girls were white, 20 Spanish, and 20 Filipino. The native girls all come from very wealthy families, and their society is very formal. I met a girl here that came out with her family from Holland 8 years ago. Here in Manila they have 50 men for every girl, so the girls all have dates for at least 3 weeks ahead. I had a date with the young lady last night. We went to the Jai Alai Club which is the nicest place in the city. We had a beautifully served dinner with fruit drinks, filet mignon steaks, dancing and a view of the Jai Alai for only $4.05 American money.

I am glad you are all enjoying the car. You should be getting some mail from me in about a week

NICHOLS FIELD *Thursday, Nov. 20, 1941, Thanksgiving Day*

Dear Bud,

~ I am sorry I have not answered your letters before this, but I haven't felt in the mood. Today is Thanksgiving, and I am not quite sure what I should be giving thanks about. Certainly not that the army sent me back to the Philippines. But I am alive and well, and I suppose that is a moral victory over here. Your last letter came on the Clipper by mistake. What do you think of that? You had it marked airmail in the states, and they apparently did not check too closely and over it came. I felt quite guilty about receiving it, and am just about ready to confess the whole thing to the postal authorities. I haven't told you anything about this pearl of the Orient yet, have I? Well, here goes......... I have been here almost three months now. For the past month, I have been at Nichols Field, taking a special practical course in Aviation Medicine preparatory to becoming a full-fledged Flight Surgeon. Prior to this I was over at Fort Wm. McKinley, with Philippine Scout troops in the 12th Medical Regiment. That was really something. Maneuvering through the rice paddies, and hiking 5 to 10 miles with a steel helmet (that is the style here for all those who may be allergic to Japanese shellfire). Fortunately, I was able to come over here, and it has been much more pleasant. This is one of the main airbases, and there is a good deal going on. In fact, right now lunch is going on the table, and I will have to leave you. Will you excuse me?

~

NICHOLS FIELD *Friday, Nov. 21, 1941, mid afternoon*

Dear Bud

Here we go again. I will try and finish this time, but it will be difficult. That Clipper just arrived with three letters for me, and so I feel pretty good. Not that I had any more mail from you, but I won't complain yet. Not until I have not received an answer to this one. Let me see, I was going to tell you about the Philippines...It is indeed quite a place, one that has become quite an arsenal, albeit. By the time this reaches you in Chicago, we may be hard at it. In fact, since the U.S. gave Japan an ultimatum two days ago about getting out of China, we have been on a constant alert here at Nichols Field, no one being allowed to be farther than one hour from the Field. Kind of tiresome down, dontcha know. Things may explode in a bit of a hurry. Troops, planes, and all kinds of tanks and ammunition have been pouring in to Manila just as fast as transports can bring them over. Why, there are so many damn Army and Navy Officers over here now, a man has to petition Congress to get a date with a white girl. The present ratio is one white girl to 50 officers, and it is getting higher with every transport. And with each succeeding month that I stay here, the native girls appear lighter and lighter. All the Officers, on arriving in the Islands receive a square of black paper to carry in their wallets. As soon as this square of paper looks white to them, it is time to return to the States. They tell the story of the Officer who, on returning to the states from a tour of foreign duty in the Philippines, checked in to the St. Frances, took the best room in the house, and insisted on having black sheets. When questioned about this, he replied that he had been seeing brown on white for so long he wanted to try some white on black... Do you think that a bit risqué?

But at fifty cents a half-ounce, this is no time to tell stories... This is really quite an experience. Over here American Officers are very well liked, much more than in the states. Because of the large native and cosmopolitan population and the markedly low wage scale here, plus the exchange rate of two Filipino pesos for one American dollar, the American Officer is the big spender in the Islands, and we live very well. For example, here at Nichols Field, I live with two other Officers in a large home, furnished by the government. And we have 4 servants. A number one boy who is cook and general manager. A number two boy, who cleans the house, makes the beds, waits on table, and has a cold drink whenever we come in. Then we have 2 lavenderas or laundresses who are here six days a week, and as we wear only white suits and have them washed every day, so they are kept fairly busy. For work, we wear service uniforms of Hong Kong khaki, which are also laundered every day. These women receive the stupendous salary of 10 pesos a *month*. That is five dollars in Gold or American money. The cook receives 35 pesos, while the houseboy gets 15. So my share comes to about $11 a month for 4 servants around the house. I personally think we are overpaying them, and am going to begin a new stringent economy policy. And let me add that our cook has been working for Army Officers for over 20 years, so he is pretty good. As to our duties, we start about seven but everyone is usually through for the day by noon, as it is too hot and humid to work in the afternoon. Of course, now with things starting to get a bit tense, a little more work has to be done. Recreation is encouraged for all Officers, and at McKinley, where I was stationed we had everything at the Officers club. A swimming pool, badminton, tennis courts, 18 hole golf course, horse back riding, bowling, and a gymnasium. After paying the monthly dues of 5 pesos, everything is free.

But to get back to topic A, Women… As I said before, it is a very sad situation. All the families of the Army, and Navy Officers were evacuated last June, which left things in a very sorry state. I am telling you, when the Asiatic fleet is in Manila harbor, and the Army is not out on maneuvers, Manila is just overrun. I was very fortunate, let me say in passing. About two weeks after I arrived, I received an invitation to a Formal Red, White and Blue Ball, given for the Army and Navy Officers at the swanky Manila Polo Club. At these affairs, 75 officers are invited, while over 60 girls are asked. Twenty white girls, 20 Spanish girls, and 20 Filipino girls, all from the best families in Manila. In fact, these 60 are just about all the presentable girls there are in Manila. Well, Lady Luck was watching over me, and I was asked to have the opening dance with a tall, dark, very beautiful young lady, whose father is a member of the exiled Dutch Consulate here in Manila. Our friendship has ripened rapidly under a tropical sun and moon, and since then I have seen a good deal of her. In fact, yesterday I took her to Thanksgiving dinner here on the post, and last night we went dancing. The only trouble is she is much too popular with all the rest of the Officers in the Army and Navy. I get ambushed every time we go out. A girl here in Manila really has things her own way. They have dates planned for every night three weeks in advance, and never miss any kind of an affair or party. And let me add something that sounds unbelievable. This girl is 21, and had never been kissed. I have been out with her probably a dozen times, and I am willing to testify that this is a true statement. I have checked into this very closely from a psychiatric point of view, believing that no person could be completely normal with such a history, but she is quite adamant about the whole thing. And the odd part of it is that I just come back for more. I must explain that she is a very lovely young lady, quite beautiful, and had a good deal on ye old ball. She feels that when she finds the young fella she wants to marry, she is quite sure she will be quite anxious to kiss him. Sounds reasonable, doesn't it?

Well, Bud, they just finished taps, which means eleven o'clock has rolled around again. I have sort of rambled on, but then, I have been meaning to have a long talk with you for some time. I was very glad to hear that your father and mother are well in L.A. I dropped them a card. Please let's have a long letter now, and ask Louisa to put in an enclosure. See if you can sneak another one over on the clipper. By the way, you can use the address on my new stationary.

NICHOLS FIELD ***Saturday, Nov. 22, 1941, mid afternoon***

~ Bud, I have just had a bit of siesta, and now I am well fortified for whatever may arise. The Clipper leaves at dawn tomorrow, and if I decide to squander a peso to mail this to you, I must have it in the bureau of posts by seven tonight. I don't know whether I will finish it or not. And on thinking it over, I have so much to tell you, that I will wait for the next clipper… now I will dash off a short note to the family as I write on every clipper. Be back soon.

~

THE PHILIPPINES ***Nov. 23, 1941, Sunday Morning***

Shall I add a few words before closing? For the past 48 hours we have been on a constant alert. I guess the Brass Hats are expecting the Japs to come over any minute. Anyway it keeps us quite confined and on the jump.

I guess that's all I have to say. When you begin reading the latest reports from the Eastern front just think of me under a steel helmet making the USA the home of democracy. By the time this gets back to you we may be at it hammer and tongs over here. So tell the girls to begin knitting me some socks.

Say—How about giving that gal Bobby Newman my address so she can cheer a lonely soldier up.

Let me hear from you soon, Bud.

NICHOLS FIELD ***Nov. 23, 1941, Sunday Evening***

Dear Mom,

It is almost seven o'clock on 'Sunday evening, and as the Post Theatre doesn't begin until seven fifteen, I thought I would drop over to the dispensary, and dash off a few lines. I didn't receive a letter on this last clipper that came on the 19th, so I am expecting one on next Tuesday. By this time you should be writing to Nichols Field. Yesterday I received your radiogram which you sent out on the 15th telling me that I didn't have to worry about the car. I sent Kay my power of attorney and she can do anything that is necessary.

Mom, so you wonder what I do with myself all the times? I wonder myself where all the time goes. Unless we are unusually busy, we are through at noon, unless I am medical officer of the day, and that happens every four days. Otherwise we have all our afternoons and evenings off. Usually I try to get some exercise. It is difficult to find someone to play tennis with, because it is too hot. The rainy season is just about over, and the sun just cooks one if he is out in it very long. Last night they had a dinner dance at the McKinley Officers Club, and although I am over here at Nichols, I was invited, as I still have to pay dues over there. At all these affairs they have about 10 officers to one girl, but I was one of the lucky ones, as I was able to bring a girl. Then after that we went downtown, and went to Jai Alai, which is an air conditioned night club that is the nicest place in Manila. Let me tell you how much time I spent in a taxi yesterday. First I went downtown to mail some Christmas cards and packages, and what with running around back and forth, before I returned to the field, I had used the taxi for three hours. Then I had to hake a cab back downtown to Jai alai, then back to the girl's house, and finally, a cab back to Nichols Field again. Your see there isn't any other way to get around. The only good thing about it is that the cabs are so inexpensive. We can hire cabs here at the field at one peso and hour, which is $.50, so I had a taxi for three hours for a dollar and a half. I guess one couldn't do much cheaper with a private car. This morning I went down to the Manila Polo Club, and played tennis, but it was so hot that we only played a short time. After a very delicious lunch, we all lay down and slept. I slept for two hours and still was the first one up. Now I will round the day out by going to the post movie to see Abbot and Costello in Hold That Ghost. Not too exciting a day.

NICHOLS FIELD *Nov. 28, 1941, Nine PM, Friday Evening*

Hello Momsie, I have just finished reading letters from you and Kay. Kay's was mailed on the 15th from New York, and yours wasn't mailed until the 20th, but they both came on the same clipper, and it felt wonderful to get them. The mail was three days late, originally scheduled to come in on the 25th, but now I don't mind. But no matter how much you write, it never seems long enough. I am very glad to hear that you are well, and that the rest of the family are well to. I know that I couldn't be feeling better physically, although I guess I do get to feel just a wee bit blue every so often. This morning I received letters from Adele and Marjorie, and also one from Les Martinson who is at Fort Devons.

Tomorrow I finish my six weeks course here at Nichols Field, and then I am supposed to go back to McKinley, my old assignment. But I have requested permanent transfer to the Air Corps, and I am waiting daily for an answer. Now that I have finished this course I am pretty sure that they will transfer me here. The only thing is that they are constructing six new airfields here right away, one as far as 500 miles from Manila, and they may decide to send me to one of those. I wouldn't be too crazy about that. But there is no use of worrying about that until it happens. As to what I do here; I report at the dispensary at seven fifteen and begin sick call at 7:30 AM At sick call, all the soldiers who don't feel well on the post report, and with 2000 men here we may have from 50 to 100 men report. I see each one, and find out what is wrong. If it is something minor, then I treat it right here. If anything serious, then I send them over to the McKinley hospital, as we don't have a hospital here. I may not finish this until nine o'clock. Then I have the special examinations to do for applicants for Aviation training. While there isn't any major surgery or anything like that, at least I am getting to see some patients, and I am not out in the field drilling with troops as I did at Fort Ord, and when I was stationed at Fort McKinley. When I am Medical Officer of the Day, as I am today then I am the only Doctor on the Post, and take care of any emergencies, until seven the next morning. At night, I get called because some soldier has been drunk and in a fight, and I get to sew up a laceration on his head or something like that, but there isn't much to it. But I am not complaining. I received a long letter from Les Martinson, and he is a private in the Army. He said that he had to use a pick and shovel, peel potatoes, carry 85 pound drums of gasoline, and do all kinds of things, but he doesn't feel badly, and feels he is doing his part along with everyone else, so I guess I should feel fortunate that I am a commissioned Officer with all its privileges.

NICHOLS FIELD ***Nov. 30th 1941, Sunday Morning***

Well Momsie. Things are about the same except that we are on constant alert here at the post. Everything is kept in readiness for any emergency. Yesterday we had two practice alerts which consist of a cannon going off five times along with a siren. That is the signal for all officers and men to report to their stations and await further orders. One came last night about eight, so we had to blackout too. And if we leave the post we must inform them where we are at all times so that we can get back within an hour if necessary. No one knows whether we are actually going to be at war or not, but we are getting ready for whatever may happen, If you do read about things happening over here, do not take too much stock in it, as the newspapers can get things pretty much mixed up.

Has Albert started back to school yet? What is he studying? Does he keep working while he attends classes? I wrote him a long letter about 10 days ago. And I hope he received it alright.

NICHOLS FIELD, RIZAL, P.I. *Wednesday evening, 10:00 PM*

Well Albie,

What do you think of my new stationery? I want you to know that you have the dubious honor to be the first person to receive it. Your very welcome letter arrived on the 10th of November, 12 days after you mailed it, which isn't too bad, the was the clippers have been delayed, Sometimes they stay almost a week in Guam because of typhoon weather. They are very careful about their clippers, not taking any chances.

As you know I have been here at Nichols Field for the past three weeks, and the way things stand I still have 3 weeks to go. After I pass this course I can apply for permanent assignment here. It is quite a post, and getting bigger all the time. Most of the planes we have here are P-40-e and observation planes, with the flying fortresses being kept up north at Clark Field, but we do have some B-18s down here. In fact, I had a chance to fly down to Zamboanga and the southern islands in one over the holiday yesterday, but I had already made plans to go to Tagaytay for the day. I have been pretty busy in the dispensary this past week learning hew to refract eyes, and so I didn't get to do any more flying, but I hope to do some this coming week. One of the pilots that I am living with has promised to give me lessons. These new P-40 pursuit planes, with liquid cooled Allison engines are just like streaks of lightning. They can do 400 miles an hour on a horizontal. We had quite a few crackups over here since the pilots that come over have just finished training, and these ships are souped up too much for them. Every time they wash one up, it costs $40,000. The propellers alone are $3.500 which is quite a bit. Give Mom a big hug for me.

LETTERS FROM POW CAMP PHILIPPINES

1942

CAMP CAPAS *Wednesday, Oct. 21, 1942*

Dear Mom:

The Nips keep telling us we are going to be able to write home real soon, so I will get a head start on them and hope for the best. I began a long letter to you the last part of January and I was quite faithful in adding a few words each day—but on April 8th, after we had made a last stand at Km. 148 (and I thought at the time it was the last of me) I was never able to get back to my *musette bag* at the aid station and the letter went astray—so… I must begin again.

Hospital #1, Bataan, Philippines. Second from left, back row: Dr. Maxwell Andler. Second from right, front row: Dr. Dan Golenternek.

Right now I am in a concentration camp at Capas, through the courtesy of the Japanese Imperial Forces, and I have been here as a part of the staff of the General Hospital No. 1 since the 5th of July, '42. Where was I before that? Long story, but I will get to it in time. It is difficult to pick a starting point, as there are so many things I want to tell you about, but I will try and begin at the end of hostilities on Bataan, April 9th.

Following the capitulation we were told to start walking north from Merivalis, where all the American troops had collected. While hiking up the steep zigzag I became separated from the Air corps troops, and after covering about 10km, found myself close to the American Field Hospital at Little Baguio.[1] Two days before, during the retreat from Orion, I had twisted my knee, which at that time was bothering me again and they admitted me as a patient, which was a very fortunate thing for me. The rest of our troops were forced to march over a hundred km to San Fernando, during which time they had little rest, food or water, and thousands died along the way. They were then packed in closed boxcars and shipped up here to O'Donnell. In a short while I was discharged and became part of the staff of the hospital, as the Nips permitted the hospital to keep functioning under American control—we had over 500 seriously ill and wounded patients. Those who had been convalescing left the hospital two days before the end, when the whole area was heavily bombed for more than 36 hours. Corregidor was still holding out, and none of us had any idea what was going on outside the hospital.

While we were considered non-belligerents, and all Japanese Guards were removed from the grounds a few days after capitulation, we were instructed not to leave the area, and that if one patient or member of the hospital escaped ten would be shot. That was quite an incentive to keep us from straying too far.

Food was still scarce, although the hospital had some stored away, and as we didn't know how long we would stay there, we continued on a two-

[1] Note on Bataan march: After he becomes separated from his unit, Max found himself near the American Field Hospital. He looked around and as no guards were near he turned off on the trail to the hospital. After a short while he came upon a Japanese Tank unit that was stationed in the jungle. The Japanese were just sitting around their tanks eating and smoking, and did not pay any attention to him, so he walked on by. He continued on to the hospital, where he was admitted as a patient.

meal schedule, and slim ones at that. It was a relief for the fighting to be over, and not have to dive for a hole every time a Nip plane came over; but in a few days we found danger from a new source. The Japs had placed much of their artillery around us to fire on Corregidor, and that latter, in returning their fire with the long eight and twelve inch Navy rifles came much too close to the hospital for comfort. After the fall of Corregidor, things quieted down, and the Nips permitted us to forage for food and supplies all over Bataan. We were able to send details out for mangos, bananas and pineapple, as well as hunting caraboa, calesa pony and mule. We were more than willing to eat any kind of meat, although we never did get down to eating dog meat. I think the tastiest meat we had was a small calesa pony we found running loose. They caught one mule, but he tasted a bit sweet. I went on one detail up to the Damalog trail about 30 Km. from the hospital, along with seven other medical officers, and in half a day we picked up over 1800 ripe pineapple. They were delicious, too. Later, we even sent a truck north to Balanga, and were able to purchase carabao, sugar, native cigarettes, and other necessities from the hospital fund.

During this time the Nips had salvaging detail working all over, trying to get all the trucks, tanks, artillery, ammunition and other spoils of war. They were unable to drive our big army trucks, so had Americans from up at Camp O'Donnel do the driving for them. In this way we were able to hear about the conditions up there, which were described as frightful. After the long trek up there, they were crowded into Nipa shacks, with bad water, no sanitary facilities or plumbing, only rice and salt, and no medication. Malaria, dysentery and malnutrition soon became widespread with hundreds of prisoners dying daily. It sounds barbaric, and we felt the truck drivers were exaggerating, but we later found that it was all too true. Two or three times a week some Nippon Officers would come in and inspect our place at Little Baguio, and they would tell the Commanding Officer, Colonel Duckworth, that we were doing very well with the sick. They were quite impressed with the way the hospital had continued to function after the capitulation, as just about every other organization had broken up. After three months there, with little knowledge of how the war was progressing, we were informed that all our patients would be transferred to Bilibid in Manila, and our hospital unit would move to Camp O'Donnell with all its personnel and equipment in an attempt to bring down the high incidence of disease there, which was steadily increasing. This was quite a move as the hospital consisted of over a thousand beds, with three kitchens, a building full of medical supplies, the belongings of all the personnel, and most important of all, about four truckloads of food that had been salvaged from the various abandoned areas and quartermaster dumps. You see, we were still existing on two scant meals a day, and hungry most of the time. Incidentally, during the stay at Little Baguio, I had a severe attack of malaria, followed by the most intensive siege of yellow jaundice that I have ever seen—yellow as a pumpkin. My weight dropped from 180 pounds to 150 in a very short time, which was not counting the 30 pounds I had lost during the war. But since then, I have managed to put most of it back on. Regarding the actual move, a Japanese trucking company of the QM. of 33 trucks made four full trips to move us. Their plan was to make O'Donnell a concentration camp for Filipino soldiers only, moving all Americans to a new camp at Cabanatuan. The original strength of the camp had been almost 60,000 Filipinos and 12,000 Americans, in the three months before we arrived over 20,000 Filipinos and 1600 Americans had died. It sounds unbelievable.

When we arrived, much had been done to clean the place up and remedy the awful conditions, but it was still indescribably filthy. The death rate was more than 100 a day, with inadequate water, no lights, beds or medications in the hospitals, with the patients lying in their own filth on the floor of Nipa shacks. There were over 5,000 patients in the hospitals, mostly dysenteries, malarias, and chronic starvation and malnutrition, with only 13 American doctors. Most of the American prisoners had already gone, leaving only 125 sick in the hospital, if the group of squalid, filthy shacks could be called that. Apparently the Japanese authorities were becoming alarmed at the high death rate in the camps, with regard to the feelings of the native civilian population, which they were trying to placate in furthering the ideals of the Co-prosperity sphere; they brought us up from Bataan in the hope that we could clean up the camp.

The chief Japanese Medical Officer in Manila ordered our unit to come up here intact. The Commanding Officer of the camp here, told us all on arrival, that he was turning the care of the sick over to us, and from there on we were responsible for the health of the camp. Well, we had a big job ahead of us, and went right to work. Five hospitals were set up, each of 1000 bed capacity, three containing the malaria patients, and two isolated with the dysentery cases. All our equipment, including beds, mattresses, surgical and dental equipment and medical supplies were installed in Hospital I where the remaining American patients were kept. As they had many Filipino doctors here our American doctors were put to work in the other four units in a supervisory capacity. Within a week of our arrival all the Filipino doctors were removed from the camp and our staff of 60 doctors had to take care of all the patients, kit and caboodle. Medicine, especially quinine had been at a premium before our arrival and many of the Filipino medical officers had been selling the medicine to the patients. If they didn't have any money, they didn't get any medicine.

In a fairly short while, we had the hospital pretty well set up with electricity in all the buildings, adequate running water in the wards and kitchens, and the institution running quite smoothly. Our special sections included a pharmacy, laboratory, dental section with three chairs, an E.N.T. department, surgery with three operating tables, and a portable x-ray machine. I was assigned as American Supply Officer the very first day, which meant a good deal of work, plus Mess Officer which was a real headache. Briefly, my job in supply was this. First of all, I was custodian of all the foodstuffs we had managed to bring up from Little Baguio, and that was more valuable than gold. Secondly, every other day I would report up at Japanese HQ. to draw the rations for the patients and personnel of the American hospital, which amounted to about 750 Americans and Filipinos. At the same time the Filipino Supply Officer who drew for the rest of the prisoners of the camp had a ration and strength count of about forty thousand. At first, when I would go up there, it was a bit difficult, as I didn't understand any Japanese, and it was strange how they issued, and the Nip supply man spoke no English. In a very short while, I picked up the Japanese words for the different foods they issued, such as rice, milk, lard, sugar, salt, flour and various native vegetables. And I became acquainted with the Nip issue man. He would be pretty decent about things. Since I was drawing for such a relatively few men in comparison to the Filipino supply Officer, he always gave me the breaks. You see, we had no contact with the outside, and the amount of food that I was able to draw each time determined whether we would get sufficient food to eat. Rice we received in abundance, over a pound a man, but the other foods were rationed out sparingly. Milk was issued only for the sick hospital cases, ten men to a can of evaporated milk. Sugar, 10 grams a man. The meat ration varied on paper from 50 to 100 grams a day, but since we received our meat on the hoof, the final ration came to about 30 or 40 grams a day. Just the same, I used to be able to draw a good-sized cow, and that gave us some extra.

CAMP CAPAS *December 8, 1942*

Today is just a year that this war has been going on, and I am more than ready to have it stop. In fact, I certainly was not at all happy that it ever happened. While it has been over a month since I wrote, I have thought about continuing many times. There has been little talk about our receiving mail lately, although at one time rumor had it that a Red Cross ship in Manila was laden with mail and packages for us. But maybe there wouldn't have been any letter for me anyway. You might not even know whether I am alive or not. Many months ago the Nips took our names and home addresses with the theory of notifying the States, but we have no idea whether this ever occurred. So much has happened this past year that I am not sure of anything. So many strange and unbelievable experiences that I do not want their memory to leave me. At times I sit back and try to realize that it has really happened to me here in the tropical Philippines, 10,000 miles from home, bombed and blasted out of Manila, starved, bombed, starved and shelled In Bataan for three months, and now a prisoner of war in a concentration camp. Sounds fantastic to me.

I should be just getting off duty at the L.A. County Hospital after an all night session in neurosurgery, and wondering whether I was too tired to keep a date with Georgia that night. I am just getting over another good attack of malaria, the fourth, and am just finishing my course of Atabrine. Before this I knew very little about the disease, having seen only one case as a medical student, but now I have a very good idea of all the symptoms mmi

WAR DEPARTMENT
THE ADJUTANT GENERAL'S OFFICE
WASHINGTON

IN REPLY REFER TO AG 201 Andler, Maxwell M. Jr.
(11-29-42) PC-G

December 2, 1942.

Ensign Louis A. Hebert, Jr., U.S.N.R.,
District Security Office,
Building #4,
Philadelphia Navy Yards.

Dear Ensign Hebert:

Reference is made to your letter of November 29, 1942, relative to First Lieutenant Maxwell M. Andler, Jr., O-381336, Medical Corps.

Lieutenant Andler is being carried on the records of the War Department as missing in action in the Philippine Islands since May 7, 1942. He will retain that status until information to the contrary is received or until twelve months from that date have expired, at which time the War Department will give further consideration to his status.

I am sure you will understand that until a definite report is received in the War Department concerning the status of Lieutenant Andler, it will be impossible to communicate with him. Should any change be made in this officer's status, his mother, Mrs. Maxwell M. Andler, will be notified immediately.

Very truly yours,

J. A. Ulio

J. A. ULIO
Major General,
The Adjutant General.
By: [illegible]

and treatment. What is odd about it, that one day one will have a severe chill with a fever of 105, a splitting headache, backache, and probably bring up one's lunch. Then, the next morning feel like going back to work. Up until this last attack, that is what I have been doing: getting up the second day to draw supplies, and never finishing a full course of treatment. But this last time has taught me a lesson. I have been in bed for four days, and having Dan Golenternek, one of the boys from the County Hospital, taking care of me. In fact, he just came in and said to stop sitting up and get to bed so I can report to duty in the morning.

CAMP CAPAS *December 9, 1942, 7:30 P.M.*

It is colder than the devil, and what makes it worse, I am developing a good solid cold. Maybe a little codeine and aspirin will have me sweat it out. To go back to the beginning of our stay here, the time passed very quickly because I was so occupied. It was necessary for me to keep an exact account of what was used in the mess as the Japanese Medical Dept. wanted a daily record of the amount of food in grams each man had at each meal. While they were issuing a ration of 20 grams of flour a day to Americans, we didn't have any yeast, so we were unable to make bread. After I became better acquainted up at the Nip HQ., I went up and spoke to the interpreter and told him that if they would get me yeast from Manila we would bake bread for their officers every day. I was very much surprised one day by a messenger with thirty-four pounds of chilled Fleischman's yeast. We had Frigidaires, which we had brought from the hospital in Bataan, nine of them, in fact, so we were able to keep it alright, and each morning I would send a K.P. up from the kitchen with 60 rolls plus bread for the whole hospital. I had a kitchen crew of Navy Mess Attendants, who used to cook for the U.S. Naval Officers, all Filipinos, and they were marvelous cooks.

A few days later, the interpreter called me up, and said they were having the Governors of the provinces in for a luncheon, and wanted to know whether I could make them five pies. I replied I could if they would supply the materials. He asked what I needed and I told him canned fruits of any kind would do. He sent to the town of Capas and had them buy up a dozen cans of American canned goods. When I looked them over there were <u>two cans of beans</u>, and <u>two of corn</u>, along with some pineapple and native mango. I tried to explain that one couldn't use beans to make a pie, so he gave me the vegetables for myself, and with stuff like that selling at a couple of pesos a can, it came in pretty handy. Well, they liked those pies, and a short while later, they wanted to know if I could make up 200 roast beef sandwiches for them for some sort of celebration they were going to have. Well, I began to get smart then and told them that I would need a good deal of supplies. Ordinarily we received a small cow every second or third day, which gave us about 75 to 120 pounds of meat for 750 people. That isn't very much. I explained that only a certain amount of the cow could be used for roast meat, and the rest had to be used for stew. So the interpreter said that I would draw another whole cow, use what I needed for the sandwiches, and keep the rest for myself. Of course, I turned the rest over to the mess, and it amounted to over a hundred pounds. And besides that, we had all the bones for soup stock the next day. I drew extra flour, milk and shortening for the bread, so we really came out way ahead of the deal. You would be surprised to see what I know about cooking and preparing meals. I must plan all the menus and see that the food is prepared properly, and that alone is a full time job.

I am writing in dribs and drabs now, as I am Field Officer of the Day. That means that I must check all the Officers of the Day and guards of the four hospitals at least four times during the night, and I am not allowed to sleep at all. The whole thing is rather peculiar. The Japanese say that we are responsible for the guard of the Filipino patients, and if any escape they will take drastic measures. Now when we first arrived, they announced that if a prisoner was caught attempting to escape, he would be shot, the ten men in his squad would be shot, and also the Commanding Officer of his organization would be executed. You can readily see that we are not very anxious for anyone to attempt to escape. Well, each hospital is about half a mile apart, and I must check the American Guard in each building of each hospital. One round just took me an hour and a half, and I was walking fast. Three more to go tonight. The Officer of the Day is supposed to get the next day off, but since I must draw supplies tomorrow from HQ. I probably won't get to sleep until noon.

But I am over my malaria and feel pretty well. I also have charge of the commissary for the hospital, which is another long story. When we first arrived here, it was impossible for anyone to get out of the camp except the truck drivers, and they were not supposed to bring anything back into camp with them. They managed to, however, and sold the food to those who had money, for exorbitant prices. A twelve-ounce can of corn beef sold for as high as ten pesos, which is five dollars, and the men fought to buy it. And American cigarettes sold for five pesos a package, fifty pesos a carton. After a while, the Japanese permitted the merchants from Capas, the nearby town, to bring food for a camp commissary, which was a godsend. While their prices were also high, it was much better than before, and all one needed was money, which everyone didn't have, including me. You see, I hadn't drawn any pay while I was in the field during the war. In fact, I haven't been paid since last November.

Well, one day, one of the truck drivers brought in a package for Dr. Andler, sent up from Manila in some unknown way. When I opened it, I found out it was from the girl, whom I knew in Manila, whose Dad was a member of the Dutch consulate. She and her family had been interned at the Santa Tomas University along with the rest of the enemy nationals, and while she didn't known where I was and hadn't heard from me since the beginning of the war, she took a chance that I would be here, which was very fortunate. She sent me toothpaste, a toothbrush, soap, aspirin, soda bicarb, some quinine, which was so difficult to get, and also a pair of wooden shoes, which all the natives wear in the orient. It was very sweet and thoughtful of her, and in a short note she wanted to know if there was anything else that I needed, and she would try to get it for me. They were allowed to have short passes to leave Santa Tomas, and they still kept their home open. I wrote and told her about the commissary, and asked if she knew of anyone who would cash a check on an American bank. Very soon she had made all arrangements and sent me up as much money as I needed, and also told me that she would send me more if I asked for it. With this I was able to buy fresh eggs, bananas, limes, and chickens, and it made a tremendous difference in my health. I was appointed as Commissary Officer for the American hospital, so each morning I would go up to the commissary and purchase for everyone connected with the hospital, and that is quite an order. These merchants bring in all manner of American canned goods, but the price is usually prohibitive. One peso for a small can of Quaker Oats. I manage to spend close to 100 pesos a day for our personnel and patients, and that is quite a bit of food. This girl is really a godsend though. We buy duck eggs. By now I have regained just about all the weight I lost previously. I would have liked to stay thin, but extra weight here is just like insurance against disease. One bout of dysentery melts the pounds right off, and if one doesn't have the pounds to lose it isn't very pleasant.

To get back to supply, they were more than satisfied with the sandwiches I made for them, and I stayed up most of the night seeing that they were properly prepared, and from then on, any time they wanted to have any sort of refreshments for visiting firemen, they would call me up. In this way, we were able to get a great deal more meat. One time, the high mark, I made them 360 sandwiches, and had 217 pounds of meat left for the two messes. That was certainly a tremendous animal. Other times we haven't been so lucky. The other day we had a calf that gave us only 47 pounds of meat. That is pretty bad for 700 people for two days. The food that we brought from Little Baguio made a whale of a difference because it supplemented the Japanese issue, which certainly needed supplementing. But now that reserve is all gone, and my problems at mess become more difficult daily. Well, it is time for another round, so I had better be going....

CAMP CAPAS *December 11, 1942, 8:00 PM*

Well, that O.D. is over, but it didn't do me any good. I didn't get to sleep until after one this afternoon, as I was busy with the commissary and mess all morning. Then I only slept for three hours. I used to mind staying up all night while on duty at the hospital, but this is a good deal different. I made my last round at 6:30 AM and I never thought I would finish it. The hiking didn't do my cold any good either, or my disposition, for that matter.

I think I mentioned no one was allowed to leave the camp except the American truck drivers, but after a while, when I had become better acquainted with the Japanese supply sergeant, he began taking me with him to neighboring towns where he picked up supplies for the camp. Wherever I would go all the natives would crowd around and say "Hello, Joe," and just stand and stare. That helps to break up the monotony a little. As I had lost most of my uniforms during the war, I had very few clothes left, but a Filipino here, who is my orderly, gave me some khaki material that he had and I took it into Tarlac and had a uniform made. That helped a good deal. And about two weeks ago, I received two of my uniforms from Manila that I left there New Year's Eve, when I came in from Bataan and stayed overnight. I got out of there, just in time as the Nips took over the next day.

Anyway, now I have quite a wardrobe. Yesterday's Manila paper stated that the International Red Cross has received the names of all the prisoners here with our home addresses, so by now you should have heard that I am alive and well. I certainly hope so. As far as our conditions here are, as long as we have to be in a concentration camp, we are probably better off here than anywhere else. The Nips let us run the hospital as we see fit. I live in a bihay with one other Officer, and we have running water, electricity, and recently I acquired one of the Frigidaires to keep in my quarters so that I could take care of the yeast and see that it is kept cold. One couldn't ask for a great deal more except a ticket home. A little before Thanksgiving I went up to HQ. and explained that the holiday was an American feast day, and would like permission to buy a caribou so that the men could have plenty of meat for one day. The adjutant spoke to Colonel Ito, and he instructed them to buy a caribou and give it to us for a present on Thanksgiving, which was pretty nice of him. We were able to bone it and get 210 pounds of meat, and fed the whole thing at one time to our 203 Americans who are attached to the hospital. For once all the men had enough meat to eat. Our biggest problem is getting enough protein in our diet. If the Nips finally pay the Medical Officers as they say, 20 pesos a month, all will donate half the money to the mess, amounting to about 400 pesos, and with that we should be able to buy sufficient meat. I want to go back and tell you what happened during the war since the last time I wrote, but I will wait until another time when I feel a little peppier.

CAMP CAPAS *December 14, 1942, 8:30 PM*

Here I am in O.D. again. I am not supposed to be on again for another three nights, but I have arranged with Jack Gordon to split the shift with him. I go off at 3:00 AM and he comes on for the rest of the night. That shouldn't be so bad. I haven't fully recovered from the last tour of duty yet. Well, today we received official notice that we would be paid in three days. And they are going to give us four months back pay. The only catch is, they are subtracting 60 pesos a month for subsistence and clothing. (So far they haven't issued any clothes.) Then, they say we must save a certain percentage of our salary, so they take some more back. We finally wind up with 20 pesos a month. No one is complaining, as we never believed we were going to be paid at all, and back pay comes to 80 pesos. Sounds like a fortune now. Everyone wants to splurge. The next thing I hope they do is permit us to write home. Yesterday was Sunday, and through the commissary I ordered 20 kilos of caribou meat, and we had roast beef for supper. And now that we will get some sort of salary we should be able to supplement the mess pretty well. I suppose we shouldn't figure on this money until we are actually paid, but they had us sign the receipt for it, and that should mean something.

The day the war began we heard rumors, and here a year later we are still hearing rumors. Now someone tells us that American bombers hit Nichols Field the other night. I can recall very vividly the first time Nichols Field was bombed by Japanese planes the first day of the war. The last clipper letter I sent off to you was about three days before the beginning of the fireworks, and I had just returned from a flight to Del Monte, Mindanao. Sunday, December 7, 1941, I borrowed Bob Wray's Buick, my roommate, and took Alice Werff up to the Taygaytay Ridge Hotel for lunch. We came back to town that evening, went to the movies, and then had supper at the Sky room of Jai Alai. A quite enjoyable day—I was beginning to enjoy the Philippines. The next morning, a few minutes past eight, I reported over to the dispensary at Nichols field, and Major Morehouse greeted me with the phrase, "Well, the Nips did it. They bombed Pearl Harbor."

I was very skeptical until he showed me the headlines of the morning paper. Just then the All Alert signal went off, with a howling of the siren, and three shots from the 75. A glance out the window showed pilots racing to their P-40s deployed around the field, mechanics revving the motors, checking the machine guns, and the Field Guard taking their posts. The whole scene sent a shiver through me, and I could almost see enemy bombers in the sky. Fortunately, it was a dry run, and as I hadn't yet received official orders from Washington assigning me to the Air Corps, I reported back to the 12th Medical Regiment at Fort McKinley. I hadn't been there half a day, when Major Morehouse called me and said that I should return to the field immediately, as they were shorthanded. They had just received the news that Eba had been leveled, and the Medical Officer there killed. He had already sent out the Nichols Field Medicos to take care of the injured there, and he was trying to cover the field with just himself and Captain Noel. He told me that he would get verbal orders from the Commanding General to authorize my return, so back I went. By the time I had returned, it was almost five o'clock, and all personnel were ordered to evacuate their quarters as an air raid was expected momentarily. More news had revealed that Bauio had been bombed, and Clark Field had been demolished at noon, with most of the heavy bombardment on the ground. We had a total of 34 B-17's here, and 17 were smashed by the first attack. Some feel this first devastating raid determined the eventual downfall of our troops. Many and varied stories are given to account for the planes being on the ground.

One version has it that they were all loaded and ready to take off for Formosa, but were kept grounded by order of the Commanding General of USAFFE who said we would not make an overt act of war until actual war had been declared. Whatever the cause, the result was a severe blow to our air strength in the Pacific Southwest. Be that as it may, we at Nichols Field felt pretty sure we were next on the list. We set out three auxiliary aid stations on three corners of the field, me drawing the spot by the water tower, a tall affair painted yellow and black, so that it could be seen from the air, which didn't make me feel any too comfortable. There were some P-52s cruising around, and our machine gunners were so nervous that they fired on one and brought him down. Two separate alerts were false alarms, and I had just about decided to get a little sleep it being already three in the morning. Three enlisted men constituted my staff, and we had dug a narrow trench about a foot deep, against the side of the swimming pool, in the shadow of the water tower, a very poor place for an aid station. A hit of the tower would have demolished us in short order. The 75 went off again, but we heard nothing for probably 25 minutes.

As the first sounds of the planes' motors came to me I tried to get as close to the ground as I could. Just as I noticed numerous flares go up from the south end of the field, the ground commenced to heave, and I heard and felt four tremendous explosions. At the same time I saw some more flares from the northeast end of the field, and the planes sounded as if they were flying in that direction. I checked my area and found no casualties, but in a few moments I received a message from Major Morehouse to report to the dispensary immediately, as they had hit hangar four. As I jogged over, a tractor hauling a bomb rack loaded with wounded men swung around the corner and stopped in front of the dispensary, which was blacked out so that we could work at night if necessary. I rushed inside, and there were wounded all over the floor. The Major had his shirt off, and was patching them up as quickly as he could, so that they could be sent to the station Hospital at McKinley. Some of the injuries were brutal, with large masses of tissue blown away, limbs torn off, and nasty shrapnel wounds of every description.

The remarkable thing was the quiet in the room, hardly a sound. Padre O'Brien, a Catholic priest with whom I later spent most of the war, was helping, and every man that was able would tell me to help someone else first, he would be able to make it all right. We didn't have time to be shocked by this first picture of a horrible war, as we were too busy giving hypos. Before we had finished, we counted seven dead and 17 injured. One bomb had landed square in the room of one of the Officers, killing him outright. After getting them all off to the hospital we went back to our stations to wait developments, but there were no more raids that night. The next morning we received orders to deploy all troops around the field, abandoning all quarters, and prepare for parachute invasion, which didn't sound too enticing. All was quiet that day and night, and the next morning, Wednesday, the 10th, we decided to move all our medical supplies out of the dispensary, and set up a new place at the edge of tent city, northeast of the runway, on a slight rise overlooking the field. Two ambulances were backed up against the first row of tents, which we had filled with supplies and equipment. Between the ambulance and the opening of the tent ran a boardwalk on which I was standing, giving instructions to five of the corpsmen who were arranging the supplies...about twenty minutes to one. Throughout the morning P-40s had been taking off and landing, doing patrol work, and there were some overhead almost continually.

Suddenly I heard a plane whine in a deep dive...looking up I saw a P-40 diving for the south end of the field, followed by two ships that I thought were also P-40s, until I saw the tracer bullets making a livid streak on either side of the radial engine. Finally realizing what was going on, I yelled to the men to take shelter under the ambulances, and I dove under one myself. As I did, I could see the machine gun bullets kicking up the dirt in front of the ambulance, and as the planes came out of the diver not more than 150 feet from the ground, I felt they were going to fly right through us. By this time our ground machine guns opened up, and the Nips' planes circled and came back again, strafing the area. One could feel the *poom poom* as the 37 mm shells struck the ground, fired through the nose of the enemy fighter planes. The place sounded like a boiler factory. Looking out from under the front of the ambulance I could see a parachute floating down, and immediately thought of parachute troops hitting me. Suddenly, the ground heaved like an earthquake, and I was bounced up against the bottom of the ambulance, while tremendous explosions broke out. There was only one soldier under the ambulance with me while four had taken cover under the other one. I was certain that was the end of us, and only prayed that it would be over soon. We were covered with clods of dirt and debris in spite of being under the vehicle. I hugged the ground as tightly as I could, momentarily expecting a bomb to blow us to kingdom come. The terrific thumping and shaking of the ground lasted about three quarters of a minute but seemed an eternity.

Gradually, the sound of motors became more distant, and when I finally ventured to stick my head out, the planes were quite a distance away. A scene of desolation greeted my eyes. A stick of 500 lb. bombs had hit parallel to the front row of tents missing the ambulances on each side by 10 feet. A deep crater about 18 feet in diameter was 10 to the left of the ambulance I had been under, while a similar crater was on the other side of the second ambulance. The bodies of the vehicles were pierced with machine gun bullets and shrapnel, while the whole roof of the one I was under was crushed by a large mass of rock and earth thrown out from the bomb hole. Continuing in the same line off to the right, a bomb had hit a water main, and a fountain 50 feet high was spurting, and the next one had torn a large crater in the road, the next a square hit on the Engineer barracks. Another parallel stick of bombs had done an equal amount of destruction. The first part hitting in the front row of tents, setting them on fire, and demolishing our newly placed supplies, a direct hit on a large gasoline trailer which was burning freely, two more craters along the roadway, and a hit on a fully loaded B-18 which had been prepared to take off from the south end of the field. The Post Exchange showed only smoking walls, the whole building having disappeared.

I hopped on the running board of an engineer truck, and we rode all over the post checking up on casualties. Surprisingly few casualties were found on the field itself in spite of the wide destruction. While riding around the runway, we could still hear the far-off drone of the twin motor bombers, and we expected them back without warning, so I kept one eye on the heavens and one on the field. Over thirty men were missing, and we were unable to find their bodies until the next day. They had tried to get shelter, in the slew surrounding the post, and a whole stick of bombs had landed in this area. Their bodies were badly bloated, putrefied from lying in the sun, and identification was possible only by going through their pockets. This nauseating job fell to the medical officer, of course, as it was necessary to have a complete record of all casualties. In some cases, insufficient evidence remained to make any identification possible.

Following this raid each squadron was assigned positions surrounding the airfield as a defense against parachute troops. Major Morehouse established a field aid station about a km. from the north end of the field, and kept the major part of the medical detachment with him. Since Headquarters squadron had been assigned the guard of the south end of the field, I took three corpsmen with me, and set up an aid station in their area about a km. south of the field. After each air raid on the field, I would start from one end, and Major Morehouse would start from the other and we could cover the whole area to check on casualties. There would be at least one raid each day, usually fairly close to noon. By this time, most of our men had learned to dig themselves in pretty well, and we experienced relatively few casualties. One raid missed the field entirely and landed their whole load in the nearby barrio of Parenaque, causing heavy civilian casualties and starting extensive fires. We helped the civilian Red Cross unite with the injured, and then went back to wait for the next one.

We remained out there for more than two weeks, sleeping on the ground, eating whenever there seemed to be a lull and bathing every four or five days. While our quarters at the field hadn't received a direct hit, the building had been strafed many times, the water and electricity were off, and with clothes and pictures knocked down by the heavy caliber machine gun bullets, the place was a shambles. About the 14th, we collected all our clothes that weren't ruined and took them down to put in the cold storage plant. On the way down in the Command car the sirens announced another air raid, which caused all civilian cars to stop. We were thus able to cruise undisturbed through the streets, and the planes did not show up. I stopped in at R.C.A. and sent a wireless home saying that while the Nips had hit the field they had missed me…so far. I also decided to get some of my money out of the Philippine Trust Co., so I sent Kay 600 pesos, and later events proved this to be a fortunate thing. After the first night, all bombing attacks had been limited to daytime.

The Major permitted us to leave every fourth night, each Medical Officer taking his turn. This made a lot of difference. I would manage to go in with Kirk, the CO of the HQ Squadron. First we would go into the Army & Navy Club, and take a hot shower and shave. Putting on a clean uniform, we would leave our dirty clothes there at the laundry, and they would be ready for us when we returned in four days. The Werffs would insist on our eating dinner with them whenever we managed to get in, and that was really comforting. In spite of the bombings, these interludes comprised some of the pleasantest times I can recall in the Philippines. One night when I was off, we went to the Manila Hotel for dinner and dancing—Bill Kern, who has since died at Camp I, both the Werff girls and myself. We had cocktails at sundown on the terrace overlooking Manila Bay, and that is an experience long to be remembered. We would have no reminder of the war if the earsplitting motors of PT boats hadn't come ricocheting across the Bay. The dining room was completely blacked out. The sight of women in slacks, and men in field uniforms on the dance floor was an occurrence new to the swanky Manila Hotel. About this time the headlines screeched that 80 Nip transports had landed at Lingayen, but everything was under control. Trying to calculate the number of troops that could land from 80 ships gave us the cold chills.

We were still expecting hourly, our help from the States. One rumor had us unloading dive-bombers at Pier 7, assembling them on the dock and flying them off from Dewey Boulevard. Other stories were just as fantastic, but we wanted to believe them so badly, that nothing seemed too improbable.

Our Engineers continued to work on the new runway in order to be ready for whatever came in. The Philippine Air Depot moved out to Santa Ana and set up, and we continued to act as a guard against parachute troops. The Werffs asked both Captain Kirk and myself for Christmas dinner if we could make it, and I was looking forward to that. About 4 o'clock Christmas Eve, Noel decided he didn't want to go into Manila, and the Major said I could go in if I wanted to. I had just arranged a ride with Kirk, when Padre O'Brien came steaming in from the Post Headquarters to tell us that orders had been received to abandon the field within one hour, and for all personnel to report to Pier 7 immediately prepared to embark on a transport. He was pretty sure we would go to Bataan, but that wasn't official.

To confirm this, the Major ordered me to report to Major Maverick at the C.P., but the explosion of the gasoline bodegas was sufficient confirmation. Prior to this there had been talk of declaring Manila an open city, and the Usaffe retreating to Bataan according to an old defense plan of a generation ago, but we kept hoping and wishing that it was only talk. The orders to evacuate made this decision appear quite certain. Our equipment included two ambulances and a G.I. truck, which carried our medical supplies and litters. The Major also had a new 1941 Hudson that he had received a few days before from the downtown motor pool to replace his personal car. Our orders were to take all our equipment to Pier 7, load it on the waiting transport, and leave all motor transportation on the dock. We loaded up and went down the pier, but the Major realized how badly we would need the ambulances and truck in Bataan, so he decided to send some of the supplies and the detachment on the ship, and the ambulances would drive down. I would also drive down with him in the Hudson.

I called Alice to say we were leaving. She could see the gasoline fires out at Nichols, and also the squadron of 14 P-40's zooming overhead to cover our retreat, and she was more than curious to find out what was going on. I knew that the city would be declared *Open* as soon as we left, but I felt that her family would worry unduly and try to leave their home in the country if they knew. I decided they would be better off if they stayed in a large city like Manila when the Nips came in, than in a small town, so I told her to sit tight and I hoped I would be back in a few days. I felt a bit like a heel running off that way, but when Uncle Sam gives the orders, there isn't much a First Lieutenant can do about it. The Major and I saw the boys well loaded on the ship, and then we went over to the Army and Navy Club where we left boxes of our clothes and personal belongings. The main ballroom was almost half filled with boxes and luggage that Officers had left before going into the field. We went into the bar and found Officers stocking up on whiskey before they left for Bataan; it was quite a busy place. We had a last drink there to punctuate our leaving, and 6:30 PM found us driving north over Quezon bridge toward San Fernando, where we had a rendezvous with our ambulance drivers.

While the road was good, driving without lights forced us to keep a slow pace. We didn't know where in Bataan the troops would dock, so we decided to stop along the road and sleep as soon as we reached the cutoff to Olongapo. By the time we reached San Fernando we had run into a continuous convoy of transportation from H.P.D. and USAFFE. I had to stand out on the road and try to identify our truck as if came through. We finally reached the cutoff just at midnight, and after wishing each other a forlorn Merry Christmas, we tried to get some sleep curled up in the car. Periodically we were awakened by the noise of either a tank or a tractor rumbling by. The next morning we found that the noise emanated from tractors dragging the heavy 155's into Bataan.

After getting a start at 6:30 AM we headed south, and found many evidences of the long night convoy with vehicles turned over on both sides of the road. In a stretch of 10 km. we saw an average of 30 trucks or cars, some large 10 wheel QM, trucks, others jeeps and command cars. As we didn't know where the ship was scheduled to dock, we decided to check first at Limay where the first dock of any size was located. We found that the hospital group from McKinley, augmented by other medical personnel had moved in the day before to set up General Hospital No. 1 with Colonel Duckworth in command. They informed us that the ship would dock at Marivelis. Major Morehouse decided we had better have breakfast there as we had missed supper the night before in the flurry of evacuation. We stepped into the chow line, and told our enlisted men to get in the line also to get some hot food. While we were talking there to some of the medical officers and nurses that we knew, the mess sergeant came out and reported to the adjutant in our hearing that he had already fed more than a hundred more than he had drawn rations for, and new people were coming in all the time to be fed. Well, that made both the Major and myself feel a bit uncomfortable, so we agreed to move on without eating.

On the way out of town he stopped and bought some bananas from one of the barrio stands and as it later turned out that constituted my Christmas fare for the day. Leaving our ambulances to follow on slowly with the equipment, we headed for Marivelis. Hiking north along the road, we encountered our Air Corps squadrons struggling up the steep zigzag with the tonnage, as there was no transportation for the troops when they landed. We managed to get down to the dock at 10:30 AM and they were still unloading supplies. The Navy Commander informed us that the whole area must be evacuated by noon as an air raid was expected. That made us hustle a bit. Colonel Churchill, former CO of Nichols Field was with Air Force HQ at a spot in the road about a km. about Little Baguio, an Engineer's post that had been built before the war. We moved back up there and waited for things to get settled. Since Major Morehouse didn't know into what position the personnel of the 20th Airbase Group would be placed, we were unable to choose a place for our medical headquarters and dispensary. Just as Colonel Churchill was passing around some C Ration for lunch, the Major asked me to go over to the Engineer HQ at Little Baguio and check up on water and lights for the possible location of an aid station. So I missed lunch.

While planes had been flying overhead throughout the morning, there was no bombing in the Bataan area, something I can't understand to this day. With cars and trucks tearing up and down the dirt road, there was a constant brown cloud above the trees to indicate the troop movement. Heavy bombing seemed to be coming from the east, in the direction of Manila, but we later found this to be caused by exploding gasoline storage tanks, which were blown by the Engineers before leaving the City. After I had made arrangements for us to use temporarily the medical facilities at Little Baguio, I returned to Major Morehouse and he informed me that the 20th Airbase Group would bivouac around km. 140, by the town of Pandan. I have probably mentioned that a medical detachment does not have its own mess, and is usually carried by one of the companies or squadrons on the post. Well, by the time we managed to get back up to km. 140, it was dark and it wasn't possible to locate any of our squadrons. Some of the men opened some wet O Ration, but I was so tired that I laid out a stretcher, hung my mosquito bar, and put away a good night's rest.

And so Christmas Day passed. A day that in no way resembled the one I had planned. Christmas dinner at the Werff's was not to be. During the night we were again awakened by the roar of tractors, and found the 86th Heavy Artillery moving into the same area. In fact, one of their vehicles came very close to the Major's recumbent form. The latter straightened them out in no uncertain terms. Morning found me checking the locality for potable water and also locating our line personnel so that we could chow. The 2nd Observation Squadron was less than a km. west of us, and we decided to grace their table. By this time a little order had developed from the chaos of the evacuation, and after the first mad dash from Manila, civilian trucks had been commandeered to haul supplies up from the dock at Marivelis.

As soon as the realization developed that Manila was not yet taken, a constant stream of trucks began hauling supplies down to Bataan. Some trucks went back to Fort Stotsenberg to get food and equipment from the post there, others went to Fort McKinley and Nichols Field. As a result, in the first few weeks of the war, food of every description was available. Vast stores of supplies and cigarettes were also available to anyone with a truck and the proper initiative at the port area. I recall one truck from Headquarters Squadron returning from there with a load composes solely of Piedmont cigarettes. The first few days on Bataan were hectic. Major Maverick informed us that the spot we were now in had been designated as the advance line for our heavy artillery while our line of first defense was still falling back from Northern Luzon and southeastern Luzon. The 34th Pursuit Squadron was the only outfit of ours assigned to operate from Orzni, and we had a medical officer assigned to them.

The rest of our personnel was scattered from Cabcaben Field to Pandan, and it would be necessary to make morning sick call in an ambulance, first checking out Aviation Engineers working on the Cabcaben field, then in turn stopping at the P.N.A.D. 27th Material, 17th Pursuit, HQ Squadron and the 2nd Observation. The latter had no planes left, the last one being smashed before we left Nichols. The daily call at the Cabcaben field was the one I liked least. The Engineers were dug in at the extreme west end of the field, and it was necessary to drive the full length of the field to get there. I would give the driver of the ambulance the all-clear signal, and then we would make a dash for it. Although we had some close ones with the dive-bombers, we had no actual trouble. On the 29th, four days after our arrival, Capt. Noel got restless to see his wife, a Red Cross nurse who he left in Manila. He had an old Buick sedan, and asked Major Morehouse if he could go back to Manila overnight, as there was no news of the Nips entering Manila. The day before we had seen the planes bombing over the Manila area all day, and he was worried about her. When the Major gave him the O.K., I immediately put in my bid to go in with him as I was worried about the Werff's, too. He grudgingly permitted me to go, but he warned us to start back the first thing in the morning. It was almost three in the afternoon then, so away we went.

Across the bay only two of the three towers of Cavite could be seen standing, and tall columns of smoke hung over the whole city. Once we approached San Fernando, it was cluttered with Army traffic carrying supplies and food down to Bataan, with empty vehicles returning for another load. We encountered some flights of enemy planes, but they were all concentrating over Manila, and weren't bothering the automobile traffic. When we finally entered Manila about 6:15, we found the Walled City surrounded by firefighting equipment and erupting dense clouds of black smoke. Inquiry revealed that for over three hours, low flying bombers had been hitting the port area, shipping in the bay, and boats along the docks of the Pasig River. In attempting the latter, some of the bombs were dropped not too accurately, and they hit in areas of the Walled City. We drove down to the port area and it was a scene of desolation. A whole city block of supplies opposite Pier 7 was burning. A single civilian guard in the port area, semi-hysterical and dazed was found walking up and down by Pier 1. He told us the planes had flown low enough to see the faces of the pilots. In all probability the Pasig and the Walled City would not have been bombed if the owners of the river boats had followed orders to get their craft out into the Bay when Manila was declared an Open City. Instead, they opened their valves and tried to sink them right there in the river by the deck. From the air they must have appeared to be tied up in to the docks and still functioning, and so were legitimate targets.

Noel drove me over to the Werff's, and said he would pick me up about 8:00 AM the next morning. The family welcomed me with open arms and insisted on my staying there overnight, although I had planned to go over to the Army and Navy Club. Noel and I were a bit wary about being seen in our Army uniforms, as Manila was supposed to be an Open City, but we saw many American Officers still there, so we relaxed. As we were eating dinner, the Manila radio announced that beginning that night there would be no more blackout in Manila since it was an Open City. He described the bombing that had been going on all afternoon, and decried the wantonness of attacking a defenseless city. The civilians were close to panic. The Americans had left them with no protection, and they felt helpless. After eating, we took a walk over to Manila Bay, and watched the hulks burning themselves out. There was still a glow over the Port area and the Walled City. The gleaming lights of the autos along Dewey Blvd. were startling after the three weeks of blackout. Before returning to the house we went over to the Army and Navy Club, still blacked out, and had a dish of ice cream, which was the last I was to have for many a month to come.

No trouble getting back to California Street and the Werffs with the blackout lifted. Mrs. Werff wouldn't permit me to take my laundry over to the club. She said her lavendera would have it ready for me when we returned to Manila in a few days. And I was naïve enough to think that we would return in a few days. Noel picked me up at eight the next morning and we started back. Mrs. Werff gave me a large piece of plum pudding she had prepared for the Christmas dinner that Kirk and I ran out on. We had no sooner headed for Quezon Bridge, when the sirens began to wail. We pulled over, but it was only a single Nip observation on reconnaissance, and we returned to Bataan without further difficulty. We found little change in conditions there except that the artillery were taking positions around us, and there was talk of our moving further down the peninsula. What struck me as peculiar was there was no evidence of any front line defensive positions of our troops. We could see troops bivouacked in areas along the highway, but that was about all. As far as they were concerned, if we had been Nips there would have been no one to stop us from driving right down to the point of the peninsula.

Another peculiar business was the complete absence of any air activity over Bataan. We could see their planes over Manila and the Bay, but they didn't seem to want to bother with us at all. No one had had a chance to dig in. They passed up a golden opportunity to catch all the troops and supplies pouring in on the one dirt highway. We were getting almost no news of activity in the north with the exception of the fact that the enemy was getting little opposition from the newly activated Philippine Army divisions. Vehicles on the 31st were still getting as far north as San Fernando, and heading south to Manila without obstruction, and Noel decided he would like to spend New Year's Eve with his wife if it was all right with the Major. Of course, I put in my bid too, but the Major put his foot down and said he didn't care about our getting captured so much, but he hated to be left behind to take care of all those troops for the rest of the campaign. He told Noel to take off, but that the Lieutenant would stay right there. And that was that. So Noel took a Sergeant with him.

That evening, the medico from the artillery came over and said quite a few of his friends from the hospital at Ft. Stotsenberg had taken over the district hospital at Balange, about 6 Km. north of us, and asked me to go up there with him and have a drink on the New Year. He had managed to salvage a fifth of scotch. We jeeped up to the hospital just in time to witness a flight of dive-bombers give the nearby civilian's barrio a going over. Within fifteen minutes they began bringing in the casualties. It seemed they would never stop. Within a few minutes the treatment rooms and corridors were filled to overflowing, with mostly women and children who had been squatting by their nipa shacks, as is the custom and were caught in the strafing fire. Only two soldiers were hit, walking down the road. A rather unpleasant way to begin the New Year. There were the first civilian casualties we had seen and it just didn't seem fair. They all appeared stunned, helpless, extremely quiet, frightened. After the Stotsenberg staff had assisted the civilian doctors with the emergency treatment we went out in the patio and in the bright, clear moonlight, tried to get a news broadcast from a shortwave radio. No luck.

Some of the Stotsenburg boys had been at Clark Field for the first big raid and we compared notes. They said our fortresses were liked up like ducks on a pond and that's just the way the Nips hit 'em. It must have hurt to see those beautiful four motor jobs destroyed. It hurt just to hear about it. We didn't even wait for moonlight to see the New Year in, but headed back for our bivouac area and comfortable litter. 1942 arrived along with orders for us to move back to km. 162. Noel hadn't returned, but we had to move back without him. There we found all Air corps personnel were going to be organized into provisional Air Corps infantry regiments. This was a blow as we had heard all trained Air Corps would be evacuated to Australia.

Every man was issued a rifle. Most of the Air Corps personnel hadn't felt a rifle for ten or fifteen years, having been employed as plain clothes radio men, coaches, and highly trained technical men. To get them back in the swing, the men were taken down to the booths and permitted to fire five rounds. I went down and fired a Gerand rifle, and also let go of my 45. That just about knocked me over.

We were assured that our provisional regiment was being formed only as a reserve, and there would be no question of our taking any frontlines position because of our inexperience. Colonel Richardson was put in command, and as soon as this happened everyone recalled all the scatterbrain stories they had ever heard about him. The stories weren't very encouraging; one had the very uncomfortable feeling that our new leader, an Air Corps officer with no infantry experience, was under the delusion that he had the unexpected opportunity to be a new Napoleon. This was very shortly confirmed when we heard that he had requested our outfit have a chance to "do our stuff." We didn't even have time to voice our chagrin before we found ourselves moving up. How far up we were going we didn't know. A meeting of the officers was called. We were informed that our troops would form a reserve line at Auregon Tuamado 36, and dig in. The advance position at this time was at Abuki, about 15 kilometers north.

On the 2nd of January we moved south to kilometer 163. On the 3rd, Noel showed up. They had had quite a time in Manila. Early on the 1st of January they heard the Nips coming in from Paranaki, so they lit out for San Fernando and Bataan. But they soon found that our demolition crews had been at work and all bridges were out over the Pasib River. Noel thought the Nips were too close to take his car back to his wife, so they abandoned it, and found a Filipino with a *banta* to bring them down the east coast to Keela . The man would only go at night and it was necessary to hole in the rest of the day under the cover of one of the grand bizas. But he made it without further incident. The civilians in Manila, he said, were just about frantic. They didn't know whether to flee to the suburbs or stay, or to board up their homes or leave them open. I could well understand.

It was about the 6th of January when we began organizing our provisional regiment with troops from both Clark field and Mikets field. Only two battalions with four squadrons in each, a skinny regiment. We had received orders to take a reserve position at Orea, another went to Colonel Bill Kennard, senior flight surgeon in the islands, and said, "Say Bill, I never liked the infantry, and if it's all right with you, I'll stick around Cabcaban field and help out. If there was anyone they could stand behind, it was Major Morehouse. He had been a flight surgeon for years and years. When Kennard asked Morehouse if he wanted to stay, the Major replied that he would stay with his troops. Since we had no infantry equipment, the material squadrons took their 50 caliber machine guns from the wrecked P-40's and welded them to tripods, rigging up a good twin fifty machine gun. In fact, when we had our lines set up with all these heavy caliber machine guns, there was more firepower than any infantry outfit. Just before we took up our reserve positions, Colonel Brady, from the 31st Infantry came over and gave us an orientation talk on stringing barbed wire, crossfire, control, digging fox holes, and tank defense with homemade Molotov cocktails. But I will say one thing: he had an eager audience, as we could hear the artillery booming just north of us. The point he stressed most was a properly dug foxhole, wide enough only to couch in a deep enough so that a man could cover his head. He described a four-hour artillery barrage, which the battalion had gone through the day before by the Nips against the third battalion of the 31st regiment. The only man hurt was one who had left his foxhole.

Three or four times in the next week we were alerted to move up. Each time it was a false alarm. Finally it came. Colonel Richardson himself got the word. A whole Filipino division on the left flank of the 31st Infantry had disappeared, and the Nips were already filtering through. We would move out at ten that night—where, no one knew except that it was north, and no one seemed to have too much enthusiasm for this move except the Colonel. We moved up in stops and starts all night, to the accompaniment of intermittent shellfire, until we were quite sure that we had reached Lindian on the other side of the line. This was the first visible night of artillery we had seen, and it was quite a spectacle. Shortly before dawn, the road petered out and the men had to carry the machine gun tripods and ammunition thru a 40 mile trail in the jungle. Dawn found us crossing the Abo Abo River, and still no contact with our main line of resistance. About this time our staff convinced the colonel we should hollow out and wait in Olos a bit. While this was taking place, the men cut a road through the brush so our vehicles could come up, and we took a very indefinite position in this area. Here we stayed for three days and nights, and it was truly a madhouse. We were never sure where the enemy was, or where our own troops were. Someone would start shooting and in a few moments there would be fire coming in all directions. The Nips would fly over at night dropping firecrackers from the planes, which sounded just like machine gun fire, but no one in our group had yet seen an enemy troop.

We finally received orders to fall back to our reserve positions at Orion to form a new main line of resistance, so the other troops could fall back. The whole left flank had collapsed. The Japanese had managed to cut a path through the mountain jungle on our left and were bringing up artillery, which would have an unobstructed fire down on our main line at Golanga. The only bright ray in this gloomy picture was the assignment of Colonel B, infantry officer of the 31st as our CO now that we had suddenly graduated to front line troops.

Back we went, and filled in our old position. For the next four days and nights troops and supplies strained south by us in a jumble of disarray. Philippine army, 31st infantry, south tracks, tank units, and finally the engineer demolition units. In fact, they brought one tank crew into our aid station the last day that had been caught on the wrong side of the bridge by the demolition boys. Someone got the signals mixed and gave the order to blow her up before our troops were over. The same thing had happened early in the game, near Stossen, and it was necessary to abandon 17 tanks, a crippling blow, equal to the loss of our flying fortresses at Clark field.

It is hard to go back to these days on the line. Our men were called the Provisional Air Corps Regiment. We found ourselves the only American troops on the new line. The light 31st Infantry Regiment had been put in reserve to bolster up any new breaks along the line. We were flanked on both sides by Philippine positions. This was quite an experience. They were even more poorly trained than our men, if that is possible, and their equipment was ludicrous. Their helmets were cardboard, they wore khaki shorts, socks and tennis shoes, actually, and they resembled a company of undeveloped American Boy Scouts, and were about one-fifth as efficient and in most cases as dependable.

As we learned later, the Nips left only a holding force on Luzon and pulled out more of their planes and combat troops to attack Malaya and Singapore. We couldn't understand the lull. Each day three or four dive-bombers would come over and drop a load. By this time we were well dug in and had gained some experience in this sort of thing. We could tell pretty well by the location and height of the plane where their tokens would drop. If they weren't heading for our immediate area we would carry on and watch the festivities. Every day an observation plane would come over for a look. We were sure these planes used a Maytag motor because of the way they sounded. One day one of our men caught a group of Filipino soldiers napping. They were gathered in a clearing dividing a freshly killed animal they had been fortunate enough to catch. They weren't paying any attention to "Joe" as we affectionately referred to our daily call. The observer dropped a small 20-pound fragmentation bomb over the side of the plane, and it struck an adjacent Mango tree. It just about cut those boys to pieces.

Things were fairly quiet until the Japs came back from Singapore. They had managed to keep the bay pretty well blockaded up to this time. A chow was brought up to us from the rear twice a day between artillery barrages. The last few weeks before the capitulation, I computed our rations as varying between 900 and 1000 calories per day. We averaged a one-pound can of salmon for eleven men, which was made in gravy for the rice. In addition, up until close to the end, we were able to get a slice of bread to go with it. The men's weight dropped rapidly after the first six to seven weeks. As things became tougher our sick call became larger. Medicines were more than inadequate. The quinine tablets held out for about six weeks, and then we had to give the men powdered quinine. That was pretty rough.

No one in Bataan was getting prophylactic quinine except those stationed in general hospital Nos.1 and 2 in the rear. Along with the acute malaria, which was becoming quite prevalent, the men were developing dysentery. The combination of the two on a soldier who were getting a thousand calorie diet was lethal. Those men who were able to come back from patrol would come in after a patrol to the outpost line of resistance and report off duty with a temperature of 106. They had only the barest knowledge as to how to take care of themselves on this dangerous type of infantry work, and they knew only the elemental principals. They were ambushed efficiently by Jap patrols and didn't stand a chance of getting back. An aid station of necessity was quite close to the position of our troops, as we had no means of evacuating them any great distance. We had dug a square hole about fourteen feet on side sufficiently deep, so that we could work during shelling and air attacks. Usually after the festivities, we were able to hold our sick parade on deck. About March 12th Major Morehouse received a call direct from Yusaki on Corregidor. He was ordered to report as soon as possible without his equipment to Headquarters on Barock. On the flimsy excuse of trying to get some medical supplies from the depot, I went to the rear with him and went over by boat to Corregidor. We landed at the dock, and General Sutherland was waiting for the Major. He called him Colonel, and told him that McArthur would have lunch with him—Morehouse would have lunch with McArthur the next day at twelve.

We had been on Tumboka Bay for so long we hardly recognized the place. The personnel on Corregidor all wore starched uniforms. One of the medical officers took us in hand and took us into the mess in the hospital area. We sat at the table with regular dishes, sugar and cream on the table, and had all we could eat, including dessert. It seemed like a different world. To complete the picture, we were able to have a hot shower and slept in a hospital bed. The hospital on Corregidor was in a tunnel that was over a hundred feet below ground, so there wasn't much to worry about. I hadn't shaved for almost three months, and so I was sporting a pretty good sized beard and mustache, which I was becoming quite attached to. But the next morning on walking around the hospital and seeing everyone so clean-shaven, I went to the hospital barber and had my face re-exposed. I did manage to save myself a small mustache in the deal.

My uniform, having been washed in the river over the past three months didn't quite come up to the hospital staff dress, but I think they understood the situation pretty well. They even had a commissary still going on Corregidor, where one could get cigarettes, Hershey bars, candy, and chewing gum. Before I left the line I had to promise that I would buy all the cigarettes

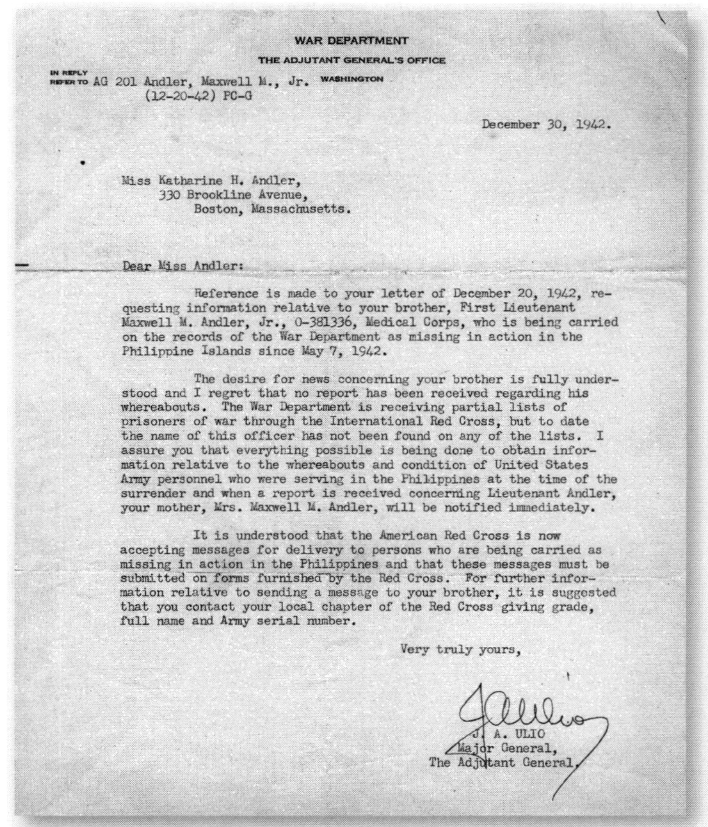

WAR DEPARTMENT
THE ADJUTANT GENERAL'S OFFICE
WASHINGTON

IN REPLY REFER TO AG 201 Andler, Maxwell M., Jr.
(12-20-42) PC-G

December 30, 1942.

Miss Katharine H. Andler,
330 Brookline Avenue,
Boston, Massachusetts.

Dear Miss Andler:

Reference is made to your letter of December 20, 1942, requesting information relative to your brother, First Lieutenant Maxwell M. Andler, Jr., 0-381336, Medical Corps, who is being carried on the records of the War Department as missing in action in the Philippine Islands since May 7, 1942.

The desire for news concerning your brother is fully understood and I regret that no report has been received regarding his whereabouts. The War Department is receiving partial lists of prisoners of war through the International Red Cross, but to date the name of this officer has not been found on any of the lists. I assure you that everything possible is being done to obtain information relative to the whereabouts and condition of United States Army personnel who were serving in the Philippines at the time of the surrender and when a report is received concerning Lieutenant Andler, your mother, Mrs. Maxwell M. Andler, will be notified immediately.

It is understood that the American Red Cross is now accepting messages for delivery to persons who are being carried as missing in action in the Philippines and that these messages must be submitted on forms furnished by the Red Cross. For further information relative to sending a message to your brother, it is suggested that you contact your local chapter of the Red Cross giving grade, full name and Army serial number.

Very truly yours,

J. A. ULIO
Major General,
The Adjutant General.

I could get, so I managed to purchase a carton for each one of the boys back at Orion. Colonel Morehouse told me that he had been instructed to find a tie because everyone who sat at General McArthur's table was supposed to be in correct uniform. After lunch, he saw me and said that he had orders that were top secret and he couldn't tell me what they were. But he could say that he was going to do what the birds did in the winter. Even I could figure out that he was going to fly south with McArthur. For the two weeks prior to this, rumors around Bataan had been that McArthur was going south to Australia. This apparently confirmed it. Colonel Morehouse asked me for my family's address and said if it were at all possible he would get in touch with them as soon as he could and let them know that I was still okay. I was scheduled to go back to Bataan on the five o'clock boat that night, and how I hated to leave. Before coming to Corregidor, while I wasn't satisfied with my lot on the front line of Bataan, at least I felt everyone else was in the same boat. But to come over here and see people getting all they want to eat, living like human beings with 120 feet of earth above their heads to protect them from any injury, justice just didn't seem to be in evidence.

LETTERS FROM POW CAMP PHILIPPINES

1943

CAMP 3, CABANATUAN *February 17, 1943*

I have just arrived in Camp 3 of Cabanatuan for the second time. Much has happened since I last was able to write. All of us had been getting along extremely well at O'Donnell as a great deal of food had come in from both the British and American Red Cross along with individual Red Cross packages. Christmas time we had more food than we could consume, which had never happened since the war began. About this time we began to hear rumors again of the camp closing, but this had occurred so many times before, and we didn't give them much credence. Filipinos were being released sporadically, and some stories had the American civilians from Manila coming to O'Donnell as soon as the camp was emptied. All of us had received a salary from the Japanese for two months, 20 pesos per month, which helped a great deal as we were able to take advantage of the camp commissary. Colonel Duckworth appointed me commissary officer and we organized a cooperative mess for both the Officers and men. Each day I would place a large order of fruit, eggs, and caraboa for the messes, and in this way we had an excellent mess. But that was too good to last. About the 10th of January, we were informed that the camp would be closed on the 24th, and that we would all go to Cabanatuan except for the two full Colonels who would go to Bilibid prison in Manila prepatory to going to Japan.

There were probably a thousand Filipinos who were not to be released because their homes were in provinces in which gorilla activity was still present, and we heard that they were also to go to Cabantuan, but to Camp 3, while all the American prisoners were concentrated at Camp 1. We didn't know whether we were supposed to go up to three and set up a new hospital for Filipinos or stay at one with the rest of the Americans, but we were moving all our hospital equipment with us. Thirty-nine Officers and seventy-three men left on the 23rd of January, while fifty men and three Officers stayed behind to load all the equipment on the train the next day. O'Donnell Camp was 7 km. from the railroad station at Capas, and while they took our luggage on the trucks, we all marched in carrying our bedding rolls and a bunch of sausages, we pulled up at 7 AM. While Cabanatuan is only about 45 km. directly east of Capas, no railroad goes directly, and it was necessary to go almost all the way into Manila and then return back north, over 160 km., and we arrived at Cabanatuan eleven hours later.

But it was quite a trip. We stopped at every station and when the local Filipinos would see Americans in the boxcars, they would run up to say hello even though there was a Nip guard with us, and some of the children would throw food in to us. At the larger stations we were able to buy anything under the sun from fried chicken to hard-boiled bolutes. The latter is a fertilized egg, almost ready to hatch, and is supposed to be quite a delicacy in ye old Philippines. I wasn't hungry enough for that, but we had plenty of fresh fruit, chicken and other native dishes, which we have learned to appreciate. Temporarily, our Commanding Officer was Major Kallus, but he wasn't feeling too well after the trip, so I took over when we came to the station, and as I knew some of the Nips who met us, made arrangements for our trip to camp. We were informed that our destination was Camp 3. Two trucks were there to take the baggage and those who could not walk, and as soon as they unloaded, would return and pick up the rest, as it was 20 km. to camp. After loading eighteen of the weaker men on the trucks we started hiking without our packs, which wasn't bad at all, and after walking for 1.5 hours, were picked up by the trucks and taken to Camp 3 about 9:30 PM. As we had over a hundred men to feed and take care of, I decided to see the Camp Supply Officer that night even though it was late.

Taking the Mess Officer, Tucker, with me, we went down to the bihay of the Sergeant Major, a Socho, and the first thing he told us was to take off our shoes before we came in. I informed him that I had been the Supply

Officers of General Hospital No. 1 at O'Donnell, and that we need certain things to get started with until our own equipment arrived two days hence. He felt it necessary to call in an interpreter in order to get things straight, but he was quite cooperative, even having his Japanese houseboy, called Tubang, get us some warm tea (without sugar). The next morning, I took a detail down and received all that had been requested. In the same manner we opened our mess and then waited for the others to show up. A visit to the Japanese Camp doctor revealed that he had expected only twenty Officers and fifty men, and he did not understand why so many had come up. Well, that afternoon the Sergeant Major came over and asked me to submit a plan for the hospital area, designating the location of that various departments, wards, living quarters for personnel and the use designed for the many buildings in the area. Well, that had me hustling around and in the midst of it all, patients began turning up. Although we had no equipment except for the individual medical kits that the Officers carried, we informed the Japanese that we would have to open up at least one ward to take care of these sick Filipinos. The next day, Dr. Nagata asked me to make out a master requisition listing all the equipment necessary to set up a General Hospital. That was another real job. We had the heads of each department make out their lists, and then consolidated them all with Capt. Bulfomonte on General Surgery, George Chamberlain on E.E.N.T., Dan Golenternek on Medicine, Pizer on Lab and Pharmacy, Neil Burr on Office, Lt. Whiteneck on electrical equipment and myself compiling the utilities. Oh yes, and that incomparable Tucker for the mess. A really tremendous and imposing list, and then I had to sit down with the Medical Sergeant (Japanese) and try to explain all the terminology so that he could rewrite the list in Japanese.

CAMP 3 *March 14, 1943*

Almost a month later. I simply can't keep up with the way things happen. I keep meaning to write, but there is always something I have to do first. But this is a fine spring morning in the Philippines and we shall see how far I will get. Yesterday I went shopping in Cabanatuan with Kumagami Socho for the fourth time in the past two weeks. In fact, I think I have been out of the camp here more than I have been in. But I will try to keep the continuity and go back to my first stay here. While the rest of our personnel was supposed to arrive two days after us, they were sidetracked at Camp 1, and we went ahead and opened two more wards, handling over 250 patients. We thought we were getting along quite well when I was called up to the Japanese Medical Office at 10:00 AM on the 1st of February and informed that we would all return to Camp 1 at 1:00 O'clock that day, and ten other doctors with thirty corps men would replace us. They had no explanation, but said they were the orders received from Camp 1. That made us feel a bit low, as we had all been working quite hard to set up the hospital. Everyone packed and lined up, waiting for the trucks to take us back about 13 km. Just as we were ready to leave and after we had had our baggage inspected, the Socho said that I would be the only one who would not go, as someone had to stay who knew how to take care of the hospital records and supplies, and I had also signed for all the equipment in the hospital. Well, with everyone else leaving I didn't want to stay, but I didn't have a great deal of choice. The forty new men who arrived had no idea about the running of the hospital as it was all strange to them, so in addition to taking care of the supply, I also worked out the daily statistical records and war medical supplies.

This continued for four full days and had me running around with my tongue hanging out, which precipitated another attack of malaria, a mild one fortunately. On the 4th, Dr. Nagata returned from the Japanese Headquarters in Manila where he had gone to find out about the change, and told me that he was sorry but that I too would have to return to Camp 1, even though he and the Sergeant Major wanted me to stay very badly. He asked me how long it would take for the others to learn how to take care of the office records and supply details. I replied that Officers had been assigned to various departments, and I was quite sure all would be ready for me to leave by the day after tomorrow. He invited me to visit him at his house the night before I left to drink beer with him. You know how little I care for beer, but to be sociable, I managed to do away with a couple of bottles and I spent a pleasant evening discussing Japanese medical training and education. When I told the Socho that I was leaving, he insisted that I would be coming back in a week and told me to leave my footlocker in his storeroom until I returned to save carrying it back and forth. And he promised that he would send it down to me in a week if I didn't return. This arrangement was rather fortunate as the group of our men who went down before I did were pretty badly shaken down. All their footlockers were taken away from them for one thing. Also, all their medicine and any electrical appliances, and some of the boys who had their own personal footlockers felt a bit put out about it.

On returning to Camp 1, I was assigned to the hospital and appointed welfare and morale officer, both job that I thought were rather important. The former had to do with a welfare fund, the money for which came out of all the postal savings books of the field officers. You see, while our Officers were being paid salaries by the Japanese comparable to their own Officers, they actually paid the Field Officers only 25 pesos a month, putting the rest of the money in a Japanese Postal Savings account, and this is theoretically returned to the individual if and when he leaves the Philippines. Company Officers like me receive only 25 pesos a month. Since only Officers and Medical Corpsmen get paid, a large percentage of the enlisted personnel received no pay. American Headquarters requested permission to use some of the money in the postal servings to buy food for those men who received no pay and this was granted, the total coming to about 5,000 pesos a month. Most of this was spent on special food for the welfare patients in the hospital, and I was in charge of distributing it to the various wards and kitchens. For the three hundred odd seriously ill cases there would be about 6,000 eggs a week, tomatoes, bananas, limes and other essential supplementary foods, and this addition to their diets was showing results. The other half of my job entailed the morale of all the patients and personnel in the hospital area, about 2400 people, and that was a large assignment. It included having entertainment programs two times a week in the evening, daily classes in history, music, languages and other subjects.

We also tried to have simple contests with cigarettes as prizes for such things as fly killing, beautifying the area, woodcarving, writing and any other kind of competition that would stimulate their interest. As a whole, the spirit and morale of the patients and men were remarkably good when one considers what they had gone through. I am quite sure that that Red Cross food and supplies were a big factor. A great deal of very needy medicines had also been received. In a very short while I had settled into the routine of the hospital and was very comfortably settled. Within a few days after I arrived, we received our double-decked hospital beds from O'Donnell, and although we were twelve officers in a *bihay,* everyone was quite comfortable. Two weeks had passed since I left Camp 3, and my footlocker still hadn't come down which worried me a little bit as I had most of my possessions in that box. I checked with the ration truck driver from there and he said he would find out about it. A few days later I bumped into the Socho from there and asked him about it. He mumbled something about my going to Camp 3, but I replied that I was sure to stay in Camp 1, and the American Headquarters had verified that there would be no change in the personnel in Camp3. He finally agreed to send it down the next day.

That night we put on a musical program with the camp orchestra and it was the best we ever had. Electric lights had been put up that day, and everything went perfectly. Just as the program finished I was called into the Headquarters office and found quite a few of the Officers from O'Donnell. We were all informed that we would be transferred to Camp 3 the next morning, as the orders had just come through from Japanese Medical Headquarters in Manila. We all really hated to leave as if felt good to be back with Americans again, but again we didn't have any choice. The list included twenty Officers and fifty Corpsmen, and was the original list that had been prepared at Camp O'Donnell by Colonel Duckworth and Dr. Nogi. This moving was getting a bit tiresome, but off we went again and I kept hoping that my footlocker wouldn't pass me on the way. Fortunately it was still there, and apparently Kumagami knew I was coming back and that was why he hadn't sent it down before. February 17 found me back at Camp 3 as Supply Officer.

The Commanding Officer, Lt. Makisima spoke to us on arrival, thanking us for the good care that we have given to the Filipinos at O'Donnell. He also said that we were not soldiers like the prisoners at Camp 1, but members of the International Red Cross, and it was our duty to take care of the sick no matter what their race or color, that being the reason for our assignment to Camp 3. He warned us we should be kind to the Filipinos, but should not attempt to affect them politically since the Philippines were no longer a colony of the US. Then he called for me and told Major Berry that I had been here before and knew all about the camp. So we started off on the right foot.

Well, we went to work, and there was plenty to do. There was a great deal of construction work, as well as labor details, such as digging latrines and sumps, building the kitchen and professional departments, and, of course, the care of the sick, which amounted to about 280 patients. A large portion of these patients were not very sick, and consisted mostly of recurrent malarias. All the prisoners in the camp were brought up from the southern Islands, and had not gone through the brutal starvation period of the Bataan campaign. In fact, we have had only two deaths to date, one, epidemic meningitis, the other a malaria complicated by intestinal parasites and scurvy. We have been here about a month now, and everything has progressed much better than we could have expected. The Supply Sergeant, who was a Civil Engineer in civilian life, and has the rank of Master Sergeant, has been more than cooperative. To me personally, he has been very accommodating. As far as request for material and supplies for the hospital, he has given us every single thing that I have requested, as long as I was able to show him what we were going to use it for. As a result, we have been able to construct and organize a good general hospital in a fairly short time. When we first arrived, our kitchen consisted only of a Sawalli roof. Since then, we have built walls, tin-covered sinks and drains, lights, three stone cauldron ovens, and Sgt. Kumagami brought us two G.I. stoves from the Japanese supply in Camp 1. And down at Camp 1, they still don't have a single G.I. stove in any of the American kitchens. At the present time, we are putting in sheet tin on the ceiling, walls and floor of surgery to make it dust proof. In fact, in the time we have been here, we have been able to get a score of things that the Americans at Camp 1 have been trying to get for almost a year.

CAMP 3 *March 21, 1943*

Have only recently returned from Manila, and still haven't entirely recovered from the trip. During the last month I have been very fortunate. The Socho has been taking me down to Camp 1 any time I needed to go.

And as we have to use the Camp 1 commissary, I arranged with him for our commissary Officer, Captain Burr, to go down there on the ration truck every Monday, which gives us pretty good contact with Camp 1. And I have been able to visit neighboring towns in the area for various and sundry reasons. As long as I had a purpose, I could go with him.

One morning, I went to Bongobon with him to get some calimensi for a scurvy patient, and when they didn't have any, we turned around and went directly into Cabanatuan to get some there. He took me into a Chinese restaurant for lunch, and it was the first time that I had been in a restaurant since the war began over a year ago. It is very odd every time I walk around in a Filipino town, the whole populace stares. The little kids run all around me and I feel like a one-man show.

They all seem friendly, but hold back because of my company. One time in the market, even though a Japanese guard was with me, one Filipino insisted on giving me a cookie, and I was afraid he would get into trouble. These trips have helped a great deal to break the monotony of the camp, and I have been able to get things such as toothpaste, shoelaces, and other things for the command that we weren't able to get from the commissary. Last week the Socho said that he was going to Manila by train to get some parts for the camp water pump. I told him that I would like very much to go so that I could get my eyes refracted for a new pair of glasses as I had been getting headaches from close work. He referred me to Dr. Nagata, the camp doctor, and said he would be glad to take me if the doctor gave me permission to go. Major Berry asked him, and he in turn went to the Camp Commander. Then they called me in to say they were going to let me go, as long as I was going with the Socho, of whom the CO thinks very highly. I was to stay at Bilibid and have my eyes refracted there. Well, I was getting a little excited about that time, especially when the train left at 5:30 AM in the morning. I was afraid of oversleeping, and woke at 2:30 and stayed awake until we left at 4:30 AM. Cabanatuan is over 20 Km. from the camp, and we rode in the command car. That also was an experience that I hadn't had since the capitulation. All I took with me was my mosquito net, towel, and toothbrush. The train was a small, wood-burning engine with sparks flying back all the time. As per usual, all Filipino trains were jammed, and we stopped at everyone's backyard. It didn't get light until after seven o'clock, and from then on at every stop, a score of little Filipinos would run up and down by the train window selling all manner of edibles and things I considered not edibles.

A tall Filipino padre was sitting close by me, and when we stopped at one of the stations, he offered to give me some money so I could but something, but I gestured to him not to do it, as the Japanese would be very angry with him. Although it was only a little over a 100 km., it took us until 9:00 to reach Manila. I wasn't quite sure what we would be able to do in Manila, but the first item on the program was a calesa trip to the Japanese Headquarters. We went thru downtown and Taft Ave, and it was quite an enlightening ride. One is quite out in the open, riding in a calesa, and as soon as one person on the sidewalk or street would see me, he would nudge the person next to him to look at the American. Very few autos were on the streets; either Japanese Army vehicles, or long, sleek black civilian limousines, sheltering rich pro-Nipponese Filipinos. I was hoping very much to see the Werffs, but HQ very definitely told the Sergeant that I would go directly to Bilibid and stay there until we left. But we did stop for lunch first, and it was the second time that I had been in a restaurant since the war began. Before the war, Bilibid had been a prison, and since the capitulation it has been the only military concentration camp in Manila. The greater part of it is hospital, run by the Navy Canacoa staff that remained behind when the Usaffe forces retreated to Bataan, so they have been captured since the 2nd of January.

I stayed there for a day, only as Kumagami was ready to return to camp on the 4:30 train the next day. Both Colonel Duckworth and Colonel Shock were still there, not having yet been sent to Japan, and they insisted on my eating with them. Although the issue food wasn't very good, the commissary at Bilibid supplied just about anything one could pay for, and I dined very well. I saw a good many people there that I hadn't seen since the end of the war, including Max Pohlman, an ENT man from the county hospital. I had my eyes refracted by Dr. Clyde Welch of the navy staff, who said he could only find a quarter diopter correction in either eye, and he thought my headaches much be caused by the strong sun, so he ordered me a number two Crooks lens. He then telephoned my prescription down to a Filipino optometrist, and they said the glasses would be ready before I left.

Just as Kumagami called for me the next afternoon at 3:30 PM, the lady brought my glasses into the office. Dr. Waterous told me not to worry about paying for them, as he would take care of it, which was fine. Well, I went to get my things together and when I returned to the office, I found Sgt. Kumagami paying the lady 32 1/2 pesos for my glasses. This was an unexpected turn of affairs, and I tried to tell him that I didn't want him to pay for them, as I would rather pay a little at a time from my salary. But he told me not to worry, that I could pay him back the same way. There wasn't much that I could do but take the glasses. I spent most of the trip on the way back explaining how I would not have had to pay for the glasses, and finally convinced him that I should write a letter to Dr. Waterous explaining what had happened, and that he could probably be able to send me back the money. The sergeant was trying to be so kind and helpful. I had a few things I wanted to do while in Manila, and as I wasn't able to get around, he told me to give him a list of the things I wanted, and he would try to get them for me. He did get a razor blade sharpener, an elastic supporter for my knee, and a volleyball. I also asked for some second hand American magazines for us to read, and he tried to get those too, but apparently they aren't permitted to sell them anymore, and instead he got me some books approved by the Japanese Military Administration that he thought the boys would like. Among them was Gulliver's Travels and Little Men, and I thanked him very much for being so thoughtful.

I hated to leave Manila, but I considered myself quite fortunate to have been able to go at all. We reached Cabanatuan at 9:00 PM that evening, and although we had been gone less than forty-eight hours, I felt like I had been gone weeks. Since then, little unusual has happened. I suppose that we are as comfortable here as we could be any place and still be prisoners. About two weeks ago, we were able to send a second postcard home, and I crammed anything I could on the back of the typed form. I don't even know whether the first one ever got through. We get little news about the progress of the war and have no idea how much longer we will remain in the present situation. At Camp 1, rumor has it strong that all healthy American POW's will leave for Japan within the next two weeks. How much truth there is to this, and whether they will take any Medics with them it is hard to say. As far as the Filipino camp is concerned, I think there are only about 750 in the camp here, including the Hospital. Groups have been sent out on various labor details, and no one knows whether more guerillas will be brought here or not. This territory is a hot bed for guerilla activity, with quite a bit of commotion centering around Laur last week. I think some Japanese casualties were received, but things have settled down again for a while.

CAMP 3 *March 26, 1943*

The hot season is with us in earnest. In spite of the mountain breezes, the sun is prostrating. Yesterday they had some Filipino entertainment come from Manila, sponsored by the Chaplain's Aide Association, but it was so sweltering out there that no one enjoyed it. We have moving pictures twice a month now, but mostly Japanese propaganda is shown. They did show a Laurel and Hardy picture last month, which wasn't more than ten years old. But we enjoyed it.

CAMP 3 *March 29. 1943*

Here comes another week, and I can see no hope of it being a great deal different from the past weeks. Now that most of the construction and organization of the hospital has been completed, our routine has settled down to rather a monotonous grind which keeps me restless all the time. Yesterday we spent the best part of the day playing volleyball, and the rest of the time I used planting onions. Each one of us has a little plot of ground behind the barracks, one growing tomatoes, another peanuts, and a few nursing along some papaya trees. Our camp population has dropped to approximately 700. Groups have been sent out to work as labor details on civilian Japanese projects, and although a few guerillas have been brought in, the strength is much less than the opening of the camp. Down at Camp 1, rumor has it that there is still strong guerilla activity in various parts of Luzon which ties in with the excitement we have had in the surrounding barrios here. I have tried to review some of my medicine, but it is oh so difficult to keep interested in what I read when I haven't any idea when I will get back into medicine. I have been a Supply Officer for so long now, that I will probably come home and open a grocery store instead of a medical office. I have just finished reading *Gone with the Wind* for the second time, and last week I reread *The Patriot*, which I enjoyed much more than the first time I read it. I think that I have a much clearer understanding of the Japanese people now than when I first read the book. Reading material is at a premium here, and that is why I tried to get some secondhand magazines from Manila.

CAMP 3 *Friday, April 2, 1943*

Down in the dumps again, and if it holds on much longer my chin will be scraping the ground. I can't understand it either, except that I don't have enough to keep me busy. About 125 guerillas were brought in from Pampanga and some of them had some pretty rough treatment. One man had a wet gangrene of his right hand and forearm, from having had his hands tied behind his back for two or three days. It was necessary to amputate above the elbow. His left hand wasn't as bad as we may still be able to save it. Little else has happened besides it raining for the first time today, and since that is most likely a precursor of the much-dreaded rainy season we must see to our nipa roofs. I was so hoping that we would be all through with this business by another rainy season, but I am afraid not. The way I feel now, I had better not write anymore, or I'll have my hair down.

CAMP 3 *Monday, April 12, 1943*

Here comes another week with the same routine. Went down to Camp 1 last week, and everyone is upset about the general exodus to Japanese territory. One list of 1000 was already made up, and told to wait in readiness to leave at any time, and rumor had it that another 3000 would be leaving within the next six weeks. That would leave only the sick and hospital unit, which would probably be moved to Manila before the rainy season. I was moved up here just in time to miss the detail. Nine doctors are being sent, and all are men who were with us at O'Donnell. I am quite sure that if I had remained, my name would probably have been on the list. On the other hand, if we are eventually going to wind up in a prison camp in Japan, now would probably be the best time to go, I should judge. We have no idea how long this Filipino camp will stay open. I suppose that it would be best for our unit if it stayed open indefinitely, but I am getting so tired of it that almost any change would be welcome. We really are quite fortunate here in our location, in that we have springs and mattresses, showers, and fairly good kitchen facilities.

In fact, yesterday the Socho took me out with a detail, and we located eight barrels of cement so that we could cement the kitchen floor in readiness for the rainy season. He has been a real friend to us all. We have started a cooperative mess here, with all the detachment putting in one half of their salary. With this, we have been buying supplementary foods from the commissary to go with the issue food and the Socho has been instrumental in getting us some things that we couldn't get through the main commissary at Camp 1. He likes hot cakes, and the other day I made up a batch for him that really came out good. Of course he had to supply all the ingredients, but they couldn't have turned out too badly, with five eggs, a can of evaporated milk, wheat flour, and plenty of sugar. Milk sells at the pretty sum of one peso fifty, and that is quite a few centavos. Better get to work now.

CAMP 3 *April 21, 1943, Wednesday morning*

The rains have come! Everyone insists that the rainy season won't begin for another two months, but when I see a deluge every day lasting for an hour or more, that's convincing enough for me. Our buildings with nipa roofs are standing up quite well and I only hope our shoes will do the same. We all wear wooden shoes or skivvies a great deal of the time to save our leather ones for the future. I am still fairly well fixed since I salvaged some shoes down on Bataan after the capitulation. The 9th of April marked the year's completion of our captivity, and for the first time these conditions are getting almost more than we can stand. It really isn't so bad, except that it is difficult to keep our minds occupied. Last week we began to take lessons in Nippongo to try and make the days a bit shorter.

I find myself at odd times of the day, and before I fall asleep at night, thinking back to my experiences at home and in Los Angeles. Last Saturday, the Women's Federation from Manila brought some of their junior leaders from Manila down here to put on a show for the Filipinos. The President is Mrs. Escoda, whom I know. While the girls are made up of the nicest of Filipino society in Manila, some of them I met before the Red White and Blue balls that I attended. While most of the songs and entertainment was in Tagalog, they sang a few American songs that the girls said were dedicated to us. We aren't supposed to talk to any Filipinos except the ones we take care of in the hospital. But the next morning, they all managed to come down to the hospital area for Mass, so I was able to see them all. Incidentally, they have done a great deal for me when I was at O'Donnell. These same people run a Filipino commissary for the prisoners here three times a week, but the Americans are not allowed to use it. I am the one who takes the prisoners over, so I get to see them fairly frequently. Our hospital unit is the only group of Americans who have any contact at all with any of the Filipinos in the Islands, since we are running this hospital in the Filipino prison camp. In Camp 1, large signs are up saying, "do not speak to the Filipinos," and no one does. We have been taking care of them since last July 5th, when we first came to O'Donnell and while we started with over 5500 sick there and over 100 dying daily, we have only 130 patients here, and a death is quite unusual. In fact, in the two and half months that we have been here, there have not been more than five deaths.

Last week we had an interesting case that did die. The patient, a 24-year-old Filipino, came into the hospital more than a month ago complaining of a pain in the right lower quadrant. He was examined by the surgeons and placed under observation. He felt better shortly, but over a period of a month he had recurrent attacks of abdominal pain, none very severe, and lasting for a fairly short time. Four days ago the ward surgeon questioned him, and as he felt fine, was scheduled to be discharged that afternoon. When the ward man came to get him, he found the patient vomiting. He was put back to bed and examined completely. His abdomen was completely negative as was his neurological. During the examination, the patient appeared to be voluntarily unresponsive, and the medicos felt that he was malingering so as not to have to leave the hospital. He did not vomit again, and although examined each two hours, no positive findings were elicited. At 9:00 the ward man reported that the patient was dead. During his stay in the hospital, his recurrent malaria had improved, his beri beri had cleared up, and he had put on weight. We received permission to do a post-mortem, and the only two findings were an enlarged thymus, and an enlarged old splenic infarct. With my job as supply officer, I don't get to see much medicine, but a case like that gets one to thinking again. It even stimulated me to read a little medicine.

CAMP 3, BOGABON, P.I. *April 25, 1943, Easter*

Easter morn! And I think that we will break out our Easter bonnet on the main thoroughfare of Camp 3, Bogabon, P.I. We celebrated a bit early due to circumstances. A truck was going into Cabanatuan yesterday morning, so I arranged to have them get us 20 kilos of caribou meat, so that we'd have a big dinner, and I think everyone had as much as they could eat last night. Usually, we are fortunate to get a single chunk of meat in the stew. We have been buying eight-ounce cans of native corned beef, at 90 centavos a can, for the mess, but that is awfully expensive. Let me briefly explain our mess arrangements. All medical personnel received a monthly salary from the Japanese, and, incidentally, I am the pay officer in addition to my other duties. A Major receives 25 pesos a month, Junior Officers get 20, sergeants and corporals 10, and privates only 6 pesos a month. We have organized a cooperative mess where everyone puts in half his salary and we supplement the issue food with foodstuff purchased from the commissary. The trouble with this is the commissary does not carry any fresh meat, and that is the thing we need most. But as usual, my ever-present contact has come through to help us with sugar, milk, cocoa, camotes, and now fresh caraboa for Easter. At eighty centavos a kilo, it helps no end.

This morning we had hot cakes made from rice flour, which weren't bad at all. Yesterday we had a fruit salad, made up of fresh pineapple, papaya, mango, banana and cincamas. The latter I think is a cross between a sugar beet and a turnip, the result tasting something like an apple. Such a combination makes quite a dent in our monetary reserve and can be indulged in only on rare occasions. The other night we had a treat. Twice a month we have a movie program. For the last two months it has consisted of newsreels in Japanese and Japanese propaganda films. Very boring indeed. When we were told the other night, the 22nd to be exact, that there was another program we were sure that it would be unintelligible again, but as there was little else to do most of us decided to walk up to the stage. We were more than pleasantly surprised to run into an all-American program consisting of a Terry Toon cartoon, a short on midget racing and a 20th Century Fox picture with Lynn Bari called *They Go Fast.* It was a good class B film but we couldn't have enjoyed more if it had been an epic. Just to see American streets, American people, hear American music was like a tonic. Every American girl in the picture looked like a beauty.

It's going to be a wonderful sensation to get back home. That's all we talk about. We wonder how much change we will find. There shouldn't be a great change in the autos since they stopped making them just a short time after we left the States. I like to think of that long grey Buick of mine. I hope you still have it and I am very thankful that I wasn't able to bring it over here with me. Everyone that did have a car here lost it. Are you able to use it? We have heard about gasoline and rubber restrictions that must have affected civilian personnel and their cars rather seriously. How about Albert? I wish I knew he was safe. I am quite sure that he is also in the Army by now, but I have no idea where he could be. American soldiers are all over the world now and I suppose he could be in a dozen different places. We all wonder whether our people know about us being alive here in the Philippines. Although we have sent two postcards, I don't have much faith in them. I still don't understand why we aren't permitted to receive or send letters home. In any respectable prison camp, POW's are supposed to be able to write twice a week. That will be the day...when our mail boat comes in. I'll expect at least a hundred letters...

CAMP 3 *April 29, 1943, Emperor's birthday*

Today is the Emperor's birthday and so the Nips are making quite a day of it. They are giving their soldiers a regular banquet and as they don't have any G.I. stoves in their kitchen, they have been roasting chickens in our two stoves ever since yesterday afternoon. The chief cook gave me a small one yesterday, which certainly tasted good. This morning they are down cooking omelets and fish. They also issue beer, peanuts, mangos, bananas and cigarettes to their garrison. They haven't said anything about making this issue to us so I assume they don't expect us to celebrate with them. Last night I was able to listen to some popular recordings from Shanghai and they certainly make me nostalgic. Especially when they played *Oh, Daddy*. I think those songs bring one closer to home than almost anything else as they bring to mind places we have been and good times we have had associated with those melodies.

In the evenings we usually get together and try to second-guess the Allied strategists and Roosevelt as to what their plans are. Some feel that the European front will have to be completely finished before the U.S. will begin a major offensive in the Southwest Pacific. Others feel a second front in Europe and an offensive here will be launched simultaneously. A review of the present status reveals that our major offensive effort is now in North Africa, and we are only carrying on a holding action in the Southwest Pacific. I feel that our present strategy includes the immediate capture of Rommel and his forces with the subsequent establishment of heavily supplied embarkment ports all along the coast of North Africa, meanwhile carrying on a constant bombardment of all possible invasion ports on the south coast of France and Italy.

At the same time the west coast of France will be battered in preparation for invasion from England. At the opportune time, tying in with the Russian offensive, a concerted invasion attempt will be made on all available coastal ports from Dunkirk on the west around to the western border of Italy. This would probably consist of ten or twelve spearheads, and future action would depend on where the weakness should be found. In these areas the initial attack will be followed up by heavy invasion forces, which should be sufficiently well-reinforced to accomplish their objective: a successful invasion of the continent.

Such an attempt must of necessity spread the Nazi defense too thin to be effective, and I think the end result of such an attempt would be a speedy end to Nazi resistance. Once the European front is decided, I don't expect the Southwest Pacific to continue for more than 90 days. The release of Russian force along the undivided attack of the Allied nations should be more than sufficient to convince the opposition of the futility of further conflict. All this is probably only wishful thinking on my part, but I will be very curious to see how close this comes to the final story. I would be more than willing to admit I was wrong if it would hasten the finish of this business. That the Russians have finished their winter offensive and are still managing to carry offensive action against the Germans I think is quite significant. Almost the first of May, and the Nazi Juggernaut in not under way. I hope the Russians can keep it up...

CAMP 3 *May 12, 1943*

The above seems a bit prophetic now. From what we can learn, both Bizerta and Tunis have fallen. Big news! And we hear also Russia is still forcing, forcing, forcing, and driving the Nazis out of their last stronghold in the Caucasians, the Kuban Bridgehead. Germany can't let down for a moment on this active front, and now she must consider a wide flung defense of both coasts of France. While we have heard many rumors, some much more optimistic than the news from Africa, we all feel that this is authentic. The *Manila Tribune* of two days ago is supposed to have admitted it. The Allies apparently have a tremendous force there, more than well supported by air superiority, which is essential, a lesson we learned so costly here in the Philippines.

The newspaper mentioned that British fighter planes and pilots had been released from the African theatre to assist in the defense of Australia, and the Nips claim that their pilots were able to shoot down over forty of these seasoned pilots without losing a single Wild Eagle. Remarkable, eh! We shall see, we shall see...We haven't been paid for this month yet. For some reason, they had insufficient money at Camp 1 for the payroll and we may possibly get the money today. If they call from down there, I will go down with the Socho to get the payroll for our 70 Americans here as I am the Pay Officer. Even though we haven't received our money, we have been able to get things from the commissary, so it hasn't bothered us a great deal.

K. has managed to help us a great deal again by getting us some supplies at the need of the mess at much cheaper prices than we would have been able to get through the commissary.

About once a week we get things from Cabanatuan that we couldn't get through the commissary at all. While I was down at Camp 1 about three weeks ago, I heard that Captain Kirk had come in to camp, and was resting in the guardhouse. On inquiry I found that he had been the CO of an American detachment at Clark Field for more than a year, and getting along very well, until one of the Americans decided to escape. For a while they toyed with the idea of exterminating old Weldon for this breach of faith, as it were, but after being tied up for a while, they sent him to Camp 1 with a 20-day sentence. I wasn't able to see him the first time, except through the wooden bars, but he looked awfully thin so I sent him down some canned stuff with Neil Burr when he went down with the commissary order the next day. I saw him the other day after he had been released and he looked a bit better.

Before the war, as you recall, we lived together at Nichols Field and all during the fracas on Bataan, I was the Medical Officer for his squadron. He will probably remain at Camp 1 until they send a detail out. Here at Camp 3 there is little new. They began a new training program for the Filipinos the day before yesterday, and I think they take three or six weeks. Tomorrow evening we have another movie that I hope will be another American film, and the 15th the Women's Federation is going to have another program. Captain Makasima asked me if we had any Americans who could sing on the program. I replied that we did, and that I would check with Major Berry. The arrangements have been made, and we are going to have a quartet of the corpsmen do a few numbers. That should be quite a program. The other day one of our patients was found over on the camp side playing tennis at 6:30 PM while the rest of the camp and the Nips were having their evening Bango. So now, everyone in the hospital including the Medical Officers must stand Bango at 6:30 morning and night. It makes the mornings quite long. And last night I sat up until after 1:00 AM reading *Anthony Adverse*. Harvey Allen has a power of description, which can only be described as bountiful and lush. Any other readings seem flat and bare after it. I don't

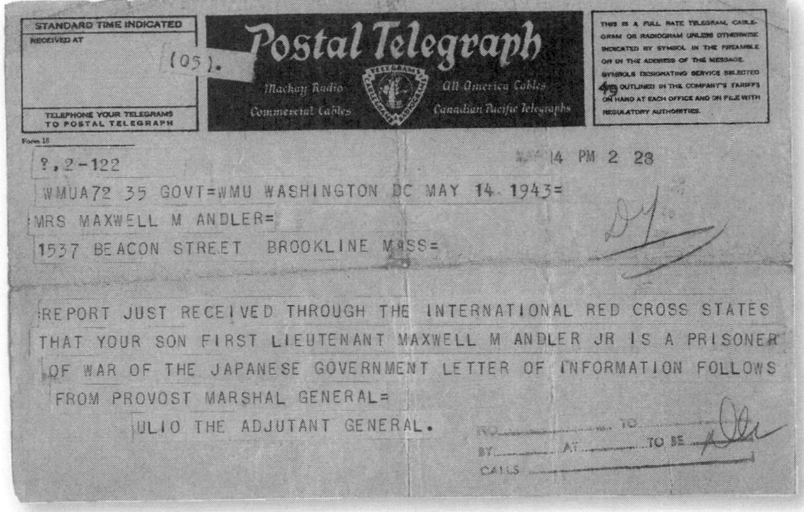
STANDARD TIME INDICATED
RECEIVED AT
TELEPHONE YOUR TELEGRAMS TO POSTAL TELEGRAPH

Postal Telegraph

Mackay Radio — All America Cables
Commercial Cables — Canadian Pacific Telegraphs

THIS IS A FULL RATE TELEGRAM, CABLEGRAM OR RADIOGRAM UNLESS OTHERWISE INDICATED BY SYMBOL IN THE PREAMBLE OR IN THE ADDRESS OF THE MESSAGE. SYMBOLS DESIGNATING SERVICE SELECTED ARE OUTLINED IN THE COMPANY'S TARIFFS ON HAND AT EACH OFFICE AND ON FILE WITH REGULATORY AUTHORITIES.

(05).

?,2-122 14 PM 2 28

WMUA72 35 GOVT=WMU WASHINGTON DC MAY 14 1943=

MRS MAXWELL M ANDLER=

1537 BEACON STREET BROOKLINE MASS=

REPORT JUST RECEIVED THROUGH THE INTERNATIONAL RED CROSS STATES THAT YOUR SON FIRST LIEUTENANT MAXWELL M ANDLER JR IS A PRISONER OF WAR OF THE JAPANESE GOVERNMENT LETTER OF INFORMATION FOLLOWS FROM PROVOST MARSHAL GENERAL=

ULIO THE ADJUTANT GENERAL.

know why I am rushing through it when one of the big things I have is time, but I hate to put it down. Well, back to the prosaic business of working out the daily menu in grams, calories, and vitamins.

CAMP 3 *Saturday afternoon, May 22, 1943, 3:00 PM*

Three o'clock...recall an hour away...time to add a few lines. Last week, the 14th, the girls from the Federation with the Escodas put on their show in the evening, and I wasn't able to get very close to them. But the next morning, while I was up at the supply office, they all drove up in their little bus to get some gasoline. I managed to go down to the garage with K, and so was able to say hello to everyone, including the Escodas. We couldn't say very much, but it was good even to talk with someone whom I knew before the war began, an era that seems years and years ago. The 9th of May, the conclusion of my second year in the army passed without my realizing it. I received quite a few things from the Werffs the other day, including milk, sardines, peanut butter, potted meat and other delicacies. I also heard something from Alice Sanders, whom I have never met, but I was able to help her husband in Camp 1. She was very appreciative of it.

I had a bad time of it a few days ago. After finishing three strenuous games of volleyball, I jumped rope for a while. Then I went into the barracks, and bent over my bed to pick something up, something caught in my back, which felt like a sharp knife, and I couldn't straighten out. Instead of working out in a few minutes the pain persisted, and I was unable to change my position without experiencing a stabbing pain. They put wooden planks under my mattress, which helped a good deal. I about went mad for two days and nights. Then I finally took a gram of codeine and 1½ grains of Nembutal so I could get some rest. I woke eight hours later without a twinge. It was miraculous. I haven't had a bit of trouble since, but I am plenty careful.

CAMP 3 *Thursday, May 27, 1943*

Back still O.K. In fact, I have been playing volleyball again, with no recurrence. I still keep my fingers crossed. I suppose one shouldn't talk about hot weather in the Philippines, but I can't help it. The heat envelops one like a blanket, which can't be pushed aside. While it rains for a short time each day, the torrid feeling is relieved only momentarily. The old adage of a two-year hitch in the tropics being sufficient receives enthusiastic support from me. I think I have already mentioned that all twenty of the officers stay in a single long barracks, and as a result live quite intimately.

We have a good crew here and manage to get along extremely well, considering the circumstances. Our CO is Major Berry, a regular Army Officer who has done a fine job up here. He has kept the organization working together, gets along very well with the Japanese HQ, and is very pleasant to live with. The rest of us are Captains and First Lieutenants. We have one Navy Officer with us, Lt. Fraligh, a dentist, who is our chief construction man. I get him the materials and then he manages to do wonders with it. He is detachment Commander and with his 50 picked enlisted men, has built us a fine general hospital. Captain Hudgins is our dentist who keeps busy all the time, one of the hardest workers in the place. Captain Bulfamonte is Chief of Surgery, and since we have built a dustproof surgery completely lined with tin, he has done a fair amount of major surgery, along with some elective work on the command, such as herniorraphies and a simple mastectomy for a recurrent cyst. Captain Pat Omeyla is in charge of the admitting room and out patient clinic, which keeps busy most of the morning. Lt. Jack Gordon, a little tyke from Iowa, is his assistant. Dan, Captain Golenternek,the O.B. resident from the L.A. County, is chief of the Medical Service, he is a good man in whatever he does. We now have only four wards open as our patient count has dropped. Our ward surgeons include Captain Al Poweleit, Lt. Kelly, Smith, DeBacker and Palermo, all conscientious men. Lt. George Chamberlain is our ENT man, and he has kept busy with many T. & A's along with a daily clinic. Charlie Armstrong, also a Lieutenant, is in charge of the laboratory and that takes pretty well care of the professional assignments. Lt. Brown was helping Bulfamonte in surgery, but since he has had his tonsils out he has taken over the commissary and Capt. Neil Burr is working in surgery. He still goes to Camp 1 every Monday to straighten out our commissaries. Capt. LeMire leads the Administrative staff as Adjutant and Lt. Perilman is his assistant. Lt. Tucker is mess Officer, and he has been doing an excellent job ever since he began at O'Donnell. Now that we have our cooperative mess he has a big job on his hands.

I have been taking care of General Supply and this includes everything under the sun that anyone may want. Colonel Duckworth and Major Berry picked this group of Officers to come up here from O'Donnell to set up a new hospital and I think they made a good balanced choice. As to how long we remain here, no one knows. Their training program is just about finished for this group, and I think another three week course begins on the 10th of June. After that, more guerillas may be brought in or the camp may close. If the latter occurs, we have made certain conclusions as to our next destination. Some think we may go down to Los Banos and set up a hospital for the crippled Filipino veterans who are located down there. Others feel we may do the same thing for the American Nationals who have been moved to Los Banos from Santa Tomas.

There is also talk of our going to Davoa to set up for the American prison camp down there. And, of course, we can always go back to Camp 1, our last choice. Why don't we want to go back there? For many reasons. First, they now have more medical officers and corpsmen than they need and we would have nothing to do...a very serious situation. Their patient count at the hospital has dropped to 1200 from over 2000. Then the camp is too big and as a result it is very difficult to get anything constructive done. Here if we need anything I just go up and see Sergeant Kumagami and explain what we want to do, and that's all there is to it. Capt. Lemire went to Manila a couple of days ago with Dr. Nagata to see Dr. Noga and he may bring us back a little more information...the news has been more that scarce. Down at Camp 1 the other day the scuttle had American troops landing on Atuta Island from the opposite sides and driving the Nips out of prepared positions. They were also supposed to have captured an airport two thirds completed. Who knows?

Another story has us putting out planes three times as big as a B-17 with a cruising range of 10,000 miles. That sounds like a real dream, but one can't tell. We have been gone almost two years now and there must have been many advances in military aviation. They can't advance too fast for me. In fact, we have been waiting for an American advance now for over a year. We have just finished another postcard home. I keep saying the same thing, as I don't know whether you have ever received any of them. I wonder how much longer it will be before they permit us to get mail. Another rumor at Camp 1 had 1500 bags of mail coming in. But down there they make up stories to fit the occasion. That's one I certainly wish were true. I want to know where Red is. I know he can take care of himself, but I think I would be a little less anxious if I knew what he was doing. I hope that Kay has remained in her teaching capacity at the hospital and is now roaming around the world somewhere with a hospital or ambulance unit. I was convinced before I left the States that was no place for a girl, and after seeing what occurred over here, I am doubly convinced of it. A medical soldier can do everything a nurse can do and in the field can usually do it better. I suppose that Kay won't agree to that.... getting tired of saying nothing.... more later.

CAMP 3 *June 9, 1943*

Wednesday afternoon and the heavens have opened. I don't think there is much doubt about the rainy season having arrived. It has been wet almost continually for the past week. It cleared up just long enough this morning for one of the Filipino Social Groups to put on some very fine entertainment. They brought up a young lady referred to as the songbird and Deanna

Durbin of the Philippines, Fely Vallejo, and besides being quite attractive she has a very lovely voice. The rest of the talent was also quite professional and we all appreciated it. It is revealing to see how little it takes to please a group that has been confined for more than fifteen months as prisoners of war. And the thing that would please us most need not be written. We began a bridge tournament a couple of nights ago and somehow I find myself in it. At home I played very little and over here I haven't played at all. But it helps to get by the long evenings so I will try. Last night we have our opponents 700 points because I pulled a prize boner. My partner opened with a two-diamond bid. I wanted to show him that I had a bust so I bid two no trump. He bid three diamonds and instead of passing as I should have, I said three no. Well that threw him off 100%, and he began the Blackwood Convention for slam possibilities, bidding 4 no trump to find out how many aces I had. By this time I was so mixed up I never gave the Blackwood convention a thought and in order to stop the holocaust and put him back in his original suit I screamed five diamonds. He interpreted that as my having one ace and bid five no trumps. That finished me off. I wanted to quit the tournament right there. I said I wouldn't bid any more and passed. Our opponents said I couldn't pass in such a spot and I said I was going to anyway. Fortunately, they doubled and my partner was able to slide into 6 diamonds. W went down four tricks doubled. In spite of that we won two out of three rubbers and went down about 800 points. Very lucky…

CAMP 3 *Monday, June 21, 1943*

My fading memory recalls that today introduces the first day of summer, and as a small indication the sun has consented to peep out of the rain clouds for a short while. We are in the midst of inaugurating a new semester at the Bongabon Educational Institute. For the past three days the Nips have been bringing in a goodly number of guerillas from Ilocussur. It is about time for us to start the rushing season and line up a few pledges. But seriously, I think these new admissions have given the camp a new lease on life. Apparently, the guerrillas have been finding it more difficult to exist in the mountains because of the rationing of rice and food by the National Association. Each individual must call for their own ration or they are investigated and severe hardships have been endured by innocent people because of this. Anyway, quite a few have been turning in and amongst them have been Americans who are taken first to San Fernando and then to Camp 1. We now have here the Governor of Cagayan, one of the northern provinces, and his son. And yesterday they brought in a doctor who did his medical work at the University of Cincinnati, and spend a good part of his life in the States. Yes, we have students from all walks of life. For the past two days the Manila paper has been running over with the momentous news that Japan will grant independence to the Philippines within the next six months. If this independence corresponds to that of Manchukuo and China, I don't think this will bring about a marked change in the status of the Islands. As far as it will affect the American prisoners it is difficult to decide.

I think the Nips would like to get us out of here and safely salted down in Japan, but at present their bottoms are too busy hauling the necessities of war. Even if independence is granted I feel quite sure that Japanese garrisons will remain in the Islands to "assist" in the maintenance of peace and order. In that way, they could keep us right where we are without too much difficulty. News of import has been unusually scarce. In face, we haven't even had a wild rumor of late. Things have come to a pretty pass when there aren't even any rumors floating about. In just about ten days I am going to bump into another birthday and I hate to see it happen. Twenty-nine years will be upon me. That is getting awfully close to thirty, and old age itself. But there isn't' much use of bemoaning the fact since there is very little that I can do about it. I will just keep waiting and hoping like everyone else....

CAMP 3 *Friday, June 25th*

The sun is out in all its splendor which means a steaming hot day for us. The day before yesterday we were informed that General in Command of all Japanese prison camps would make an inspection of our camp yesterday. Well, we primed and spruced and just about dismantled our *bihay* to hide all the *quan* and paraphernalia that we had accumulated. Then we lined up in the hot sun and awaited the inspecting party scheduled at two o'clock. At 3:30 we saw the General leaving without having set foot in our area. So we declared a holiday for the rest of the day.

CAMP 3 *July 1, 1943*

Tomorrow, the 2nd of July, commits me to twenty-nine years of age. I certainly hate to see it happen. It will be my second birthday in the Philippines and I truly believe the last. Latest rumor has the Chinese accomplishing prodigious feats and getting quite close to Nanking. Italy is supposed to be getting a continuous merciless bombing which is driving the people to revolt and necessitating the intervention of Nazi division to preserve axis order. The beginning of '43 would leave us with 100,000 planes. I think the pleasantest rumor has Roosevelt promising that all American prisoners in the Philippines would be returned to the United States by the end of the year because Americans couldn't live more than two years in a tropical prison camp. I am beginning to agree with him. Monday I went down to commissary at Camp 1 as Captain Burr was sick and instead of stopping there we went right on in to Cabanatuan. I hadn't been in there for a couple of months. We went to the Food Control Association to pick up the vegetables for the camp and then over to the Iceplant. I went in the cold storage room for a few minuets and it felt so cool I hated to leave. Also went to the market and I had a chance to snoop around, but there wasn't anything I wanted to get. Took 42 to Camp 1. About ten days before, 38. Altogether, probably 200 which is a goodly amount. Was able to get some horseshoes made which should help a bit. Have just finished a singles and doubles cribbage tournament which also assisted the rainy evenings to sluice by. At the present time I am in one of my depressions. I have just completed a bi-weekly check on all the equipment and three washbasins were missing. Two weeks ago two were missing. I tried to explain that I hadn't eaten them, but explanations don't go very far. I was very close to telling him what he could do with the rest of the basins, but I restrained myself. I will probably feel better tomorrow.

CAMP 3 *July 4th, 1943!*

A very quiet fourth. My birthday slid by just like any other day. I did manage to borrow a phonograph and some American records from K. so we had a concert of American songs that was appreciated by all. The only trouble was the songs just brought back old memories more clearly. Tonight we are going to have a big dinner with plenty of caraboa roast. I asked K to get us 20kg of meat in the market at Cabanatuan along with some onions and camotes this morning, which should make a pretty good supper. It isn't very often that the men can get all the meat they want to at a meal. Went down to Camp 1 yesterday to see about our salary but they hadn't been paid down there yet. Found out that some of our doctors had been sent out on a detail to Bilibid. Three doctors, three dentists and a flight surgeon were needed. There isn't much question that I would have made that one if I had been there. This place looks like it will continue indefinitely, but one never knows. As far as I am concerned each succeeding day couldn't be longer, which is a good solid pessimistic outlook. I am developing a bit of prisonitis. After becoming accustomed to the great open spaces of California this is rather confining. At present we are quite enthused in a large scale garden for our mess. Lt. Fraleigh, Capt. Golenternek and six enlisted men have laid out a large area of onions, camotes, cucumbers and beans, and start work every morning at 6:30. I helped them with a pick and shovel for a half hour but that was enough for me. The blisters haven't gone yet. It rained ten days steadily before we began the thing, but or the past six days we haven't had a good rainstorm. Old man weather is crossing us up. I think Sunday is the hardest day of the week to spend since there is just nothing to do. I get so restless I can't sit still. And that's the way I feel right now so I will continue later....

CAMP 3 *Saturday, July 17, 1943*

I begin to write with renewed hope. Last week one of the Officers, Lt. Tucker, received a letter from home. It was mailed April 30, 1942, only fifteen months to get here, but he was plenty tickled to get it. I used to chafe at the delay of the clipper mail but after two years of waiting with no results, I won't say a word of complaint, no matter what the date of mailing. I spoke a bit prematurely about the absence of Mr. Pluvius. Since then we have had a few cloudbursts that have just about washed the whole garden away, as well as us. *The Manila Tribune* has been quite full of the exploits of the Wild Eagles in recent encounters around the Solomons and New Guinea. After getting through most of the eyewash, we gather that we have taken about four more of the Solomons and are in the process of cleaning up the rest of New Guinea. In Europe there seems to be a confirmation of my predictions made about two months ago. For the past six weeks, the allies have been pouring supplies into all points of embarkation along the coast of N. Africa and now we are just beginning to hear about a mass landing on Sicily.

While *The Manila Tribune* has said little about it as yet, local scuttle has us landing parachute troops, taking airbases, landing a half million men with a fleet of 3,000 vessels, and meeting no resistance. We are also supposed to have taken the city of Messina, closest point to the mainland of Italy itself. In Russia, the Germans were supposed to have started their summer offensive on the 3rd of this month, but in the last ten days have been able to make no advances and in most sectors counter-offensives by the borscht consumers have driven them back as much as a hundred miles. With general reports coming of progress in the China Field of Operations, we might be heralding the long awaited Allied offensive from all sides. Our hospital routine continues unchanged. Another bridge tournament is in progress. I have finally been made a Captain—of the Officers' volleyball team, no less—and we all have a difficult time keeping the days filled. For the past week my gastric mechanism has been on the fritz, with a G.I. history typical of a G.I. tract neoplasm. But I will probably be back to a full mess kit of rice three times a day very soon. I haven't said much about eating rice as the main part of our diet, every meal every day for the past eighteen months. For breakfast we have just rice and sugar called lugao because it is wet. Also tea without sugar. Lunch we have a mess kit of boiled rice with either a meat stew or vegetable stew. Supper is pretty much like lunch, only more rice. It really isn't as bad as it sounds because we supplement it with commissary things we buy such as duck eggs, fruit, etc.

CAMP 3 *July 27, 1943*

Things are happening…things are happening. Even though the Japanese Military Administration edits the Manila paper, one can follow the trend of the news. The paper of the 22nd is up in arms because of the ruthless bombing of Rome by the Allies. Popes all over the world deplore the barbaric slaughter of defenseless civilians. How easy it is for them to forget the not so distant bombing of English cities, with the destruction of churches, homes, whole districts. Hitler and Il Duce have just had a hurried conference thought to be concerned with the recent landing of Allied troops on Sicily and the activity on the Russian front. In the Pacific Southwest, the paper ridicules the idea that the Allies have taken Java already and warns the Filipinos that they shouldn't get the wrong idea about the advance of the Americans in the Solomons. They wouldn't affect the general picture. Locally, efforts at Independence have been hindered by a wave of banditry in Manila whereby influential Filipino citizens who have been cooperating with the present administration, have been assassinated. The editorial department of the paper warns that if this attitude persists, the Nipponese may not grant independence. At Camp 1 a 500 man American detail has just left for Japan. The 1000 man detail scheduled to leave more than two months ago never did. Again there is talk of sending all the healthy Americans to Japan, leaving only the amebi cases. How this will affect our unit it is difficult to say. Here at Camp, they are about to wind up another three-week training period for the Filipinos. Next month no training is scheduled, but there will be another three-week period in September. That keeps the camp open at least another two months. Our reading material has been exhausted. There is just nothing left to read which leaves much too much time to think. The first and biggest mental problem—how much longer will this last? Months or years? And when it is over...then what? Three, maybe four years older, can I still go back and consider the plan of study begun before the war...three or four years work in an institution, tied down, no salary, no home life, not to disregard the possible difficulties in getting back into a good residency. What alternative? General practice? I fear few of us are qualified as a G.P. without at least a year's institutional work to dust off the cerebral convolutions, hoping there is no residual atrophy from disuse. Probably it is much better for our peace of mind not to look so far ahead permitting the future to develop unmolested as destined, but after the many years of conditioning in cerebrating, it isn't possible to keep the mind a pleasant blank...

CAMP 3 *August 8, 1943*

That last paragraph appears almost pathological now. How did I ever get to looking so far ahead? Had better cut that out. Much better to go from day to day. The day following the recently mentioned conclave between the Duce and Hitler, the former resigned in Italy and the King Emanuel has taken over with complete clean house. The Allies have offered them terms of surrender that have been refused but the pot boils. Latest reports have just about the whole of Sicily in anti-axis hands with the exception of Messina. Rommel has been sent down to make over command of the German troops in the Balkans…in anticipation of a second front. The bears are still pushing, hardest in the southern area, with great possibilities in the offing. In the southwest Pacific the paper tells us that a great battle is taking place at Munda Bay, the outcome of which should decide the fate of the whole Solomon group. We are certainly beginning to push from the south and appear to have plenty of stuff to push with. I have been fortunate. Last week Major Berry asked if I would like to assist in General Surgery in addition to my other duties to sort of get my hand back in it again. I, of course, replied in the affirmative and it has been quite enjoyable. I will probably be in surgery for two or three months and that will help some. It is alarming to see how much of my surgical technique has slipped away from me. It makes me feel like a medical student again.

The food situation is becoming a bit acute again. While the regular ration has fallen off in regard to vegetables because of the season, the commissary has also taken quite a drop. No fruit has come in for almost a month and prices of other articles are going up steadily. Canned food of any kind has become prohibitive. The worst thing has been the eggs. When we first came here they were as low as ten centavos apiece. Last week they were 20 and yesterday the bill was 25 per egg. Since my stomach has been upset for almost a month, eggs are about the only thing that I have felt like eating, but if the price continues to rise I will have to get over it. I haven't yet been able to find out what's wrong with my G.I. system, but it gets no better. I had a complete blood study, which was essentially normal, and repeated stool examinations have not shown anything positive. I am a little afraid that I might have amebic, but so far the laboratory says no. The only good thing about it is that I am losing a pound a day, and I can afford to do that for a while longer....

CAMP 3 *August 19, 1943*

Little more than a month and Sicily is supposed to be ours. I hope the paper confirms that. That puts the boot in a shaky position. The tempo is increasing steadily. This is evident on all fronts. Here at Camp 3 there is supposed to be one more training period next month. After that we don't know what will happen. Most probably we will go back to Camp 1 and we are not looking forward to that. But other things may develop to change the present plans and we may stay here a great deal longer. I am feeling much better...beginning to eat rice again. I suppose it will put back the weight I lost in no time. My mornings have been more occupied since the first with surgery. We have been limited so far to herniotomy and rectal surgery with some circumcisions, but at least I am getting to feel a bit more comfortable with a pair of gloves on and a suture in my hand. Evenings we have all been playing a fair amount of bridge. I had played very little before winding up here, but I am learning a bit about contract now.

It has been so long since I have received a letter that I have lost the drive to write one. There just doesn't seem to be anything of interest to write about. The life in a concentration camp is not conducive to occurrences of interest. The days are pretty well stereotyped. The bell for bango rings at 6:30 AM It is awfully hard to wake up, but we roll out and count off. Some go back to sleep until breakfast at 7:30. Others like myself try in vain to sleep, then get up to shave and wash. Breakfast, without variation, consists of lugao with sugar and salt and tea. Of late I have been plunging and having an egg because I haven't been able to eat rice. Our day's work begins at 8:30 AM and everyone is supposed to be at his or her place of business by then. I usually go over to surgery to do the dressings and no matter how low I am, they are over in half an hour. I then manage to take care of any supply business well within an hour and as a retreat isn't until 11:30 I have 1.5 hours to mutilate. This can become a very difficult task with reading material as scarce as it is. At retreat we have a half hour to lunch, which we utilize by lying down and discussing various phases about anything in the whole wide world. After lunch, which usually consists of rice, tea and a vegetable such as corn, greens, or *gabi,* we have until 2:00 o'clock to siesta. When the bell rings to go back to work, it is just about as difficult to get up as it was for morning *bango*. Back to work until four. But what to do?

Since I have been assigned to surgery I can go back and forth from the supply building and that puts a few kinks in the afternoon. Retreat rings a four and we are officially through work for the day. Supper at five, with delicious rice, and if an odd day, then carabao meat; if an even day, one can never tell. Today for lunch we had camote greens, something like turnip tops and tonight we will have eggplant. Also rice bread. *Bango* again at 6:30, and we can bathe before or after. And then we have lights in the office until ten o'clock where everyone usually gathers for bridge or checkers. You can see how in 16 or 17 months such a regime can become a bit tedious. But I am sure that once we get back home it will all be very easily forgotten. That is what I am looking forward to with a great deal of pleasure.

CAMP 3 *August 28, 1943*

Just two years ago today I arrived in the Philippines on the USAT Cleveland. Not a day to celebrate, but we did nevertheless. We have six officers who came over on the Cleveland and this morning we had a bit of a commemoratory breakfast to mark the passing of the day. Quite different from our usual repast of lugao and tea. The meal consisted of hotcakes made with rice flour, good coffee with cream and sugar, an omelet, and fried bananas. Oh yes, syrup on the hotcakes. I still feel a bit stuffed. Gastronomically speaking yesterday was also a big day. We butchered the proverbial calf, which in this case happened to be a carabao calf we bought through the commissary at 33 centavos a kilo on the hoof, and as he came to over 150 kilos, the meat ration was more than ample. Two hamburgers for lunch, a large order of roast carabao for supper, and scraps in the rice for lunch today. That is more meat than we get in a regular week's ration. My weight was down to 190 three days ago, but I fear I will be putting it back on rapidly if we can manage to get more meat.

But to get back to our little reunion. Those present included Joe Bulfamonte, that old desert fighter whom I am now assisting in surgery, George Chamberlain, Pat Cmeyla, Neil Burr, Harry Brown and yours truly. We are all looking forward to a future get together in the States when we can look back on this occasion only as a pleasant memory. We all expressed the wish that we would not be here for another anniversary of the same event. There are quite a number of officers who came over with us on the Cleveland who were killed during the Bataan campaign or have died from disease since then. All of us here feel quite fortunate that we have been able to come through as well as we have to date.

Last week Captain Makashima came down and informed us that we would have to consolidate our positions as 400 Nips were moving into the adjacent area and would need four of our buildings. The only rub was both the buildings that we were living in were included in this area, but at least we aren't moving to Camp 1, so we got right to work to fix up the new buildings that we are to move into. It was necessary to get permission to change the plumbing, dig a new latrine, and also try to get wiring in the new building, and I think we will be able to swing the whole deal. We were also led to understand that we would be here until the end of this year, which is longer that I expected. Don't know how it will be to have the opposition as such close neighbors, but I think we will get along alright as long as we keep away from them whenever possible.

CAMP 3 *September 5, 1943*

Sunday afternoon, and we are waiting for an inspection party which will include Dr. Nogi from Manila. We have had quite a bit of excitement these past few days. Three days ago, on the 2nd, we were paid our monthly salary. As there was an error, I arranged to go down to Camp 1 that afternoon. A few minutes before lunch Major Berry informed us that he had just been ordered to send twenty-four men and twelve officers back to Camp 1. This was depressing news as we are all better off up here at Camp 3, and we had just finished rearranging ourselves. And every time we have to move it means losing a part of our belongings. While I was gone during the afternoon, the Major picked the men who would stay with the exception of one

Officer, and when I returned he told me that Capt. Burr and I would draw to see who remained. I drew first and the slip said go, so that took care of that. Down at Camp 1 they told me that an 800 man permanent detail was being picked, in all probability to go to Japan. It looked like we would get down there just in time to make the detail, which didn't make us feel any better. All the boys started packing right away, but as we would not know when we were leaving until Capt. Makashima returned from Manila I decided to wait. I would have quite a bit of cleaning up to do, as all the supply would have to be turned over to another officer who was remaining. The thought of leaving here made me feel a bit blue as I was one of the first to come here and helped set the place up. But there isn't much one can do about it when one received an order in the Army. I felt the same way when I was ordered over here. Last night Capt. Makashima returned and the Major saw him this morning. He then came back and told us that Makashima wanted us all to stay right here and he was going to do everything he could to keep us here. It was just like a reprieve from the Governor. And if Dr. Nogi is satisfied with his inspection this afternoon, I think we will have a very good chance of staying here for a while longer. We are certainly keeping our respective fingers crossed, especially since there is talk of another training period in November. Yesterday we heard the long awaited announcement regarding the project of putting a hole in the toe of the boot, but more of that at a propitious time.

CAMP 3 *September 21, 1943*

Since our last contribution we have been told to go and stay three different times…to Camp 1, I mean. At present we think we will go within a week, but have no definite word as yet. I don't care if we never get the word. The longer we stay here the closer to the end of the affair. It has been almost three weeks since we first received notice about leaving. Dr. Nagata still says to be ready to go at any time, but I haven't yet turned over the supplies. One thing we are a bit worried about: up here we have been fortunate enough to have beds and mattresses, quite a luxury in these times. I have been hoping that we will be able to take the mattresses with us to Camp 1 when we do go as the bamboo is very hard; but I don't know whether we will be able to swing it or not.

This past month the commissary supplies have been awfully slim and along with a slim issue ration our chow has fallen off a good deal. What with our intended move, the mess hasn't purchased anything, so all in all, we are just about ripe for another round of Red Cross food. We received the previous load just before Christmas, and I never expected then to be looking forward to the same thing almost a year later.

The local paper is quite interesting. In relating the surrender of the traitor, Bagdolio, to the Allies, it expounds the good fortune of the Axis in getting rid of a cancerous growth like the Italians. One doesn't know whether the Duce is going to try to rally another group around the Fascist banner or not. The Storm Troopers are alleged to have rescued him from the clutches of an International court-martial at the hands of the allies. The Nazis are putting up stiff resistance in southern Italy, but I can't see how they will be able to hold their positions for any length of time. The whole business is pretty well mixed up and we probably won't get the straight of it for a number of weeks. The big thing is there is one less axis in the axis. The Russians are apparently still pushing, having taken Briansk, and also area on the Black Sea. I got a bit huffy in the barracks last night and wagered a few of the boys at ten to one that the whole war would be over by this coming New Year's. I didn't want those boys discouraging me.

Tonight I am looking forward to rice hotcakes for supper. It is quite an affair. First the rice must be pounded into coarse flour in a large wooden mortar and pestle that we have constructed. Then...with a few dashes of almost nothing we have hotcakes. Either we use one egg, or a small amount of evaporated milk to hold the stuff together, a little sugar and baking powder. And of course, they are delicious. At least they taste awfully good now. These last few days I have been sprouting mongo beans and after three days, frying them up with rice. Almost like fried rice on Tyler Street. Our ration today consisted of rice and tea for breakfast, rice, tea and camote leaves for lunch, and rice, stringbeans and tea for supper. It figures out to about 2100 calories, including the 40 grams of sugar, which we are very fortunate to get. Utilizing 500 grams of rice, almost 1800 calories are included there, but

I still have plenty of reserve to go on. And, too, I have good friends, which I will say more about later. I heard from Freddie and he gave me a hundred, as well as E. who sent me 50. That makes a lot of difference with an egg costing 26 centavos.

CAMP 3 *Tuesday, September 28, 1943*

The evening before the day before we go to Camp 1, Captain Makashima informed us that we would go down there on the 30th. And I think this time we have really received the word. Tomorrow General Morimoto, he who is in command of prison camps, will make an inspection of this camp. Such an announcement causes quite a rumpus in our regular routine. For some reasons whenever a general inspection is expected, everything must be hidden. There must be nothing on or under the bed, on the shelf or hanging on the wall. Over a period of months all sorts of articles tend to accumulate, such as *quan chans,* clothes, shoes, bananas, an egg or two, toilet articles and such. Each finds a place to which it becomes accustomed. Then the order to prepare for inspection. Everything, no matter what, must be put up on the bamboo catwalk running down the center of the building. This cannot be seen from below and so much bears the brunt of just about everything we all have except the beds themselves. When the barracks is finally ready for inspection, it appears like a vacant building…but very neat. It couldn't' be otherwise…there's nothing in it. And to cap it all off, the General probably won't even get down here for inspection at all tomorrow. He hasn't for the last two scheduled appearances. But he may fool us this time. As soon as he completes his visit I will get busy and turn over the supplies and equipment to Major Berry who will have to take care of this job along with many others. As things stand, we will get to take our mattresses with us. A break indeed. Especially as I understand we will not be assigned to the hospital in Camp 1 as they have sufficient personnel already.

By the by, before I go any further, I have a complaint to lodge with the family in general. Yesterday quite a few of the Officers received radiograms from their families, and my name was not included in the list. I can't understand that. The one good thing about it is that their messages mentioned that our postcards that we have been sending out periodically are getting back to the States. I really do understand that the only reason why I haven't heard from you as yet is because of the inadequate mail service. I expect to get a flock of mail one of these days. These radiograms were received in Tokyo in June and July so it took three months to get them from there to here. For the past five months I have been ordering a duck on each weekly commissary order, but I was never able to get on and had just about given up. Last week I not only received one, but two, and they were four pesos a can. Last spring they had been a peso. But since a 12-ounce can of corned beef has skyrocketed to nine pesos a can, I figured that the price of ducks wasn't so bad. I annihilated one of them for lunch yesterday along with a couple of friends, and it was certainly a treat. We stuffed the bird with rice, flavored with a bit of onion, and then roasted the whole business. Very nice indeed. The second one will follow tomorrow probably unless someone changed the plans...again. If we don't go, I will let him get a little fatter around here. But I am inclined to think his number is up. I think that that I will go down to Camp 1 tomorrow and straighten out a few things. First of all I will tell the Finance Office that part of us will be down there for our next payday on the 1st of the month. Also our commissary order will have to be separated and not sent up here to Camp 3. And I may be able to get some information as to where in Camp 1 we will be assigned. This may well be the last entry that I will be able to make for many a day. The last news that we have describes the Germans falling back to Naples, the Russians still driving, and the SWP, Burma and China fronts gradually showing progress....

CAMP 1 *October 10, 1943*

Camp No. 1! We have been here for 10 long, long days and what days. As before at Camp 3, we were informed on the 29th our leaving would be delayed another two days. So bright and early on the morning of the 30th, I went up to HQ to check up on our supplies. While I was fooling around up there Neil Burr came steaming up to tell me that we must be ready to leave for Camp 1 within 2 hours. That didn't give me much time, as I had never gotten around to packing. Fortunately I had turned over all the supplies and records to Major Berry the day before just in case. It didn't really take me long to toss my things into a barracks bag and by 11 AM we were all lined up on the road waiting for Capt. Makashima to go through the formalities of a Japanese farewell. He mentioned that he had tried his best to keep us there but Manila HQ gave him no choice. On the other side of the camp a Filipino band was rehearsing and as we piled on to the truck they broke in to *Auld Lang Syne, Aloha,* and finally *Don't Give Up The Ship.* A lump filled my throat for the next 15 minutes. It made us feel close to home for just a moment.

All the officers had their mattresses with them, but a rude shock awaited us at Camp 1. Our mattresses were confiscated along with our extra blankets, shoes, and medicines. The EM lost their mosquito nets, all their clothes except what they had on and just about everything else. At the conclusion of this little ceremony we were assigned to different barracks in the camp area.

CAMP 1 *November 3, 1943*

There isn't much use in trying to keep this up to date. For one thing there is no typewriter or convenient place to work it is difficult to write more than a few lines at a time. I have made many transfers since I stumbled into this camp, the last one being from the hospital staff to general farm duty, on the camp side. That was four days ago, and I fear that it is a permanent move.

When we first came down here a little more than a month ago we were all listed as casuals and assigned to general duty which means any kind of manual labor. The Nips said that no more medical personnel could be added to the hospital staff which left us out in the cold. As a casual officer on the camp side we would be available at all times to make up 100 man labor battalions. On previous visits to Camp 1, while I was still supply officer at Camp 3, I had made frequent contacts with Col. Schwartz the CO of the hospital at Camp 1. I used to bring down many of the notes, medicines, and funds of personnel of Camp 1 to him for distribution and so he knew all about our work with the Federation girls and Escodas in regard to the supplies coming up from Manila through Camp 3. He met me the 1st of Oct. while we were lining up for our pay at American HQ and mentioned that he had requested my transfer to the hospital but didn't know whether the Nips would agree. I didn't' know how much good that would do either, but I was hoping.

The following day I was initiated into the ways of massaging a hoe handle. Quite an experience! Incidentally, I have learned the sweetest sounding word in the Japanese language, "*YASUMAY!*" If I never hear any other word, I will be more than satisfied. It means "rest" in the broad sense of the word. When a work detail is cancelled for any reason it results in a *yasumay* day. Likewise on Friday, the Nips have their weekly holiday, which gives us one too, and Friday is referred to as *yasumay*. The only catch is that Sunday is just like any other day of the week—we work. My first job with a small clubby group of 99 other men was hoeing on the farm. One man—one row. I was fortunate in that I worked only a half-day, but that was enough. My back was broken, my hands blistered, my clothes filthy, and mentally I felt just as badly. Just about this time an unusual request came through from the American work detail office. All men with a presentable khaki uniform were told to report to Japanese HQ. We found out that a Japanese picture company was filming a drama, *Down with the Stars and Stripes,* and they were going to use American prisoners to make some of the battle scenes. Just like that I became a Japanese actor. The director was a graduate of USC, a Mr. Abbe who had worked in the studios of Hollywood for 15 years. The main theme of the story seemed to be the brutal treatment of the Filipinos by the American soldiers.

This man Abbe was very decent to the Americans. The picture company had brought up a lot of props including American uniforms, shoes, leggings, and musette bags. Abbe had the men whenever possible, leave their old tattered clothes and keep the good equipment that he had brought up. Quite a difference from our local brigands, who hadn't been exposed to the U.S. for 15 years.

Two days later I found myself again one of a 100-man detail—general duty. This time my specialized type of work consisted of carrying boulders weight about 25 lbs back and forth to help build a road in the camp. Very stimulating work! But when things seemed darkest my reprieve came through in that I was ordered to report to duty in the hospital that afternoon. It seemed too good to be true. One the camp side, I was sleeping, or trying to sleep on the bamboo slats along with two others in a bay 72 inches wide, trying to bathe out of a canteen cup, having no place to keep my gear and all in all an extremely uncomfortable situation. On the hospital side I was assigned to quarters with double beds in a wooden building with shelves, space to walk around and most important, a shower. Shades of Camp 3. Chamberlain, Bulfamonte, and Golenternek also moved down with me. But this was too good to last. We had been there less than one week when Nip HQ ordered Col. Schwartz to discharge 500 patients from the hospital to duty and cut the medical staff from 86 to 31 officers. This didn't sound possible but the Nips were still running the show and that's all there was to it. Two days later Officers Call blew and we gathered to hear the announcement of who the 31 medical officers would be to remain. The majority of the officers had originally been at hospital 1 before the war, and then at hospital 2 on Bataan before coming to Cabanatuan. As I had been with the organization less than a week I was quite sure that I would be one of the first men crossed off the list and I was quite resigned to the fact that I would be right back on the farm. I was truly astounded to hear my name included with the 31 to remain. I am quite sure that everyone else was surprised as I.

I was assigned to Ward 3 as ward surgeon, a dysentery ward for seriously ill cases with 75 men. It felt good to be working with patients again. But this was too good to last too. One week later a new order. 240 more patients must be discharged to duty plus 7 medical officers. I spent 3 full days sifting over my patients trying to find the 23 men bet fitted to stand the grueling work on the camp side. When I turned my list into the hospital office I was informed that I would be leaving with them. Sad news indeed! That explains how I moved up to barracks 37, Group 1 with the rest of the casual medics. I reported up here on the 31st of Oct. and strange as it may seem, I have worked less than ½ a day in the past 11. Either it has rained, it has been a Japanese holiday or a Japanese funeral, have contrived to cancel the work detail. As a result rumors run rife. They include the camp closing, our sailing to Japan, and our going to one of a dozen different places on the Island. In fact, the roster of all the casual medical officers who were not amoebics was made up including their specialties and experience. This immediately started off some new rumors. The medics were going, the medics were staying and everyone else was going. The medics were being sent to Australia, the medics to Japan to work in civilian provincial hospitals, and the upshot will probably be…nothing. Personally, I feel that they have found some use for us and they will let us know about when they are damn good and ready. Until they do I am afraid that I will be available for general duty on the farm. Thinking about going to Japan gives rise to many possibilities and queries. How will we go, when, what will we do when we get there, our final destination and most important, the chow? With this vegetable farm here we are probably getting better chow than we could get anywhere else while a prisoner of war. Last week I volunteered for a local detail, destination unknown, but the Nips asked for a Captain which, cut me out, and Bulfamonte went instead. I understand that he will probably be at Corregidor taking care of a work detail there.

CAMP I *November 7, 1943*

The charm finally broke yesterday and I went out on the corral detail. Most of the day I spent planning Johnston grass, which consisted of wielding a pick. The remainder of the afternoon we did what always has to be done around a corral, cleaning up. I really appreciated my canteen cup bath when we finally returned. I hope my blisters will heal before we go out tomorrow.

CAMP I *November 11, 1943*

Armistice Day. We can see no sign of one in this fracas; in fact we are looking forward to more intensive action. Yesterday I put in a full day's work as a carpenter. We began an hour early and we quit an hour late because the Nips wanted the work finished that day. In the middle of my endeavors, while on a ladder, I fell out of a window backwards, landing none too gently on my head. Nothing broken but I was badly shaken up. The Nip sergeant in charge of the detail was a softie—he let me rest for 15 minutes.

General Moremoto, the joker in charge of all prison camps in the Philippines, inspected the camp the day before yesterday, which necessitated the usual routine of hiding everything in sight. Also, everyone on the farm had to go barefooted to show the general they weren't bruising the tender little plants with our shoes. The big news of the camp arrived yesterday when American HQ was notified to clean out a warehouse for the purpose of storing Xmas packages. Momentous news! There is supposed to be a good deal of shoes and clothes, which will certainly be appreciated. Most of the camp is in fairly good shape, under the circumstances, with the exception of vitamin deficiencies, which are beginning to develop again. The packages will have arrived just in time.

I haven't mentioned the patient who escaped from the psychopathic ward about a week after I was transferred to the hospital. He was an attempted suicide and managed to slip away just as they let the psycho patients out for the morning *bango* (check-up, roll-call). Since the inception of the camp, the men have been divided into shooting squads of 10 by order of the Japanese. If a man escapes, or attempts to escape, the other nine men in his squad plus his barracks commander, are supposed to be shot—a very unpleasant policy. This doesn't apply to psycho patients fortunately. The man couldn't be located in or around the camp. The Americans on duty at the time were put in the brig indefinitely.

Eight days later while a group was out working in the camote section of the farm, the patient was found laying on the ground gnawing on a raw camote. He was stuporous and one of the men notified the Nip guard. It was necessary for him to be carried in on a litter. From here on the story reverts to rumor. Some say he died before they could shoot him; another story had him pistoled in the back of the head. Whatever the outcome, he has attained his wish—to die. Some feel that the present small details laboring on the farm are due to the escape of this man since they haven't enough guards to watch us. I don't know the true reason for all the *yasumay* but whatever it is I like it.

CAMP I *November 14, 1943*

Almost time for supper, and we have just finished up *quanning* up a salad, slice banana, shredded coconut, and a little brown sugar—a tasty bit to wind up the evening meal of rice and camote leaves. I feel that I have gained at least 10 lbs. since I have been down here at Camp 1. Apparently this manual labor agrees with me. This afternoon I was initiated into the complex machinations of the camp library. It is run on a cooperative basis. One must first turn in a book to receive a library card. For newcomers like myself who have no books, books belonging to men who have gone out on details can be purchased and donated to the library. Price 50 cents. This sounded like a pretty good arrangement to me, so I went down to buy one. One of the assistants said that I could buy *He Walks by Night*. Fine. I paid the 50 centavos and requested the book. The clerk said he was sorry but the book was out and I would have to apply for it at the reserve desk, where I noticed quite a long line. Twenty minutes later another clerk informed me at the reserve desk that I would have to pick another book, as there were too many reservations for this one. Another minute wait brought me to the card catalogue. Since a sign said that not more than two books could be reserved at one time I finally found two that I thought would be interesting and gave the clerk the two code numbers. He proceeded to point to a small sign on a table with many numbers thereon which said, "the books listed below cannot be reserved." Closer inspection revealed that the list included both my numbers. I turned back to the card catalogue, took one look at the line waiting, and gave up, a beaten man, leaving with a brand new library card, the owner of a new book but nothing to read.

CAMP I *December 4, 1943*

Many things to hash over again. I have moved again, the fifth time on this camp since arriving two months ago. This time I moved down to the other end, very close to the hospital, but not in it. The past 4 days have seen me marked "Qrs" because of a fine, juicy furuncle on my right cheek. The dispensary medico even thought it serious enough for six grams of sulphathiazol a day. That made me rest a little easier as the furuncle was located in the butterfly area within the boundary of the well-known fatal triangle. One of the boys incised it two days ago and I return to duty this PM, hale, hearty, and unhappy. Our latest work detail has been building a double barbed wire fence completely around the camp, another result of our recent escapee. This detail of course alternates with general farm duty. This is the most disliked assignment in the camp. It is real coolie labor, the men marching out in groups of 100 with one Taiwan guard in charge and every one does the same thing.

The Red Cross shipment has finally arrived and it is certainly a much better package than last year. The greatest news is that there are tons of personal letters and packages waiting to be censored. That is what I am sweating out, as the camp expression puts it. But I haven't mentioned the radiogram from home on Nov 16th. It was received in Tokyo Nov 4th, the most recent message from the States to date. It was from you and told me that you and the family were all well. That was news I was waiting a long time to hear. You also said Kay was married. That was a surprise. I didn't think there was any one left in the States to marry with nine million men in the Army. I certainly hope she is happy and she deserves it. I would like to know who it is.

The Red Cross boxes came in a 47 lb unit, each containing 4 boxes. So far we have received only one small unit, but it has been more than satisfactory. About half the units were marked invalid packages and that is what they issued everyone first. The Nips have to inspect everything and they found that the Old Gold cigarettes had a "V for Victory" on it so they decided to confiscate all the Old Golds from the packages. That still left about 8 packages of Camels and Chesterfields per man. The food contents were much much superior to a year ago, even though smaller in size. I think they are worth enumerating. A lb. can of powdered milk, a lb. of prunes, a can of corned beef, salmon, 3 1/4 lb. cans of butter, a 1/2 lb. of Kraft cheese, 2-4 oz. bars of emergency ration chocolate bars, each 600 calories, 2 cans 1/4 lb. concentrated ham and egg, 2 cans pork loaf, one can of Spam, 1/2 lb. Domino sugar, 2 1/2 lb. tins of soluble coffee, 1 can of Welch grape jam, some pate, 8 portions of bullion, a box of scorbutic acid tablets. We have still 3 more units to be issued, two of them being regular, with more solids and less soft foods. The Nips here decided that we wont' get another until Xmas, then one a month through February. That's probably the best way if this stuff doesn't dwindle down in the interim. So far our slant-eyed friends have appropriated three cases of Lucky Strike cigarettes, three complete shoe repairing outfits, 1000 pairs of shoe-laces, an unknown number of sewing kits, and I don't know what else so far. The supplies included 2600 pairs of very good shoes, a large amount of shoe repair material, and toilet articles, which we all received yesterday.

CAMP 1 *December 15th, 1943*

Wednesday morning and it is my turn to *yasumay*—quite pleasant. We get about 1Đ2 day every four days. Probably the biggest surprise of the week was the arrival of all our hospital personnel from Camp 3 on Sunday morning last. They had been given only on day's notice and they still don't know how or why it happened. Cmeyla moved into our barracks and Hudgins, the dentists, moved into the dysentery area as an amoebic. Right now the big discussion in camp is the distribution of the Red Cross shoes. Everyone who has not received a pair to date is firmly convinced there is the heaviest type of skullduggery afoot. My shoes are in fairly good shape compared to most of the boys, but I would certainly like to swap them or a pair with rubber soles. No more word about mail and parcel post packages but we are still hoping. That will be the day! In the past week they have been issuing the perishable from the remaining boxes so everyone has plenty of cheese, coffee, chocolate, and prunes.

We successfully weathered the Imperial rescript day on Dec 8th and we had a general farm detail that morning, the only place where the guards really get rough. We didn't' get out until after nine and although it was raining, there was no speedo and no casualties—in our group.

The hospital staff and the patient population were cut again and this time Nate Barshop made the grade. He moved in with us yesterday and is out on the farm this morning. I hope he has an easy time of it. Our news is rather scanty and not too reliable. The little we can tell is that we have the Gilbert Is. and are working on the Marshalls from the air. Up to the 12th we had made two heavy air attacks, the first by the navy sea-based planes, working out of 30 carriers and putting 1000 planes in the air in one formation. A second air attack by land based planes presumably from the Gilberts. No information as to results. A meeting of our four power heads at Iran has supposed to have finished in complete accord. A second front in 100 days if Germany is still holding up from the intensive bombing they have been undergoing. Turkey is expected to enter the war very soon. In Italy the Allies are suppose to have battered a heavy defensive line of the Nazis for 9 days with shelling from the sea, land, and air, finally smashing it, and they are now expected to move North with little resistance.

CAMP 1 *Sunday, December 19, 1943*

Our rumor campaign is picking up again. Last PM "a fairly reliable source" had us landing on New Britain, 500,000 landing on Malaya, and mongo beans in the commissary, the last item being the most important if true. *Yasumay* today but all casual medics are to stand by for a check on medicines. The story goes that a Nip guard was found asleep on the duty and is supposed to have received some Nembutal from an American, so—a bit of confiscation. For the past week we have been working on the park detail, which is busy fixing an area in front of Japanese HQ. This is quite close to the commissary kitchen for the Japanese soldiers and we could see them making special things for the Nips such as potato cakes and papaya ice cream. The latter really looked delicious as we were working in the hot sun.

As we lined up at the end of the day to go back into camp someone called me from a nearby *bihay*. I turned and saw the former interpreter from Camp 3 beckoning to me I went over to the house and without saying a word he handed me a cupful of ice cream. Was it good? Just about the most delectable bit of stuff I think I have ever had. It came at just the right time. I hadn't shaved for four days and I looked and felt dirty, hot, and tired. That cup of sweetened sherbet was good!

Last week Harry Levitt purchased a run down garden in our area and the company commander threatened to plow it under if we didn't' weed it. So I think I will get a little extra farming on my *yasumay* day.

CAMP 1 *December 21, 1943*

This should be the first day of winter in any normal country—but not here. Although the nights have been quite cool of late, I am quite sure the temp. hasn't dropped below 70 F.

CAMP 1 *December 25, 1943*

Christmas morning! The carolers are doing their best at the protestant church services close by our barracks. Last night we were shown an American movie after which the mess served coffee and rice flour cake. Catholic mass was scheduled at midnight and as the platform is close to us, most of us stayed up to attend. About eleven, the camp glee club, a fine group went through the area with familiar carols that made one quite blue. The mass did not impress me unduly, and I turned in shortly after twelve. The morning the mess outdid itself, serving stewed prunes, coffee, and sugar on the rice, a real Christmas breakfast. There hasn't been a meat issue from the Japs for more than three months and the piece de resistance from dinner will be baked mongo beans. I think we will *quan* up a prune pie for supper. Yesterday we received a second unit from our Red Cross boxes, unopened this time, and it was quite welcome. Food and nourishment seems to be the prime topic of conversation. We hear through the grapevine that in Manila the prices of foodstuff is rapidly becoming prohibitive, rice at seven pesos a *ganta* sounds unbelievable.

There as been quite a bit of excitement around the camp these past few days. One day last week, out on the wood detail near Camp 3, about 13 km. away, one of the officers on the detail found a note pinned to the woodpile from the guerillas. It said, "Do not trust the 'J!' Escape at once" and was signed by a Lt. in the Philippine Army. One of the Nip guards saw him pick up the note and took it away from him. The Officer has been locked up in the brig and they are convinced that he has been communicating with the guerillas in spite of everything he said to the contrary. Since we have received our Red Cross supplies, Japanese HQ issued an order stating that no RC food or American cigarettes would be sold, traded, or given to any Japanese soldiers or Filipinos under penalty of severe punishment.

Christmas card.

Also no American food or cigarettes or containers would be taken out of the front gate by details working outside the camp. Well, the morning after the incident on the wood detail I was assigned to a detail going outside to cut some sod for the park area we have been working on. They lined us up on the road, and ordered us to put everything we had in our pockets inside our hats. Guards then proceeded to pass along and inspect everyone. Any piece of paper that had writing on it was confiscated. And no blank paper was permitted, even *benjo kami* (toilet paper) as they feared we might write a note to someone. Well, one officer on our detail, Jack Lemire, Colonel Duckworth's adjutant from Little Baguio, pulled out a couple of notes from Santa Tomas without realizing it, and now we don't know what will happen. So far, we haven't heard anything, but that little slip could blow things wide open. If those jokers ever found out about the traffic we have had through the underground, I am sure they would hang us all.

The past two weeks the new RC shoes have been issued. This is being done according to a priority list, first the wood detail, then men working in Jap. Area, utilities, guard, HQ, etc. After these were taken care of, shoes were to be issued to general duty men on a 20% basis in each group. In our barracks of 34 men, 9 men were to get shoes. Well, my shoes were in fairly good shape and although I certainly wanted a pair of those new rubber sold shoes, I reported that my shoes were serviceable on the survey. About a week after, only five men had been fitted, and they had no more small sizes. Well, yesterday when our work group came back to camp after having been shoved around all morning by some unusually irritating guards, Commander George, our barracks leader told me the supply had no shoes left smaller than eleven, and if I reported down there immediately I would be able to draw a pair as they had more than 300 pairs of large sizes. I toed down there and received my shoes. They certainly look like a solid well-built shoe, and my fervent hope is that we never have the opportunity to wearing them out while a POW.

CAMP 1 *December 26th, 1943*

Another day of *yasumay*. We have just returned from signing the monthly payroll and before the vivid impression leaves me I want to tell you about the fine Christmas play we had last night, dramatized by our might Cabanatuan Art players. Lt. Al Manning, USMC. Quite a talented man in camp, adapted Dickens's *Christmas Carol* to fit the situation and did a truly noble job. The scenes Scrooge was taken to see consisted first of a corner in a Japanese POW camp in the Philippines showing three half naked men sitting on the ground eating their ration of moldy rice on Christmas Eve. The next scene was the living room of an American home, with the man of the house having just received a postcard through the International Red Cross from his son in a Philippine prison camp. "Everything was fine, Dad. Feeling fine, chow fine, morale fine. Love to the family. Don't worry." While he is sitting there by the fire, two boyhood friends of his son come in to cheer him up, one in Navy blues and the other in khaki, two of the few uniforms that have been salvaged and nursed through the fracas. That scene brought a tear and a lump in the throat of many a man there including my own. The final scene opened on a merry Senatorial reception in Washington D.C. on a Christmas Eve many years later and those present gave their interpretation of Christmas. One guest had been a POW in the Philippines. The whole thing hit us just right. It was the general opinion that this was the best bit of entertainment that has never been produced in the camp. A fine way to conclude the holiday festivities.

We still haven't received any American mail, and I am getting a bit anxious about it. It will take at least a dozen letters to satisfy me, but I will be tickled to death to get even one. I wonder if they will permit mail from anyone except the immediate family. Our camp commissary is fast becoming an extinct organization. Chicken cost as much as eleven pesos apiece, pomelos were 15 centavos and they are now 65. Peanuts increased from 50 centavos to two pesos a cup; an orange is 40 cents, a cup of mongo beans use to be 80 and is now over two pesos. Our pay is 30 pesos a month but it doesn't go very far with such prices.

A truck has just come in to camp bringing more men from Bilibid, the prison camp in Manila. There are still about 4000 men out of the camp from details in the Islands. Down at Bilibid, the condition are much worse than here because they do not have any farm from which to get vegetables. I think that the farm here has actually been life saving.

LETTERS FROM POW CAMP PHILIPPINES

1944

CAMP 1 *January 1, 1944*

New Year's Day. And that's about all I can say for it. Watching New Year's Day go by in a prison camp is a very depressing thing to me anyway. Last night the camp band and entertainment put on a very good show which was followed by coffee and cookies in the mess. I stayed up to hear them ring 8 bells for 1944, but little else. We have had no details since the 29th as it is a Japanese holiday, and we don't begin again until the 3rd—quite a long rest. Yesterday the last 15 men from Camp 3 came down and now there are no Americans left up there. I understand that a part of the Ewing Filipinos were permitted to go home for the holidays and over a third failed to return.

CAMP 1 *January 13, 1944*

Very little impetus to write, little is happening. We are working one half day every two days, which makes one want to work even less. Still no mail, and I am losing my optimism about it coming through. News is at a new low; even the rankest scuttle is not forthcoming. The people at Santa Tomas are supposed to have received some British Red Cross packages, but time will prove or disprove that. Monotony, a most prevalent situation in a prison camp is quite the most disquieting thing here. I can see one of the Medical Officers computing the amount of money Uncle Sam will owe him if he gets out of here one year from now. A couple of others are playing bridge. I am doing almost nothing.

CAMP I *Thursday, January 27, 1944*

Here's a big space to fill up. These past two weeks our details have been almost 100% on the farm without shoes. No one knows the reason why. The first week was a nightmare as the ground was hard, dry, and sharp. But the Lord must have taken pity on us because it has rained during the night for the past week making the good earth much more pleasant to the plantar surfaces, and this rain is in the midst of the dry season, too. In fact yesterday it rained so hard that all details were called off. About 3 weeks ago we received 10,000 tablets of carbasone for the treatment of Amoebic and they expect 80,000 tablets more. I don't know how effective this drug will be but they will have sufficient to repeat the course of 20 tablets if needed.

CAMP I *February 5, 1944*

Yasumay—happy is the word—Saturday afternoon. I don't know whether my feet would have been able to stand another session or not, the ground besides being dry and hard is now quite hot almost too hot to stand. I was out this AM picking *telinum,* a leaf that constitutes the major portion of our vegetable ration and my feet are still burning. I don't know how much longer this shoeless business is going to keep up but I am willing to say "Uncle" right now. Another crisis has engulfed us. Two days ago our rice rations were cut, and quite a bit to. There has been no meat in our ration for about 3 months now, but we get a small amount of dried salt fish, which is soaked and mixed with rice to make fishcakes, and they aren't bad. We understand that the civilian ration as well as the Japanese garrison rice ration has been cut, also, so we are all in the same boat.

LETTERS FROM JAPAN

1944

ISLAND OF HOKKAIDO—MURORAN *Sunday, April 10, 1944*

The Medical detail has finally materialized to the extent that I am now in Japan, which is a hard thing to realize, and the northern most tip of the island to boot. Our party consists of 50 Medical Officers and 150 Corpsmen. I find that I have made no mention of this momentous event. About Feb 6th or 7th after working on the farm all morning, we returned to find the camp in turmoil. Nip HQ had requested a detail of 40 doctors, 10 dentists and 150 corpsmen to be divided into 4 hospital groups. No other information available. Well, we were wild with joy. Our feet were sore and blistered and we were sick and tired of being a laborer in a 100-man group, one man, and one row. We didn't care where we were going or were we would work. We had all been classified as to our specialties and HQ had dropped off the neuro. to make me a surgeon. About a week later we were examined by a Japanese lab. Men were given an anal smear, throat culture, and blood smear—then nothing happened, and back to the farm we went.

Identification badge worn by Max Andler.

It looked like the detail had been called off. Rumor had us going to Japan; staying in the Philippines and taking care of American details working in four different Nip airfields; and finally taking care of Nip casualties in hospitals around Manila. With our yellow skinned friends supposedly taking such a beating, I thought the last possibility quite likely. The situation held fire for about ten days and then the examinations were repeated. We heard that the Nip medical orderly got drunk, and dropped all the culture tubes. Incidentally, no amoebics were eligible to go on any detail and this cut out Dan Golenternek, Neil Burr, George Chamberlain and Lt. Fraleigh, USN. To further split up our old camp crowd, Cmeyla, Tucker and I were assigned to Major Berry's group, while the remaining medical officers were assigned to other sections.

ISLAND OF HOKKAIDO—MURORAN *Sunday, May 21, 1944*

I have finally located a typewriter again and now I may have a chance of catching up with this wordy affair. Trying to use a pen is not satisfactory. I just can't write fast enough. This makes me feel at home. The nicest and biggest news to date is that I received another radiogram from home yesterday, and although I don't know when it was sent, it was received in the Philippines on the 19th of March, 1944 and says that everyone at home is well. Two more days will have me in Japan for two months, and I am only now beginning to thaw out. Even so, the last two days have seen the temperature remain at 8 degrees centigrade throughout the day with a nasty wind blowing down from Siberia. A great country to read about. Before going back to finish my trip from Manila, let me give a brief description of my present situation.

The prison camp I am now in is composed of Dutch and British soldiers who are working in an iron foundry close by. The total personnel numbers 479, including seven officers, four Dutch, two British and myself; quite a cosmopolitan showing. The Dutch soldiers are made up for the most part of Dutch Eurasians from Java, while the English troops hail from all parts of England, Ireland, Scotland, and Wales. As I cannot understand any Dutch I am of little help to the Dutch doctor, but assist with the British troops working with Dr. Murray, a Major in the royal Army Medical Corps. And he is actually an Irishman. A Japanese First Lieutenant is the Commanding Officer of this camp, but a Lieutenant Colonel Imoto is the High Commandant of three prison camps in this area. But more of him later.

In regard to the work the men do, they are divided into sixteen groups, and each morning at seven o'clock the supervisors from the nearby foundry come and march them off to work. They take their rice with them for the noonday meal and do not return to camp until late in the afternoon. Shortly after my arrival here I found there was a great deal of discontent among the men. They felt the rice was not being divided equally in the kitchen for them to take out to work each day. In camp, the rice was put out in buckets to be eaten in the billet and each man was sure that the next billet was getting a bigger ration than their own. The senior officer of the Dutch, Capt. Borske, and Major Murray, the senior British Officer, both asked me if I would be willing to take over the Mess Officer's job as I had had the experience in the Philippines. I had hoped that once I left the Philippines I wouldn't have anything more to do with supply and would confine my activities to medical work, but this was not to be. I agreed and they both went to the *Shoko*, as the Nippon Officer is called, and suggested that I be ordered to check the issue of food. And so, on April 30th, a standing order was issued which not only appointed me as Mess Officer of the issue, but also to receive and sign for all rations of food issued by the Japanese Hancho in charge of the kitchen.

The difference here from our camps in the Philippines, is that the Japanese are directly in charge of everything. A Japanese soldier stays in the kitchen all day and tells us just exactly what we will cook for each meal and just how we will cook it. He has an office in one corner of the kitchen, and at times can be quite difficult to deal with, although I have gotten along with him quite well for the most part. His name is Judo and each morning we go into the storeroom and he tells me in Japanese what we will take for the next three meals. As you can easily see, a great deal of the time I haven't any idea what he is saying, but I agree with him as I can usually figure out what he wants from what he issued. Well, yesterday his method of mine didn't work out so well. He had told me to put aside 13 kilo of rice for the following day and I understood him to say put 18 kilos of rice in for the breakfast meal this morning along with the bread which we have every morning.... if there is yeast. When he looked for the 13 kilos of rice this morning, there wasn't any, and as a result there was a hot time in the kitchen for a while. But he cooled down sufficiently to issue rations for tonight and tomorrow and now everything is milk and honey again...for how long I don't know. And it is five o'clock and time for me to check the issue of rice for the evening meal. To make it more difficult, each group has a different size bucket and the personnel of the groups varies from 22 to 31. I am getting more gray hairs...

ISLAND OF HOKKAIDO—MURORAN *May 27, 1944*

A beautiful day in May. One of the few nice days that I have experienced in Japan.

About a month ago, Lieutenant Colonel Imoto, the CO of the three camps in this area, came here for a ten-day stay to have a personal interview with every man in Camp. For the great part of his life he has been a teacher of English in various schools in Japan. In fact, on the 27th of March, the morning we arrived at the main camp headquarters, it was six o'clock and snowing. We had been on the train for four days and nights without being able to wash, shave or sleep. Well, we lined up in front of the Colonel and he made a speech of welcome, which consisted of a not too concise resume of his accomplishments in teaching English in Japan. He spent fifteen minute describing his unusual and remarkable methods used and how he had increased his enrollment from a mere handful to thousands. You can guess that we weren't in too receptive a mood for such a discourse and were relieved when he said he would continue at a later time after he had had an opportunity to rest and get cleaned up.

From this headquarters that same day at noon, I was informed that I would proceed with four men to another prison camp about half a day's journey away. This news just about finished me, but they were still giving orders and I was taking them, and at noon away we went back to the railroad station. A *gunso* from the new camp had come to get us, and he was quite pleasant and agreeable on the train that took about six hours. A peculiar incident occurred on the train during the last two hours of the trip. At each station, about eight or ten middle aged men would rush into the car carrying large Nippon flags. They would proceed to fling a window open on the side facing the station and outside would be a large crowd of people seeing them off. The men would be quite stimulated by the famous sake and if anyone happened to be sitting in the seat by the window, they merely climbed over them. Everyone in the station crowd was shouting and singing and the before-mentioned men would thrust their heads and shoulders half way out the windows to join in the festivities. At the end of each chorus of a very short patriotic rhyme everyone would give three *banzais* and then the verse would be repeated. This whole procedure would be repeated at each station and as there were at least fifteen stops before we reached our destination, the train had become quite crowed as well as exceedingly noisy.

I tried to find out what was going on from the Nip *gunso,* but he said he could not tell me. As each of these new arrivals would catch sight o the five Americans in one section it would stop them up short for a moment...but only for a moment. By the time we had come to Muroran where the camp was, our car resembled the tail end of an American Legion convention. The camp was about three miles from the station and after an hour's wait a small baby pickup resembling an Austin picked us up. The camp, referred to as Hakodati I, is made up of approximately 300 British troops and 180 Dutch troops from Java, predominantly Eurasians. The Officers consisted the afore mentioned Dutch Medical Officers Dr. Lutter; a British Medical Officer, Major Murray who is Irish; Lt. Wynde, a Scot in the British Intelligence corps who acts as interpreter; Captain Borske; the senior Dutch Officer who takes care of the administrative duties; and two flying cadets, both Dutch—Jonker and Jongsma, who live in the Officers' quarters and mess but work with the men out at the Iron foundry. Quite a cosmopolitan crowd when you add one Yankee from California. Each officer has a room of his own in the Officers' quarters with a common mess room. Incidentally, this is the only room to have a stove. They had a hot supper waiting for me, which tasted just about as good as food can taste at ten o'clock in the evening.

ISLAND OF HOKKAIDO—MURORAN ***Saturday, the 28th of May***

The way things have worked out we finish the rounds in the small hospital about 10:30 AM and I am free until 11:30 when I have to check the noon meal. So I will try and use the hour each day to coordinate this long story.

Dr. Murray has been perpetually helpful and that first evening he saw to it that my bed was well made; six blankets, a raincoat and two overcoats, and he advised me to sleep with my socks on. In addition they had a brick on the stove for the foot of my bed. Reville was at 5:30 AM with tank at 6:00. The thermometer read 5 below zero centigrade. I hadn't experienced that kind of weather since I was home for Christmas in 1939. An inspection of the camp the first morning revealed that there was little need for an additional medical officer. There were a total of 473 troops with 21 men in the hospital and the two doctors already here had little to do. As many of the Dutch troops spoke little English I decided to help Dr. Murray with the British troops each day, and if Dr. Lutter needed assistance at any time, to help him if I could. While still on the ship coming to Japan, I contracted a heavy cold, which stayed with me. Less than a week after my arrival I felt feverish and found my temperature to be slightly over 100. Dr. Murray had me stay in bed and in two days my cold was better, but my temperature had gone up to 101. I was quite sure that I was having a recurrence of malaria even though there were no facilities to make a blood smear. I began a course of Atabrine. Again we hit a snag. Five days later my temperature had increased to 103 in the evening and was 101 in the AM I became a bit worried about this time, especially when the local Nippon CO heard I was sick, and was quite upset as he felt no doctor should ever get sick. Fortunately, the next day the fever was close to normal and in three days I was up and about again. This little bout had knocked just twenty-six pounds off me and I was looking quite svelte again. Since that time I have felt completely healthy and put on ten pounds, and if one wished to be facetious they could say I was rounding into form again.

ISLAND OF HOKKAIDO—MURORAN

Wednesday evening, June 7th, 1944, 8:00 PM

~ I think we have finally run across some summer weather here in Hokkaido. The last two days I have been running around in my shirt sleeves and felt quite comfortable. Everyone has been informed that 3000 letters have arrived in camp today. I don't expect any as I received more than my share, but I think I will take mine out and read them again when everyone gets theirs. It isn't very often that I permit myself to think about home because I feel too blue, but hearing about this mail has set me back again. I will be over it by morning. Yesterday the medical socho took the corpsmen and myself out for a walk in the countryside and it was quite refreshing. Have I told you that I have taken to smoking a pipe fairly regularly now? I was a bit surprised to find two pipes in the box you sent me. The tobacco from S. S. Pierce's was excellent. It looks like Sonia had something to do with that. Seeing a beautiful full moon coming up, increases this restlessness that I have tonight. I haven't described to you our bathing facilities. In Japan everyone bathes in a large common tub with very hot water. Here we have a cement bath about 10 feet square and three feet deep and it is filled it hot water every three days, temperature about 45 degrees centigrade. First one soaps up and washes from a basin of water at the side of the bath, and then steps in to soak. On bath days, the officers have a bath first with the whole bathhouse to themselves, and as there are only four of us in camp in the afternoon, it is quite pleasant. I feel a great deal better. Much, much better.

ISLAND OF HOKKAIDO—MURORAN

Tuesday, June 13, 11:00 AM

Back to the pen again. This time I shall print and see if it goes any easier. I can tell already that it won't. The typewriter has gone back to the front office for some reason or other which cuts me down no end. We have a *yasumay* (rest day) in this camp every ten days now and on the last one, we put on a play. It took place in a nightclub called Maizie's Place and some of the female impersonators were quite striking. Mr. Wynd, who appears a bit effeminate without any difficulty, was Maizie, and extremely convincing he was. My part, on the male side, consisted of squiring a fluffy young thing to the club. My lady friend was a Dutch Eurasian boy from Java who had once been a dancer at the royal court in Batavia. When he finally finished dressing, in a turban and some sort of a sarong, even I was a bit confused. Remember now, we had been salted away for more than two years now.

ISLAND OF HOKKAIDO—MURORAN

July 11, 1944, Tuesday, but almost a month later, *8:00 PM*

~ All the men in camp have just finished digging air raid trenches. The Colonel from Hakodate was here about two weeks ago and overwhelmed us by telling us to expect some American planes soon, as there were no fences in the sky. He also read us some news clippings describing how cruel the U.S. pilots were and we could expect them to bomb hospitals as well as prison camps. I am looking forward to it with relish. I certainly would never say that I could enjoy being bombed, but it would be worth it, I know, to see American planes again. The second front was explained to us in the following manner. "Germany could not attack America, so they set a trap for the Americans in France. Their strategy was to have all the troops land on the coast and then annihilate them with a secret weapon, controlled by none other than Mr. Hitler, who pressed the button. He further informed us that the Americans had landed 20 divisions and five were wiped out immediately. The Colonel was quite optimistic for the Germans. He continued by telling us we could expect an attack on Japan this summer, and Nippon would use the same strategy as Germany. Perhaps this is the policy they are following in the Southern Islands. Very effective for us.

A week ago Sunday, I said goodbye to my twenties and it depressed me a bit. I don't like to be 30 years old especially in a prison camp where I have very good prospects of getting older. But considering the circumstances, I am convinced we are quite well here with our ration at least equal to the civilian population. Since the high commander has been changed, there have been constant improvements in the camp conditions. I really feel that he is pro-American and pro-British having taught the language for so many years. To stop corporal punishment in a Japanese prison camp hardly seems possible, since that is the only type of discipline they depend on in their own Army. Many of the men feel that this change of policy is because of the war trend, but I think it is the result of Emoto himself. He has permitted us to get some medical books plus a phonograph and American records which had come through the Red Cross. And yesterday we left camp for the first time, taking a walk over to the bay about two miles away and went swimming. Now Red Cross personnel can go out for a hike once a week, a good deal different from the Philippines. The Nip medico, Dr. Shiba, a hypertonic little shaver who suddenly has taken a great interest in the health of the men, arranged this. A coincidence that this occurred with the arrival of Emoto? He is very much interested in intrathecal B therapy for peripheral neuritis of Beriberi, so that he and I did lumbar punctures on all the BB cases, about twelve, and injected 1 mgm. of metaboline, Nip B1. Some of the men developed quite severe reactions with meningismus, vomiting and marked malaise. Assigned as camp surgeon, he wanted me to repeat the treatment a week later, doubling the dose. Since the patients were all British and Dutch, I and Dr. Murray and Dr. Lutter do them and we had no difficulty at all.

ISLAND OF HOKKAIDO—MURORAN *Sunday, July 16, 1944*

Yasumay day in this camp and the men need it. The hot weather is here and many of the men work outside handling pig iron and scooping as the British boys say. Most of them are on the borderline medically. While we received a good supply of Red Cross drugs and vitamins, there is not sufficient of the latter to use them prophylactically as we should. Incidentally, to put it in the record, Dr. Shiba informed me that I should supervise the use of the drugs, as they were all American products. This I thought not a good idea. I divided all medicines between the Dutch and British proportionately and turned them over to Dr. Lutter and Dr. Murray respectively. I act only as Medical supply officer issuing the drugs as they request them and keeping the records.

ISLAND OF HOKKAIDO—MURORAN *Tuesday, July 25th, 1944*

Our camp life goes on unchanged. We had another session of spinals today without any difficulties. Dr. Lutter asked me to examine a Dutchman with hemoptysis and pain by the right rib margin. I could hear little in his chest, but he had a tender enlarged liver along with an old history of amoebic dysentery in 1941. He may well have a liver abscess with respiratory embarrassment. Shall we aspirate? With what? We have just heard that Colonel Emoto will be back tomorrow to stay for a week. I am curious to see what he will have to say re: the world situation now. I doubt whether he will mention the present shakeup. Our rice ration here has been altered considerably. About a month ago we were issued one half the ration in potatoes to mix with the rice and two weeks ago 50% of the potatoes was cut and replaced with *daikon,* a Japanese type of coarse radish that is a bit hard on the digestive system. But the ration is still much superior to that in the Philippines when we left. The news permits us to think about going home with a little more rationale. After becoming inured to living under prison camp conditions for more than two years, it is difficult to visualize a normal existence again. The thought of being able to enter a restaurant and having a choice of food instead of just getting a daily ration to be divided among so many men, the opportunity of entering a store and picking out a shirt or a pair of slacks instead of hoping for an issue of old Japanese uniforms. The thought of driving a car again and going wherever one wishes is a pleasant thing to mull over. Visions of the past find me receptive with increasing frequency. I doubt whether such everyday experiences will ever seem matter of fact to me again. Me thinks I will spend the evening with Mr. Christopher and his surgery.

ISLAND OF HOKKAIDO—MURORAN
5:00 AM, Thursday, August 3rd

Last PM we had our first serious blackout with a small garrison of outside guards coming in to police the camp. As it was quite warm we decided to leave our lights out rather than blackout. I think I was in bed by 8:30 and that is why I am up so early. At 5:30 AM I go up to the cookhouse and see that the breakfast is properly and justly served. Then we measure out the rice for the men to take to work, which is another hairsplitting job. For the past two days I have been going out to the factory at 10:00 in the morning along with two men and a guard t deliver a side dish to the men for their lunch. It was quite illuminating. In delivering the food it was necessary to go to each separate group in all parts of the factory, a walk of approximately five miles. But it was a fine chance to get a first hand peek at the great war effort of our Eastern foes—not too impressive. In the factory garage the manager was wearing a pair of Chevrolet coveralls and I saw 3 Harley Davidson motorcycles in use. Apparently, the local talent (U.S.) has extended this far.

ISLAND OF HOKKAIDO—MURORAN
Wednesday evening, August 9, 1944

The Colonel has come and gone with the customary unusual results. We complained that it was necessary for the medical officers to send sick men out to work. He was quite indignant and said that in the future every man in camp would stay in if necessary but no sick men would go out to work. A big step for our side. Then the men complained about the food saying that bad potatoes and radish were being used with the rice. The colonel proceeded to line up the Japanese staff responsible for buying an issuing the bad potatoes and bawled the daylights out of them. He then told me that he had issued instruction for the POW cookhouse staff to have full say as to the preparation of the food in the future. I was also to refuse to accept or serve any food that I considered bad. Another victory for our side. He then gave us his usual talk on Japanese history, this time the Jap-China war of 663 years ago. But we didn't mind that. His brief resume of the world news included an item about the pilotless German planes hitting London. A far as I could determine they had used about 5200 of these dynamite affairs with a casualty of a little over 4000—a bit expensive. He also mentioned robot tanks but I can see little advantage in that. His theory as to the U.S.-Japan fray in the Pacific is that they are fighting a very strong foe and so must expect to get hurt. I agree with them. He told one group of men we couldn't get any more Red Cross food as the Americans were sinking every ship that tried to get to Japan. In general, the "big picture" is developing nicely.

ISLAND OF HOKKAIDO—MURORAN ***Monday, August 14th, 1944***

Have just finished playing some baseball with Major Murray and Sgt. Matuozi—a hot afternoon and it felt good to get some exercise. To inaugurate our new regime in the kitchen we turned out a vegetable loaf for the men to take to work at lunchtime—minced potato, carrots, radish, and flour. It was a big success and the men are clamoring for more. We will try the same thing with fish. Today we wrote our first letter home—still 100 words but in an envelope. We were also permitted to enclose our snapshots taken two months ago. We are getting closer to civilization every day. Must get cleaned up for the evening sick parade. We are experiencing a mild flu epidemic here in camp and as I have the sniffles tonight I will probably be on my way tomorrow. The Nippon Shoko had a meeting of all his billet leaders called Hauchos. Afterwards he came in to tell me that all the men had reported to him that they liked the new method of serving the noon day food. For the past two days we have turned out fishcakes and a loaf of bread so the men have had sandwiches. There is absolutely no grease or cooking oil available, which limits our cooking no end. We obtained grease for the trays from the bone marrow of horse bones.

ISLAND OF HOKKAIDO—MURORAN *August 24th, 1944*

And I have just 6 more days to go in the cookhouse, and then I am relieved for a month. It will be difficult to keep occupied after being wrapped up in work. These past few days there has been talk of one or two of the officers here being relieved and sent to an Officers camp at Tentugzi down south. We were even asked if we wished to volunteer. The underground informed us that Wynde our interpreter or Major Murray, the British Medical Officer would go. They both became a bit upset as neither wanted to go and wrote a letter to the colonel requesting this. But the Shoko informed them this AM that no one was scheduled to go. So we will wait and see. I am certainly the logical one to go if someone has to leave. But the boys allegedly in the know say I will stay.

Have just finished reading *Captain Horatio Hornblower*—I have been trying to read it for years. There is plenty of action and I enjoyed it all.

ISLAND OF HOKKAIDO—MURORAN *August 27th, 1944*

Have been completely off my feet these past three days. No diarrhea but nauseated from morning to night. It can't be a pregnancy sneaking up on me. We had a British soldier die yesterday from acute dysentery probably amoebic. We had given him sulfaguanidine, carbasone, plasma, and I.V. glucose, but it didn't keep him at all. One of the staff just came down and wanted to know if he had any personal belongings such as a ring, as they wanted to have something to send back to his family. Quite a different setup from O'Donnel when they were burying over 200 a day with 30 men in each grave, and the authorities didn't even want to know their names, just the total number dead. It's a fortunate thing to be a POW from a country whose position is getting continually stronger. It has certainly been reflected in the changing conditions in the prison camps that I have been in. In fact, two of the guards refer to the POWs as their guests. I have just heard there is a man in camp who was in N.Y. as late as July, 1942. His ship was a merchantman sunk by a German raider in the Indian Ocean and he and his crew were turned over to the Japanese and brought here. I am going to see him tonight.

ISLAND OF HOKKAIDO—MURORAN *September 1, 1944*

The months are sliding by much too quickly—while some say the faster the time passes the sooner the war will be finished I feel that the days of my stay on the earth are becoming progressively less. I had quite a chat with a British merchant seaman named Idle. And incidentally he was as idle as they come. Anyway he had been in Boston for Christmas of 1941 and left there in July of '42 with a cargo for India. A German raider sunk his ship and rescued the crew in Indian waters. While they were aboard, the Nazis sank two other merchant ships, and turned the captured crews over to the first Japanese warship that was encountered. Idle said he and his men were very well treated by the Nazi crew, and the German captain told them he was sorry that he had to turn them over to such a cruel and heartless people as the Japanese, but that he had no room for them on his ship. When they left N.Y. in July the only two things that were rationed were sugar and gasoline. But he thought the number of cars and taxis in the street appeared as numerous as peacetime. There was nothing to indicate the country was at war except down at the dock area. Here the workers were making **an enormous amount** per hour for working overtime loading explosives. It certainly felt good to hear about home.

We had quite an experience in camp yesterday. A member of the Swiss Consulate, a Mr. Ballard, along with some Japanese officers and interpreters, visited the camp. Interviews were arranged for the five officers in camp and some of the camp workers. We went in to the room in pairs with our names and the names and addresses of our relatives on a piece of paper. Besides the Swiss there were 8 Japanese officers and our camp commandant, Lt. Hirati. Mr. Ballard introduced himself, shook hands, said he was very glad to see us, and informed us that he had asked for our names so that he could notify our families that he had seen us and that we were well. When he found out I had come from the Philippines, he requested permission from the Japanese to ask me some questions about the POWs there. This was granted and he then explained that the Swiss consulate had managed to get permission to send money to the American prisoners in the Philippines, and he asked me how this money could best be spent. I told him that they had received an enormous supply of medicines and vitamins and what the men needed was food.

The rice rations had been cut to 400 grams a day including 40% corn. I suggested they try to buy rice and vegetables. They were going to send five pesos per man per month, which amounted to 18,000 a month. I was permitted to say anything I wished and some of the things I said the local boys didn't like at all. He asked about the health of the men and I told him that all the men in the camp were borderline with no resistance left. Their diet had no fat at all and no animal protein. We were getting new cases of dysentery and a man had died within the week. I added the work at the factory the men were required to do was too heavy for them under the circumstances and that the Medical Officers, Dr. Murray and I had decided to prohibit them men from any strenuous exercise on *yasumay* days because they were not strong enough. He asked if I personally had any complaints and I replied that as an officer I was treated quite well and had no requests to make. He stayed about five hours, looked over the camp and then left for the Grand Hotel at Noboribetsu. That was the first time I have ever been permitted to speak to any non-Japanese about this or any other prison camp. Another indication of the times.

This was supposed to be my last day in the cookhouse. While shaving at 7:30 AM I had a chill lasting about an hour and then my temp hit 102.6. I had a bad head and that's about all. I took some codeine and asa and went to bed until the interview, and felt quite well by last night. I don't understand it. And as Dr. Lutter has taken over the cookhouse I was able to rest all day today.

ISLAND OF HOKKAIDO—MURORAN *September 3, 1944*

~ I must have spoken too quickly. Had another chill yesterday morning and then the mercury hit 104. I thought it wasn't going to stop, but after a good sweat it was back to normal in time for me to help at the sick parade in the afternoon. I decided it must be some more malaria and began another course of Atabrine. OK today—just a bit weaker and a bit thinner. This is not time to be getting sick, while we all feel it is so close. Zzzzzzz…what the return home will be like. I must make a decision as to where I will live and where I will work. Also what kind of medicine to go back to—that is the question mark.

This is a big evening in camp—sweet beans for supper, and a concert. It will be music from round the world. They asked me to sing some American songs, but I felt it would be a favor to the States for me to refuse.

ISLAND OF HOKKAIDO—MURORAN *September 5, 1944*

~ Today is supposed to be the last day of a three months ultimatum to Japan. If they don't give up, mass all-out bombing of the mainland is to begin. Only the future will prove if there is any truth o this one. I don't hold out much hope for the rumor that Germany has capitulated again.

Since I have been relieved from the cookhouse for a month my mind has been much freer. Things were getting quite serious when I found myself dreaming of the rice distribution. It was on my mind all the time. Now I feel like singing again. I am reading some of the Ted Cross books, one *Three Harbors* about Revolutionary war days. I enjoyed it immensely. Physiology by Viggers is claiming some of my time. My appetite is still gone and I am losing weight, but I can afford to do that for a while yet.

~

ISLAND OF HOKKAIDO—MURORAN ***Sunday, September 9, 1944***

A good time to begin another page. Events have been happening thick and fast. First of all the Japanese doctor arrived from Hakodate. He informed us that he was quite concerned because a man had died here a few days before and he told us with a straight face that there must be no more deaths. He was astounded when Major Murray informed him that there would be many more deaths before the winter was over unless something was done about the health of the men in the camp. Since then we have been on a merry-go-round. For the past 3 days we have been on the go all day long until 10 o'clock at night. We paraded all the weak men and explained the manual work they were doing at the factory such as scooping and loading pig iron was too much for them. This amounted to more than 80 men out of 182 British troops. After he saw them all stripped he agreed that something would have to be done. We also explained that we had no laboratory equipment of reagents to do the simplest tests. I also told him that I would like to have arrangements made for me to use the surgical facilities of the nearby General Hospital if any emergency surgical cases developed. He replied that he would try to remedy everything that we had brought up. He has not left yet so I don't know what he will ask for next. We have had to compile all kinds of statistical reports for him to take back to the Hakodate Colonel. The type of work each man does, his weight for the last four months, along with the average of all the camp, the number of days sick and kind of sickness for each man over four months, and innumerable more.

It looks like the men are letting themselves go mentally. We have had seven cases in the past week. Some of them get a sudden dizzy spell and stagger around. Others suddenly become completely paralyzed from head to foot and can't talk. With each one of these, we give a complete physical and neurological examination. After we find everything normal we try some means of convincing the patient that he is alright and we know it. Most of the cases were fairly easy. One, whom we were called in to see at 8 PM one night was completely comatose, a flaccid paralysis of both arms and legs. Well, we had quite a struggle, working for two hours that night and most of the next day. First, we checked him over completely and found no evidence of pathology, then I picked up one of his legs by the knees and instead of his leg hanging as it would with a flaccid paralysis he held it straight out. That clinched the diagnosis and by putting pressure on certain nerve centers we were able to arouse him. Then we forced him to get up and walk. At first he just staggered and fell with a vacant stare on his face. We kept prodding him on the backside and slapping his legs to keep him walking and gradually his gait improved. From another source we found out what was troubling him and since then he has just about returned to normal and is back working.

ISLAND OF HOKKAIDO—MURORAN ***Tuesday, September 12***

The doctor has finally gone. He said goodbye to me five different times. As a final blow he had each one of us down separately to tell us that the British and Dutch were not cooperating.

He told me that as an American, I should be the one to bring them together. Also that all the Red Cross drugs were American drugs and that I should know them better than the others. He instructed me to be in charge of them and supervise their use. He also repeated that I was to do any and all surgery whether it was minor or major. All in all, we heaved a sigh of relief when he left this morning. We hope the Hakodate Colonel will take some actions on his recommendations.

We heard some startling news about Hakodate. At three o'clock in the morning of the day the Swiss Consulate was to come, they awakened all the officers there, about 35 including Major Lentz and Harry Levitt. They were informed that they had two hours to pack and leave and they could talk or communicate with no one. They all had a special breakfast with the Colonel and they were heard to sing, "We'll hang our washing on the Siegfried Line" and *For He's a Jolly Good Fellow*—and away they went. The only two officers left were the Australian doctor and Al Brown, the American dentist.

ISLAND OF HOKKAIDO—MURORAN ***Saturday, Sept 16, 1944***

Plenty of rain, which keeps one feeling, depressed. I have certainly been taking it easy since I have been relieved from the cookhouse, but in two weeks I will be back at it again. Just finished *Forsyte Saga* by Galsworthy—quite bulky but interesting.

ISLAND OF HOKKAIDO—MURORAN *September 18, 1944*

Well, as usual now something new happens almost daily. Last night Mr. Stirling, a Navy WO from the Hakodate camp, dropped in without a word of warning to do a stool survey. He mentioned that some Canadian Red Cross supplies had been received at Hakodate about 10 days ago, and to bear that out our shipment arrived this morning. The clothes are American from this year's supply, and most of it for civilian internees.

ISLAND OF HOKKAIDO—MURORAN *September 25, 1944*

Colonel Emoto has just arrived for a four-day stay. What will he have to say this time? Last visit he was quite intrigued with the German D 1 that has been a bit outmoded now.

Message of the War Dept.—"Public Law 490, 77 Congress, approved March 7, 1942, as amended, provides that Officers, Warrant Officers, enlisted persons, army nurses and civilian employees in active service, who are captured by the enemy, shall while prisoners of war, be entitled to receive or to have credited to their accounts the same pay and allowances, including flight pay to which entitled at the time of beginning of absence or to which they may become entitled thereafter and their allotments and deductions for dependents and maintenance of life insurance shall continue in force".

With respect to promotion of Officers, the War Department policy is that "action will be completed on a recommendation for temporary promotion in process when the Officer is reported missing in action or in the hands of the enemy but no temporary promotions will be initiated after an officer is reported missing in action or a prisoner of war."

ISLAND OF HOKKAIDO—MURORAN *Tuesday, September 26, 1944*

Last evening the interpreter came down with the above message from the War Department. It was quite a surprise to get it, and it gives me a pretty good chance of having a Captaincy since the capitulation; as I had heard that my recommendation for promotion had already been approved at Corregidor and sent back to 2nd Corps. I hope they manage to get the records back to the states and didn't toss them overboard in all the excitement. I should think they would have notified you if it had gone through. Time will tell, time will tell. We have been able to write quite a bit of mail recently, and the boys here have been getting a lot. Mr. Wynd, who has two sisters in the States, received a letter from Connecticut dated May 1944. It seems the mail is coming via the Trans Siberian Railroad across Russia, which speeds things up, a bit. My mail is still being sent down south probably, and from the action in Southern Waters recently I don't think the mails are too regular.

The boys at Cabanatuan should be feeling a bit frisky. I would certainly like to see Dan Golenteruck and Neil Burr again. I wonder if they have attempted to move any of those amoebics out of there. If they are left at Cabanatuan, they should be fairly safe. I wish I could be with them right now instead of looking forward to a cold winter on Hakodate. I am fairly safe in thinking this should be the last one here. On the 18th, Mr. Sterling, the American WO from Guam who does all the laboratory work at Hakodate, arrived here to do a 10-day stool survey. He is supposed to be quite an expert on amoeba. So far he has had eight positive stools for amoeba histolytica, and this has given me a chance to study them. We still have some carborsone and a small amount of emetine left.

ISLAND OF HOKKAIDO—MURORAN *September 28, 1944*

There is a bit of a tang in the air that bodes ill for the coming winter. My toes are cold already. And the cookhouse, with a cement floor is one of the coldest spots in camp. We received another small batch of Red Cross food, one Canadian box for 4 that didn't go very far.

I heard some interesting things about Major Lentz and Levitt from Mr. Stirling that may account for their going south with the other Officers. Emment apparently had difficulty staying off his back, the same condition that he suffered from in the Philippines. Poor Harry got mixed up in an appendix and everything went wrong from the beginning. The spinal anesthetic didn't take, but they went ahead with the surgery anyway. Then Harry couldn't find the appendix and the Nip surgeon had to step in and do the job. Then they tried to let Harry close and by this time he was so upset and disgusted he couldn't hold the needle. He had tried to explain to Dr. Shiba that he hadn't done any surgery since he had been a medical student, but that didn't seem to make any difference to Dr. Shiba. I have already explained to him that I was an aspiring neurosurgeon and not a general surgeon but I am quite sure that if an acute appendix develops, I will be the baby holding the sock. Fortunately, I have been able to study a bit of surgical anatomy...and if the appendix isn't too hot we should be able to get by. We have heard no more about the surgical arrangements that are supposed to be taking place, but obviously we can never attempt any major surgery here.

ISLAND OF HOKKAIDO—MURORAN *Friday, September 29, 1944*

We have just finished our visit with Lieut. Col. Smoto and as usual, he said the unusual. A few remarks were quite suggestive as to the trend of the war, we thought. In one case he was discussing the point that Japan was fighting a spiritualistic war and not a materialistic one. He continued by saying that if American and Britain wanted to shake hands now Japan would not hesitate for a moment. That sounds good. Another point, he said that if the cause were just, even though Nippon was sure it could not win, it would fight for the right. Very interesting! Could he be referring to the present situation—He also told us that Churchill and Roosevelt have had many meetings and they have announced that after the war America will control all the important points in the world. A big order indeed. It appears that we will be the international policemen when this thing is over.

ISLAND OF HOKKAIDO—MURORAN *Saturday, September 30, 1944*

My last day of freedom from the cookhouse for a month. But it won't be too bad. Received a *Cunningham's Anatomy* yesterday on the head and neck, which should keep my spare moments filled. I have been mulling over a 10-yen wager I made with Major Murray re: the final day. In a burst of enthusiasm I shouted by the end of this November' and he immediately took me up on it. Mr. Stirling left for Hakodate this morning, and I must admit I heaved a sigh of relief—he has been a bit trying. I fear he never has gotten over his many years spent as an enlisted man. Now that he is a Commissioned Warrant Officer in the U.S. Navy, he feels that the world revolves about him. His attitude towards any occurrence was highly flavored by his own ego. His verbose descriptions of the excellent work he had done in each and all of the Prison camps he had been in would lead one to believe, a bit erroneously I fear, that each camp had become habitable only after unwearied and time-consuming effort on his part. Along with this he has a happy faculty of gossiping like an old lady. He seemed perpetually blown up with his own importance. When we received an extra loaf of bread for breakfast he was convinced it was because he was here. When the Colonel arrived he was sure the Colonel would have him in for a personal conference to see how he was getting along, and if there was anything he wanted. Well the Colonel never even acknowledged his presence here and didn't have him in with the Officers for the conference. They had heard that he was scheduled to leave this AM. He immediately assumed that he would be going back with the Colonel and informed us that he expected to have a nice talk with the old boy, as the Colonel asked him for advice frequently. This morning he was notified that one of our camp guards would be taking him back and he would have to walk to the station. As Major Murray said, "It takes all kinds."

ISLAND OF HOKKAIDO—MURORAN
Monday afternoon, October 2, 1944

Have had a busy morning! Last week, along with the Red Cross food, we received some American Red Cross clothes, including 35 sweaters, fatigues, socks, towels, winter underwear, shirts, blue blankets, gloves and hats. Also 150 hand knitted woolen pullovers, and American Army woolen blankets. Well, the Shoko called Capt. Borski and Capt. Murray and asked them to submit a plan for distribution of the clothes. Incidentally, there are also about 150 pairs of shoes. Just before my arrival here they had received 155 pairs of pajamas, hats, gloves, socks, towels, shoes, winter underwear and woolen shirts, which the Nips distributed directly. Then in April, after our arrival, 155 fatigue suits, American Army issue were issued to the Dutch troops only as the British had received pajamas. My 4 American Corpsmen received none as they were living in a British billet. I did nothing about it at this time. The new supply of clothes was turned over to Borski and Wynd, and they arranged the distribution. No one approached me as to the need of the 4 Americans but Mr.Wynd wanted to give me a pair of socks because the officers had received socks and towels from a previous Japanese issue. I told him that I didn't need anything, and all the articles were distributed with the exception of a few blankets, and nothing had been issued to my 4 men. I had decided to have nothing to do with the Red Cross supplies, but last night after I had gone to bed, I couldn't sleep for more than two hours because I felt that I hadn't take care of my own troops. Here Dutch troops had two issues of American fatigues and my men had none. Other men in camps had new woolen sweaters knitted by American girls for American POW's and everyone but the American had them. The same with woolen underwear, socks, hats, gloves. Towels and the whole business and they had none. I determined to do what I could to change things in the morning and finally fell asleep. This morning I explained the matter to both Major Murray and Mr. Wynd, and they both agreed that there had been a mistake made and wished to do anything I suggested to rectify things. Since almost everything was issued out it was difficult. Each would get a woolen blanket. Sgt. Stevens, new shoes. Sgt. Matnozzi, a woolen pullover that Mr. Wynd hadn't yet issued—and for Cox and Fitch I asked Capt. Borski to call in 2 suits of fatigues from the Dutch men who now had two. I don't know whether he has agreed to this plan yet or not, but if he doesn't then I am going to see to it that he is forced to. Dr. Murray suggested that I, as an American officer and a member of the Red Cross, be put in charge of any new American Red Cross supplies that may arrive here, and after seeing this last fiasco, I am beginning to agree with him.

~

ISLAND OF HOKKAIDO—MURORAN ***Thursday, October 5, 1944***

No results on the coveralls from Capt. Borski. He is still "trying" to get them. But I will straighten those out this evening. Yesterday I decided it was my job to make a survey of the Red Cross clothes issues in camp. I wrote out the following statement and gave it to Mr. Wynd and Capt. Borski: "As the only American Officer and representative of the American Red Cross in this camp, I feel it my responsibility to make a detailed survey and record of the status of American Red Cross clothing in this camp for the following reasons:

1. With a complete record available stating the number of articles of clothing each man has received the future issue of any additional Red Cross clothing received can be more easily and more fairly made.
2. Since part of the clothing has been issued by the Japanese Camp Staff and recent issue handled by the POW Officer staff, such a complete record has probably not been available.
3. This record will be of value in estimating requests for additional Red Cross supplies as was possible during the recent visit of Dr. Ballard of the Swiss Consulate.
4. As a representative of the American Red Cross I may be ordered to report as to the amount, distribution and use of American Red Cross supplies sent to this camp."

ISLAND OF HOKKAIDO—MURORAN ***October 6, 1944***

I have just received a lengthy written reply from Capt. Borski to "Medical Lieutenant M.M. Andler, Muroran".

Subject: Status of Red Cross clothes.

Referring to your undated and unsigned circular letter, probably only meant for the Commandant of the Dutch and the Commandant of the British groups, I beg to inform you:

1. Indeed you are the only American Officer in this camp, which does not imply that you are also representative of the American Red Cross.
2. We would like to see it proved that you are representative of the American Red Cross. In my humble opinion you are a military medical officer not automatically member, less representative of the Red Cross.
3. Referring to sub 2 mentioned we cannot understand that it belongs to your responsibility to start a more detailed survey and record of the status of all the Red Cross clothing issues.
4. As far as I know, Lt. Wynd and I have a complete record of the Red Cross goods issued by the Japanese as well as issued by either of us. (English and American clothing.) That the issue of the Japanese was not done in the right way I can partly confirm; but what we both have issued is undoubtedly done correctly and <u>fairly</u>. That the following issue could be done more <u>fairly</u> is according to my opinion an improper insinuation.
5. An estimate of what we might need—Lieutenant Wynd and I are able to do that too, I supposed. Why does it take Lieutenant M.M. Andler to do that? Up to the present we got Red Cross without previous estimations; we <u>simply</u> had to divide a certain quantity as good as possible.
6. Your Sub. 4 I answered already; and that eventually I am only responsible to the International Red Cross, Geneva, that you have appointed yourself as representative of the American Red Cross is your own business. I and my colleagues too never will recognize you as such, unless you can show us the proofs now.

Summarizing I can inform you:

A. That I do not feel myself obliged and also do not intend to give you any justification or inspection of my records.
B. That by eventual distribution of goods which are not issued to a certain group, these will be issued at a ratio of ⅓ for the Dutch

groups and ⅔ for the British groups. Among the British groups also the American are accounted for.

C. I wish and my colleagues too, that a new shipment of goods will be put again in the hands of the POW Officers. And that the issue will be left to Lt. Wynd and me; for the issue of Red Cross goods to the Americans in this camp you may come to an understanding with Lt. Wynd in due time.

D. I would like to point out that if the Japanese hear complaints or remarks about the distribution, it certainly will have the result that in the future the issue of Red Cross goods will be done by the Japanese, what undoubtedly for us all is highly undesirable."

Quite a statement—I am in the process of girding my loins in rebuttal to show him just how inaccurate are all his assumptions.

ISLAND OF HOKKAIDO—MURORAN *Saturday, October 7, 1944*

Round three—quite a tussle. After explaining all his mistakes in detail to him, I concluded with the statement that if he didn't agree to my request, I would notify the Camp Commandant, the Hakodate Colonel and the next Red Cross Representative that came here, that I had requested to make a survey of American clothing in this camp, and while Major Murray was willing, the Dutch CO had refused. I further stated that I could cite many instances where I considered the distribution could be made more fairly—the most outstanding being the four Americans who had not received any previous Red Cross Issue and were completely forgotten in this. To all this his only reply was that I was going to the enemy, and after the war he would write to my government and tell them all about it. I finally stopped his tirade, which included telling me I would be committing treason, and explained that I had no anxiety about the legality of my actions or intentions, and if he considered the whole matter a little more carefully, he would realize that he didn't have a leg to stand on. To further knock the props out from under him, the Nips came along and told Mr. Wynd that he would leave for Hakodate this morning, and they further ordered all of the Non Coms. to make a complete survey of the Red Cross issue in the camp. This sort of took the wind out of his sails, and he wound up by saying that he wanted to speak to Major Murray first. But I think it is all over but the shouting. In fact, I have already gone over the type of forms I want to use with Sgt. Crazier, and I expect to get started tomorrow.

ISLAND OF HOKKAIDO—MURORAN
11 AM, Sunday, October 8, 1944

We have had a terrific wind and rain storm, which is still going strong—the fence along one whole side of the camp has been knocked down, and it is extremely difficult to walk facing the gale. Anyone could step right out of camp but I think, all in all, that they are much better off inside. I am sure our food ration is better in some ways than that of the civilians outside. Just as it is getting cold, we have exhausted our supply of charcoal, and as the coal stoves won't be in for another month probably. It looks like some cool days and nights ahead.

ISLAND OF HOKKAIDO—MURORAN
Saturday, October 14, 1944

We managed to get by Friday the 13th without too much difficulty.

The paper work of my survey is completed. I saw Capt. Borski again, and repeated what I planned to do, and this time he was much more agreeable, and said that I could have his records. Now, I have to see him about the overalls again. But I have changed my attitude. This time I am going to put it up to him. Some Dutch troops have been issued with two pairs of hurricane coveralls, and the 4 American troops have received none. If he thinks that is o.k., then I won't do anything more about it. Two pairs of coveralls aren't that important.

This week has been filled with *The Sun is My Undoing*. I haven't quite finished this thousand-page novel, but it is one of the most consuming stories that I have ever read. It is somewhat on the same framework as *Anthony Adverse*, but even more enjoyable. From Bristol, England to the African

Gold Coast, Barbados, Cuba, England again, Cuba, Spain, and back to Bristol. Very difficult to realize that the author was a woman.

Called down to the office a couple of nights ago and informed that the four Americans and I would be permitted to send a radio message of 40 words from the Tokyo station. Now that we are writing two cards of one hundred words every two weeks, there isn't too much left to say. I did send a card to the Adjutant General requesting that my allotment be doubled if my promotion to Captain had gone through.

ISLAND OF HOKKAIDO—MURORAN *Thursday, October 19, 1944*

As usual, when I neglect to write for a week, many, many things happen. For one thing Al Brown, the dentist from Hakodate came two days ago and he brought the news that they were opening a new camp of 300 men very close to Hakodate and that I was pretty sure to be the medical officer assigned there. So I am waiting for the word to leave. And when the two American Medical Corps men, Sgt. Matuozzi and Sgt. Stevens heard about it, they asked me to take them with me. They don't realize that I am not running this show, but the Japanese. I decided to go down and see the Shoko about it and mentioned that if I were leaving the American Corps Men wanted to go with me. He asked me if I could stay here and take care of the British troops here. I replied that I could, but that Major Murray could do it much better as he had been with these troops since they left Singapore. I also said that if anyone had to leave, I was the one, as there were no American troops here but Dutch and British. All he said was *So-ha.* It seems as if they have been considering sending Major Murray up to now, and maybe I have changed his mind. I don't want to leave here, but I wouldn't feel right staying, and having Major Murray go. There is nothing more I can do about it now except wait and see.

Al Brown is supposed to stay for six weeks, and it is pleasant to have him here after a visit from Stirling. Al says the new camp should open on the 23rd, which doesn't leave me much time. The Nip Ambei is all hopped up about the great vectoring of theirs in preventing a landing on the Philippines. He tells me that America is *wari*—which means finished. His story is that for the last 3 days, the Americans had been trying to land on the northern part of Luzon, the Wild Eagles have held them off.

We ran across a month old *Nippon Times* in camp a couple of days ago, which was quite interesting. For an English type newspaper, edited in Tokyo, it is surprising to find some of the things we read there. One article described the task force, which attacked Saipan, including 16 battleships, 50 cruisers, 300 destroyers and close to 50 carries. Comparable to our peacetime Navy—another attack by Goebbels to the German people reveals an unbelievable change in the whole mental setup of the Germans. He talks about the necessity of fighting valiantly on their own soil if they do not want the Fatherland to be completely obliterated. He recognizes the overwhelming force of the allies. Another article by a Japanese Correspondent in Bohn relates the miraculous withdrawal of the Germans from Occupied France in record time. And the Japanese attitude in the paper and editorials was similar, always mentioning the overwhelming forces and equipment of the Americans—the paper bucked us up no end. I don't think a paper at home could have seemed more important in relating adverse news.

ISLAND OF HOKKAIDO—MURORAN ***Friday, October 20, 1944***

A cold afternoon. I have sort of gone over my stuff to see what I should take and leave behind if I get the word to leave in a hurry. If I don't take my blankets I can carry my clothes fairly well. But the officers have been issued with 6 American Red Cross Army blankets—100% wool, and I hate to leave those behind. This preparation may be a bit premature, but I doubt it. And I don't seem to mind the thought of moving too much. I feel it isn't for much longer. It will be the same there as here if Major Murray leaves and I stay. Neither of us understands Dutch, and for the one who stays behind it won't be so good. Re Dutch Officers

ISLAND OF HOKKAIDO—MURORAN ***Sunday, October 22, 1944***

Sounds quite familiar, but I can't decide what it signifies. All the boys on the other team know the exact date of the coming presidential election and they are quite certain that Roosevelt will be defeated. Last night one explained that because of the recent tremendous losses off Taiwan and the Philippines, all the American people are against Roosevelt, and when he speaks they turn off the radios and newspapers.

From the way this detail was shaping up I thought I would leave before my month in the cookhouse was finished, but with only eight days to go, there will be no reprieve. But with a new Dutch Warrant Officer functioning, the place runs quite smoothly. With a cement floor, it feels like an icebox.

ISLAND OF HOKKAIDO—MURORAN
Tuesday, October 24, 1944, 5:30 P.M

In the cookhouse—We have finally done it. Received an issue of meat for lunch. Five kilos for 406 men—I can't figure out how little that is for each man.

ISLAND OF HOKKAIDO—MURORAN ***Friday, October 27, 1944***

Rain here again which makes Muroran a dismal gloomy place. We celebrated Al Brown's birthday last night by opening a can of Prem with some toast—that constitutes a celebration under these circumstances, although the diet here is not bad at all. Usually there are plenty of vegetables but little meat, and no fats. Even though the picture is good, this weather is depressing. The best thing to do is keep busy. Which I will do right now—Baking in the kitchen today. 6:30 PM—I can't eat my supper until after sick parade—as I am not very hungry. So I have a few minutes.

Saturday afternoon—Have just heard that four more boxes of Red Cross clothes have arrived. We shall see how these are going to be distributed. It's hard to forget about the cold weather.

Sunday—These entries have been a bit disjointed. Today we did our monthly inspection of the men and they look fairly well on the whole. Most of them have gained at least a kilo. There has been a great deal of polishing and cleaning here today, so everyone is sure the Colonel from Hakodate will arrive in the next 48 hours.

ISLAND OF HOKKAIDO—MURORAN *Saturday, November 4, 1944*

Another visit from the Colonel has been consummated. He read us a news clipping quoting Vargas' message to the U.S. from Radio Tokyo concerning the declaration of war by the Republic of the Philippines about the first of October. In it he mentions the bombing of Manila and other cities. The Colonel said that many men had asked for news, but he had received orders not to tell us any. One thing he could tell us was that the whole American Fleet had tried to attack some very small islands where there were just a few Nip troops, and they had been annihilated by the Nip Fleet and Air corps. The battle lasted 10 days. On the first day they sank three times as much as Pearl Harbor, and the second day twice as much. He neglected to outline the program of the last eight days. But there wasn't much doubt that the American fleet was again completely destroyed.

ISLAND OF HOKKAIDO—MURORAN *Monday, November 6, 1944*

Election Day tomorrow—How long will it take for us to hear the results of the election? If Dewey wins they will tell us about it right away—If Roosevelt stays in. they will try to keep it from us as long as possible. But I think we will manage to find out fairly quickly either way it goes. Sent another postcard last night. Have no idea whether they are getting home regularly or not since I have heard nothing since the Gripsholm mail. No, I take that back. I did get a radiogram forwarded about two months after our arrival in Japan.

ISLAND OF HOKKAIDO—MURORAN *November 7, 1944*

Election Day—Not much excitement here but I imagine there is plenty at home. Saw ice on the ground for the first time this morning at Tenko—The centigrade was at 2 degrees at 6:30 AM. I don't like this cold at all. Re: the Red Cross clothing—When Capt. Borski and Major Murray were called down to receive 4 boxes of Red Cross clothing, I went down with them. Then on the basis of the camp inventory, which I had compiled, I offered a plan of distribution between the Dutch and British, which was accepted.

Regarding individual distribution, I worked it out with Major Murray—the Dutch I left to Capt Borski. I arranged for the 4 American Corps men to get a suit of winter underwear—the two working in the repair shop to get a pair of overalls, and the two in the hospital a pair of socks. They are pretty well fixed up. We made some adjustments in the previous issue of Mr. Wynd, picking up 32 pairs of underpants that had been duplicated, and an undershirt. All the underpants were redistributed to outside workers, and I kept the undershirt as I had no winter underwear at all—it helps a good deal.

ISLAND OF HOKKAIDO—MURORAN *November 10, 1944*

Saw the first snow this morning and it didn't make me feel any better. Have heard nothing official about the election, but the way the local boys are acting, I think Roosevelt has done it again.

ISLAND OF HOKKAIDO—MURORAN *November 11, 1944*

Armistice Day—The Japanese doctor from Hakodate is coming tomorrow. His last visit left us going around in circles. The Shoko called us down to his office last night and read us a message from the High Commandant—Colonel Emoto said that in spite of point 5 on his program that no more POW would die from any cause. A man had died at Hakodate and he was quite put out about it—therefore, in the future the following action would be taken by both Japanese doctors and POW doctors. Without regard for personal feelings, the Camp Commandant must be notified under the following circumstances.

1. When a patient's illness is outside the specialties of the doctors taking care of him.
2. When a patient's condition is so serious that there is no chance of him recovering.
3. When the diagnosis is unknown.

I don't know what the Camp Commandant will be able to do about it, but that's the way it stands now. But we will see what Dr. Shiba says about the death in his camp. When he was last here he had us send the weakest men to Hakodate so that they would have better care with him there. This noon we began thinking back to our last meal that didn't consist mainly of rice, and it's been a long time of rice san kai or three times a day. I really feel that when the time comes and we eat a meal without rice, our stomachs will send off their message to the brain saying that it is still half empty—shouting for rice. I hope not.

ISLAND OF HOKKAIDO—MURORAN *Thursday, November 16, 1944*

Have been out scooping coal, which warmed me up for awhile. We have just concluded another session with the Nippon doctor from Hakodate and he is a changed man. The first thing he did when he saw us was to say that a man had died at Hakodate. He didn't give us any chance to ask any questions. He then asked whether we had received the Colonel's message. I began to feel embarrassed for him. He must have been raked back and forth over the coals ever since it happened.

Sunday—Just finished a hot bath—a moral victory for our side. I have not made myself very popular since the visit of the doctor. I told him that we still had trouble trying to get aspirin for the evening sick parade. The Socho had a Japanese sick parade every three days for those men sick enough to be kept in from work, but there was never any medicine issued for those men we saw each evening after work. Well the Doctor had a long session with the Socho and the Shoko and the result was that the Jap parade has been completely eliminated. And each day we can put in a chit for daily issue of medicine. I then told him that the Colonel had arranged for additional stoves for the men but not additional coal—Therefore the group and hospitals were cold most of the day. He replied that they were short of coal. I then pointed out that over at the factory they had coal heaps 3 stories high. He had no answer for that. As a final blow I mentioned that the Colonel had stated that we would have a bath 3 times a week, and we were getting only two. That also was straightened out. Later on the Shoko had the three doctors down to his office and informed us that if we wanted anything in the future, to ask him and not Dr. Shiba. We had only brought up the medicine question five or six times before. He also told us on the q.t. that there were many boxes of Red Cross food on the way and should arrive before Christmas. Probably some medicine also. We have managed quite well on the Sulfa drugs saving the biggest share for the winter.

Oh, yes—I asked the Dr. about the new camp but he didn't have much to say about it. I explained that I was quite comfortable here, and did not want to move, but if a doctor had to leave, I was the one. He did say that there was a new camp and they were now working on the hospital. I also mentioned that the American Corpsmen wished to go with me if I was transferred. From what he said, I think it will happen the first part of December. While I am sure that it won't be as comfortable in the new camp, I am ready to get away from here. I can feel myself getting grouchier and more irritable every day. Sometimes when I am in the mess with the four Dutch Officers and they are all jabbering back and forth I think I will explode. But so far, I have just sat in the corner and ignored them in the same manner that they ignore me. A change will do me good. Another 10 days will see me back in the cookhouse, and that is probably a good thing, as it will keep me occupied.

For the past two weeks, with this cold weather, my batman and I have been having quite a time trying to make my bed so that it will keep me warm. Every night it has been different. Since we have no mattresses it is necessary to sleep on two blankets. The chief difficulty then is to keep the blankets tucked in and the bed together. It doesn't take more than an hour for me to kick the bottom and the sides out, and from then on it's a losing battle between the blankets and me. There is always a cold draft whisking in someplace. As soon as one place is covered up another spot becomes vulnerable. For the last 3 nights I think we have hit on the solution. Paddy has made a blanket roll leaving just enough room for me to wiggle in. And although nature's calls are indeed a problem it is worth the effort. At least I am warm and I couldn't kick out of those blankets if I were a mule.

ISLAND OF HOKKAIDO—MURORAN

Wednesday, November 22, 1944

~ Tomorrow is Thanksgiving, according to Roosevelt anyway, and I have been trying to figure out some way the American Corpsmen can celebrate it. About all I can do is give them a can of corned beef and let it go at that. Did the President repeat that the American Armed Forces throughout the world would have turkey for Thanksgiving? I heard him say that last year—I fear we don't fall in that classification. But that doesn't bother me very much.

Yesterday I took out all my mail and read them through again. May 14, 1943 was the first word you had of my whereabouts. It doesn't seem possible that you had no word for so long. That's 13 months after we were captured. We still haven't had any mail come via Russia, but some of the English have received mail dated July, 1944. Just to keep occupied, I tried to write down the different ways I had gone back and forth across country, but I am having a difficult time with June, 1935, and September, 1936—Our memories for pre-war events are quite inadequate.

ISLAND OF HOKKAIDO—MURORAN *November 25, 1944*

Yesterday was a big day in the camp. Five hundred boxes of Red Cross food came into camp, which means 2000 individual boxes. American—for our British and Dutch allies—Capt. Brown insists all this food is sent for American POW only. If that were true, there has been enough food for all Americans to have two boxes a month for the rest of the war. But I think it was meant for everyone. Certainly the Dutch Red Cross is in no position to be sending food to their POW In fact, they are probably getting American Red Cross Relief supplies in Holland right now. Incidentally, rumor had the war over in Germany again last night. Also occupation of 2/3 of Formosa. I like to keep mentioning each time the rumor tells of the fall of Germany—because one of these times it's going to be the solid truth. In fact, it could be the truth this time. Roosevelt's Thanksgiving was observed by opening a can of salmon. I gave the 5 corpsmen a package of Japanese cigarettes along with their corned beef (turkey) dinner. It has been almost impossible to get a cigarette in camp, and a package of 10 was selling for 25 yen. Two and a half yen for one cigarette. Now that the Red Cross cigarettes are in the men are much better off. The boxes are changed a bit from last year. Only 5 packages of cigarettes and one can of soluble coffee. But there are two packages of Wrigley's gum in each box.

ISLAND OF HOKKAIDO—MURORAN *November 27, 1944*

We received our first issue of Red Cross two days ago and it has been a treat. It works out to almost 5 full boxes for each man. Quite a bit different from the Canadian Red Cross two months ago; one box for four men. We are scheduled to get another box for Christmas, one on New Year's Day to celebrate the Japanese Holiday, and one Feb. 15. Then 4 boxes for 5 men on the fifth box—about 60 pounds of food for each man. Each unit contains a pound can of powdered milk, a half pound of cheese, 1 can of C. Beef, two cans of luncheon meat, 4 cans (4 oz.) of butter, 1 can of jam, 1 can of pate, 1 of salmon, 1 can soluble coffee, a half pound of sugar, a pound of raisins, 2 bars of soap and 2 bars of gum, 2 bars of D. ration chocolate, and I think that's all—oh, yes—five to seven packages of cigarettes. A cup of coffee with cream and sugar is really a treat. And nothing can beat that army emergency chocolate ration. It is quite interesting to see the change in the camp morale since this food came in. One hears singing groups around the fire with men working over the stoves on new quaning combinations. It is odd to see so many people chewing gum. And many of these Britishers have never chewed gum before. Capt. Brown, the dentist, has just about finished his work. He has managed to scrape and check the teeth of every man in camp, with over 150 extractions. He and I are going to have a real Thanksgiving dinner this Thursday now that we have our Red Cross boxes.

I found out today that the 5 American Corpsmen supplemented their Thanksgiving lunch last Thursday with a small brown dog that had unluckily wandered into the dispensary. I didn't think they were that hungry. We have just had an inventory of the 600 odd library books and 3 songbooks were missing. As a result the Camp Commandant ordered that no books, games or phonograph would be issued until the books were found—not so good, as I am quite sure the books will not be found. Sent off two more postcards yesterday—one to you, and one to Sid Garfield in Los Angeles. He is probably in Washington working with the Kaiser Corporation. In just a few more days back in the cookhouse I go. It has been a pleasant month outside. Had quite a chat with the Shoko a couple of days ago during which he mentioned we would have the pig for Christmas—he also asked me to submit a plan to him for a Christmas program. Have been dreaming about getting home again—the American food must have done it. Anyway, it made me think about it today—so I thought I had better begin to study again.

Had an interesting session with Cecil on pneumonia. Am going to try and do a bit of reviewing each day. I don't want to be caught unawares when this thing is finally over. In December we shall have a hot bath 4 times a week. A really good thing in this cold weather. One feels warm for the rest of the day. And it should lower the incidence of skin infection during the winter.

Matters finally were brought to a head in our Officers' mess today. I spoke to Dr. Sutter and suggested that if the Dutch Officers would try to speak English when Dr. Murray and I were in the mess, it would be a pleasanter place for everyone. He in turn, suggested this to the other Dutch Officers who agreed and we tried it for the first time tonight. Everyone was on their best behavior, and it was quite clubby—I don't know how long it will keep up, but I think it was a step in the right direction. Ten PM and with the thermometer at 0 degrees Centigrade, the best place is bed.

ISLAND OF HOKKAIDO—MURORAN *November 28, 1944*

Received a standing order from Hakodate stating that 38 boxes of Red Cross drugs had been received, and they were being divided between four camps. This one was scheduled to get 13 boxes. We have managed to keep most of our Sulfa drugs for the winter.

ISLAND OF HOKKAIDO—MURORAN *December 2, 1944*

This has been the coldest day yet. And I am back in the cookhouse. It is colder than I expected it to be. Al Brown has gone back to Hakodate and we don't know when he will pay us another visit. He was supposed to leave at 9 AM but the motorcycle didn't show up and he began walking. Well he missed the train and they brought him back to wait for the one PM train. Must add a note to say that our mess has quickly degenerated to its former status, with the exception of Dr. Lutter who keeps trying. The two Junior Dutch Cadet Officers have apparently taken the attitude that there are four of them and only one English and one American. Wherefore, why not speak Dutch—So I will say no more about it. Still no word about the new camp—I can feel myself getting more touchy and irritable everyday. A terrible thing—I know that I must be quite difficult to live with. I know I won't be as comfortable in the new camp, but I will be extremely disappointed if I don't go. The American Corpsmen will also. Tomorrow, *Yasumay,* and we sleep until seven. I can hear that Siberian breeze whistling outside right this minute, and it feels like Michigan Blvd. on a windy day in December. The bed for me.

ISLAND OF HOKKAIDO—MURORAN *Monday, December 4, 1944*

The wind still moaning—and no warmer—Rabbit fur earmuffs were issued to all the camp tonight—an odd contraption. But they are probably quite handy when the temperature falls away from the zero mark. Last night we had a concert in one of the empty billets, and I have hardly thawed out yet. Two stoves were put in for the evening, but it made little difference. After it finished, at 9 PM, I decided to have a cup of soluble coffee to warm my innards. The coffee helped, but I had to pay the piper—by wiggling out of my warm bedding roll four times during the night—along with snow blowing in through the cracks between the window frames. Each day makes me more appreciative of my leather flying jacket and gabardine flying suit issued me from the P.N.A.D. in the Philippines. The temptation to get rid of them during many of my former moves was great, but the possibility of going to Japan warned me to hold on to them. The Navy Great coat that was given to me in Bilibid is also very warm, but I rarely wear it as it does yeoman's duty on my bed. Right now there are seven blankets on my bed plus a Japanese overcoat, and the Navy great coat. Still I am not too warm. It doesn't look like I'll ever be able to stand a good solid New England winter again. The camp is cleaning up again, which means the Colonel is due again. It seems he is always just coming, or he has just left—the boys have just written a parody—Santa Claus Emoto, everything he does is Joto. I agree with them too. Our Red Cross drugs were supposed to arrive today, and we were disappointed when they didn't arrive. My opinion is that the drug list will closely resemble that of last year—with some possible changes for new sulfa drugs.

Received two more cards to send today. I fear a review of the cards I have sent you for the past two years would show little variety. Each time I get a chance to write there are only two things I want to get across. One, to ask whether you are well—two, to tell you that I am well so you won't worry about me, all the rest is just padding. Still have heard nothing of mail coming this way.

This evening in the mess, automobiles were brought up in the discussion, and of course, the first thing I thought of was the pearly gray Buick I had for four days. It was certainly a thrill for me when we walked out of the East Boston airport that night, and Albert gave me the keys for that long gray car at the curb. Probably everyone appreciates their home most when they find that circumstances force them to leave it. But I am certain that I have always appreciated mine, and will always be thankful for those few days we spent together before all this started. It gives me many pleasant memories now.

Major Murray saw his 32nd birthday go by today. I certainly hope to be home for mine. In fact, I was a bit surprised to be a POW on my 30th. Better luck next year.

ISLAND OF HOKKAIDO—MURORAN *December 10, 1944*

Sunday evening and another *Yasumay* day has passed. This past week we have been working up suggestions for Christmas Day. One of the Bakers suggested that we try to make an individual cake for each man in a milk tin, asking the Nips for flour, sugar, soda bicarbonate and grease, each man supplying the powdered milk, chocolate, raisins and butter from his Red Cross box. It sounded o.k. to me so we threw one together to test , and after showing it to all the men in camp I took it down and had the Shoko try it. He was quite pleased with the idea and quite agreeable, but said the only snag would be getting the baking soda. That was four nights ago. Yesterday just as the bath orderly called us, the Shoko sent for me. He wished to know if we could use yeast for the cake, as it was very difficult to get the soda. I checked with the bakers and the reply was lame. I then explained that in the Japanese Medical Supplies there were now 12 five hundred gram boxes which we used very seldom, and all we would need for the whole camp would be two kilos—He decided to cogitate a bit more before making a final decision, and in the interim I was too late for my bath.

To take a Japanese bath is quite an experience. Sort of a community affair. In our bath house there are two cement tubs, one about 5 by 9 ft. and the other 5 by 15.—both about 4 feet deep. The water is heated in a large boiler in the next room, and then piped in. The temperature ranges from 40 degrees to 45 degrees Cent. Everyone first washes carefully, on the racks alongside, and then all climb in to soak. The Officers bathe first, and it is quite nice with only four or six in at a time. But then the thundering herd arrives and from there on in it is bedlam. By the time the camp is finished the water is almost black, and as thick as coffee grounds. It pays to get there early. Now that we are getting a bath four times a week, it seems we are always in to soak. I have an extremely mild peripheral neuritis, along with slight edema of the legs. When the bath is over 42 degrees Cent the burning of my legs and feet is so severe, I can hardly stand it. It is probably due to chronic hipoproteinemia. Just about the only protein we get here is in the rice. When there is meat the issue is 10 kg for 400 men. This Red Cross food should help some. The theme of Colonel Emoto's last visit, a short one of three days, was the occupation of India by England back in the eighteen hundreds. I found out that he gives the Nip staff the identical lecture he puts out for the POWs. Two hours of it. The whole thing boiled down to him being a schoolteacher and he needs a class.

ISLAND OF HOKKAIDO—MURORAN
Monday evening, December 11, 1944

Have just come from a meeting with the "talent" in the camp. The Shoko asked me about the arrangements for the Christmas concert, and so another job has developed. The snag is there must be no speaking parts as the Colonel is afraid we might slip in some anti-Nip propaganda. It is quite difficult to get any humor in a program with no dialogue at all. But we are going to try. The men are quite cooperative and if we can find a method to beat the cold it should be all right. Another touchy factor is the perpetual one of trying to do anything with Dutch and English troops in cooperation. I can see why they could never get anything done in the League of Nations. Studied some Cardiology today, but didn't get very far. These are long days, with no news and confined all the time. We still have some men who are on night work, loading pig iron from 7 PM to 3 AM. They get an extra 400 grams of rice a day, but I am sure it's not doing them much good. Some of these nights are truly bitter.

ISLAND OF HOKKAIDO—MURORAN *December 20, 1944*

I see that on Dec. 11 I was complaining the days were too long. Since then, I have hardly had time to eat. On the 13th we received 13 boxes of A.R.C. drugs, 9 boxes of toilet articles, and 41 bales of clothing, including 480 American army greatcoats, and nine bundles of assorted clothing. We have been quite busy deciding how to issue the clothes. In the interim I had another go with Capt. Borski. For the first two days I was busy taking care the drugs, and so I let him and Major Murray check over the clothes. The next thing I knew he was writing a letter to the Shoko in French giving a plan of distribution of all the clothes, and as usual there was no mention made of the four Americans. This time I decided there was no sense in being considerate of his feelings, as he didn't appreciate it. I collared him in the mess and really laced him out, in front of Dr. Sutter and Dr. Murray. I repeated everything I had had to say before, and told him that I wanted a full copy of all the articles received, and I also made suggestions as to two mistakes in his plan. Well, it was the same old story. He mumbled around a bit, and a short while later, brought me a complete typed list of everything to check over before taking it up to the Shoko.

In regard to the concert, we are in the midst of heavy rehearsals. The Shoko has been quite agreeable to all my requests. We finally worked out a theme for the affair. The setting is in the entertainment room of the high Rajah. His Prime Minister of Entertainment is attempting to find some diversion for the Rajah to snap him out of the doldrums, and then on comes our acts. To get around the cold drafts in the assembly room, we have taken over 100 blankets and erected a tent of blankets, which completely encloses the ceiling and walls. We plan to use 3 or 4 stoves inside—and do the trick. This morning I asked the Shoko is we could use the hall Christmas Eve for a final rehearsal with the stoves going, to see how it would be, and he gave us the go sign. The next thing on my mental bill of fare is the cookhouse. We are in the throes of the cake for Xmas. The Shoko has been stalling me off every day about the soda, and today, he finally decided. If I would supply one kilo from the Red Cross drugs, he would supply one kilo from his medical supplies. So we made a deal. Now we have to go about the business of collecting all the individual contributions.

ISLAND OF HOKKAIDO — MURORAN

Christmas night, December 25, 1944

And it has been a really full weekend. Wish to make a record of Xmas messages received:

Christmas cards.

One from American Red Cross—"The American Red Cross sends you Christmas greetings and a sincere wish for continual strength and courage in the New Year—" Signed Paul O'Conner, Chairman.

Message from American Government—"To every American Prisoner of War goes this Christmas message of appreciation for your steadfast courage and faith with my prayers for your well being Stop—May you find some cheer and hope this Christmas day and may the good Lord watch over you." Signed—G.C. Marshall, Chief of Staff. A peculiar thing getting a message from the C. of S. through the Nips.

ISLAND OF HOKKAIDO—MURORAN

Thursday evening, December 28, 1944

Very close to the New Year. The days have been racing by because I have been busy. The week preceding Christmas was like a permanent nightmare. Some of the people in our show were on night duty, and never did get to rehearse before they went on. Our big final rehearsal was Xmas Eve—and I was tied up in the cookhouse all day, as we tried to bake bread in the morning, and the cake in the afternoon. Two days before this I had a row with Araki Sacho because I refused to give him some bicarb tablets in return for his soda, and as a result he refused to supply any soda. Well we were in too deep to cancel it, and I agreed to use the powdered soda from the Red Cross medicines if the Shoko agreed to supply us with some for medical purposes whenever we requested it. Then came the job of collecting the ingredients from each man and checking them all. I tried to make bread with homemade potato yeast, but it was too cold and the breads looked like hotcakes when they came out of the oven. And this gave us a late start on the cake—in fact, the individual cakes were finally finished at 3 AM Christmas morning. They truly came out better than we expected. We also made one for each of the regular Nip staff—the Shoko was quite pleased with his. All the men **kept looking** in the cookhouse to be sure nothing happened to their ingredients. I had Sgt. Metuozzi take over the rehearsal, but at eight o'clock he came over and said that things weren't progressing very well and that I had better come over and line things up. I dashed over to the assembly room from the cookhouse and arrived just as the Shoko came in to see what was doing. Even though the night workers were out, we ran through a hasty show and arranged for a dress rehearsal at 1:30 PM Christmas Day. Then back to the cookhouse to see all the cakes weighed before they were baked—each 420 grams. I didn't get my supper until ten and the bakers kept right on going until three. Christmas morning I found that the program was all upset on account of the religious services which were continually being switched around.

After I finally managed to have all the services in the morning, the Nip didn't issue the meat for lunch until 10 AM, and so we didn't serve until almost two. By the time we were ready to start the rehearsal it was time for the show. In fact our cast was late in getting into costume, and the show would have been late if the Shoko hadn't come down to make some special awards to men who had worked a whole year without missing a day. One man in camp, an interior decorator in civilian life, made the costumes and they really made the show. When the Nips saw the opening scene they sent for the photographer right away and made us reenact the opening scene.

Christmas play.

Christmas play.

The sultan really looked like a sultan—and the guards and band had very good uniforms. Each part followed without a hitch, and after it was over, many said it was the best they had ever seen in this camp. The strain was over Christmas night, and I was able to relax for the first time in a week. Now, all the boys are asking for another cake on New Year's Day. I don't think we will get any soda for it.

We had an interesting time in the kitchen the day before yesterday. It is the custom each year for the Nips to make some special kind of unleavened bread from pounded steamed rice for the New Year's Day. Here all the Nip guards bring in their wives and children to help them and work at it all day. The rice is first steamed in baskets, and then pounded while hot with a large wooden mallet, until it is a gummy mass. This is then powdered with flour, rolled out in sheets about 3/8 of an inch thick and two feet square, and then cut up into small pieces about three inches square. These are given to everyone on New Year's Day, and they are supposed to represent the Emperor's Body or some such thing.

Well, these people had quite a picnic in our kitchen, about 20 of them, and we had to do our cooking around and between them. The stuff isn't bad if one has Red Cross butter and jam to put on it. And here we get another parcel on New Year's Day. What a difference they make to the men in camp. They don't seem like the same people. This will be our third parcel in little over a month. My four American Corpsmen sent me down an unusual Christmas card early Xmas morning with all their caricatures on it, along with a whole bag full of Wrigley's chewing gum.

It brought a lump to my throat. I also received some homemade cards from some of the English boys, which made me feel extremely good. And the group honchos thanked me for the effort and work I had put in for the Christmas program and dinner. It is peculiar, that this camp is made up of 2/3 English and 1/3 Dutch, and yet with the exception of the two church services, I had to arrange just about everything, from carolers singing Christmas Eve after taps, through to the supper Xmas night. Of course my being in the cookhouse for the month of December left the food angle up to me. But I am still not too sure how I became mixed up with the concert—and the latter would have been impossible if I didn't have Sgt. Coozier, the qm. man to fix up the hall and tent, plus Chinie, who made the costumes. Now that it is all finished I am working on the new Red Cross drugs that came. This time we have three critical medicine boxes instead of one. That gives us a large supply of sulfa drugs—18 pounds of sulfaquanidun, 900 sulfadiazine tablets, 3000 sulfathiozole, and three pounds of sulfanilamide, also a third box of multiple vitamins and assorted drugs—giving us 45,000 M.U. tablets.

ISLAND OF HOKKAIDO—MURORAN *Saturday, December 30, 1944*

We're off again. I dropped in to see the Socho this AM and informed him that if he would loosen up from one kilo of soda, we could make each man half a cake. He in turn hinted quite strongly that he could use a bar of chocolate or a can of powdered milk. Well, this floors me a bit, but Major Murray came through and slipped him the chocolate. From there I proceeded down to the Shoko to see what he thought of the idea. He wasn't too enthusiastic because of the sugar idea, and he was amused when I suggested that we might get some sacks of sugar in future Red Cross. We had to go up and count how much sugar there was in the stores. When we found 22 sacks of sugar and 33 of flour he said *"Yoush!"* which means o.k. in Nippongo. I then broke it to him gently that the 3rd Red Cross box would have to be issued today so that the men could get the ingredients. This stopped him as he had planned to issue the boxes on New Year's Day, the big Nip holiday. But again he came through with a *yoush* and away. I went to get the wheels of progress in motion. All men will work only half day tomorrow so that they can return and scrub up the camp for the great day. Every single thing must be washed and polished. And this finds me in the midst of unpacking all the medicines. We have had to move all the I.V. glucose saline and plasma to a warmer place to prevent them from freezing solid.

Tomorrow is my last day in the cookhouse for a month, and it will probably be a tough one. The Nip Hancho Kudo has not been there for 3 days because his baby died, and along with this there have been no vegetables coming in for quite awhile. This makes it very difficult to find something to cook. Fortunately there has been fish but the men have been spoiled by the

Camp medical staff: (back row) Schryver, Lapré, Stevens, Finucane, Comber, Matuozzi, Stern, Umehi, Ysendoorn, Meyer, Cox, Rosario, Fitch, Moffat, Weerman, Hill, Warnes; (front row) Japanese doctor, Major Murray, Lieut. Andler, Lieut. Lutter.

Red Cross food and turn up their respective noses at fish. I will appreciate the change from the cookhouse, as it is not very pleasant up there the first thing in the morning. Something always seems to be going wrong—one day the rice is short, the next day the fish doesn't get around, last night someone took the soup tub of Group 13, and they didn't have any soup. And tomorrow I will have to stay in the kitchen all day again, to see them make the cake. Oh yes, the Shoko called Sgt. Crozier after I left, and told him to see me and say that he would like me to repeat his order on the cake for him and his staff. What do you think of that?

LETTERS FROM JAPAN

1945

ISLAND OF HOKKAIDO—MURORAN

6 PM, Friday, January 5, 1945

I am waiting for my rice and Spam to fry up for my supper. Still no vegetables in the kitchen, and the soups are quite foul—dried fish and a bit of flour. The Red Cross boxes of the men are taking a beating—and so is mine. It is very fortunate that we have them now or our diet would be straight rice. But I know that when I again get as hungry as I was in Bataan, I will be glad to eat this dried fish or anything else.

ISLAND OF HOKKAIDO—MURORAN

January 8, 1945

The rising suns are flying out front again. Imperial rescript day—They shouldn't be doing that a great deal longer. New Year's Day went off without a hitch. The cakes came out even better than the last ones and all the men were quite satisfied—an unusual state of affairs. It is interesting to see the difference between the British and the American in regard to the Red Cross food. In Cabanatuan the big thing was hotcakes and everyone was making them. Here it is puddings—puddings of every description. And it is quite simple to chill them by simply leaving them in the room where the temperature hovers at minus 5 degrees. I even tried my hand at throwing together a pudding myself, and it wasn't bad at all. Sugar is the key.

ISLAND OF HOKKAIDO—MURORAN
Tuesday, January 9, 1945

Ran across an American history book in the library and ran across many dates that I did not recall. Have just heard that Lnguyan is coming back into the news. This time we are making the landing with about 800 barges, 10 aircraft carriers, cruisers and all the rest of it. And along with it, just to muddle them up a half dozen of our cruiser came down and began shelling the largest of the Kuriles. Along with this—500 planes have daily been making the lives of the Formosans a bit hazardous. The old tempo is picking up—picking up.

ISLAND OF HOKKAIDO—MURORAN
Wednesday, January 10, 1945

We are awaiting a general inspection to check up on our QM supplies, so everything has been called in, including the medical library. That doesn't leave us much to do. Five days ago we were told that a pipe burst and there would be no bath. Since then we have waited impatiently for it to be repaired. Finally, this AM, I began checking up to speed up repairs.

ISLAND OF HOKKAIDO—MURORAN
Monday evening, January 15, 1945

Having just received a Ticonderoga pencil from the good old Red Cross, I will try it out.

ISLAND OF HOKKAIDO—MURORAN
January 16, 1945

The days roll by with little or no effort on my part. Half of January is gone. Last night we had a blackout drill, and today a detail began cleaning out the air raid trenches, and getting them in shape. With the temperature hovering at eleven below, it's going to take a good deal of bombing to get me away from a warm fire into a shallow ditch full of snow. Our camp staff, as well as the civilians at the factory, have become quite *B-Ni Jeu qu* (B-29) conscious. It colors all their conversation. We had a couple of visitors drop in to see our Nip Corpsman. They are from the A.A. outfit up on the hill, and from what we can gather they aren't too well off. No overcoats, short food, little coal, and all night duty every third night. Also many cases of frostbite—we haven't had any to date. I truly think that the POW's are much better off than the civilians or troops here. Besides the regular issue we have the Red Cross food, medicines, clothes and toilet articles—which makes a great deal of difference.

Yesterday we gave everyone in the camp an injection of anti-typhoid serum and there have been a number of sore arms resulting. In fact, Dr. Lutter has been in bed all day today. Ever since I heard about the last landing on the Philippines I have been bewailing my fate that I was shipped out. To sit here in the northern top of Japan and think that hundreds of American planes are flying back and forth over Cabanatuan fills me with frustration. It must be a wonderful feeling for those fellows who remained behind. And I imagine the Santa Tomas internees are getting a bit restless, too.

Last week we had an inspection by some bigwigs and staff, and when they made their rounds of the hospital I was pointed out as the Americano—The way the game is progressing, I have a feeling that Americans are not going to be unduly popular in this part of the world. I can still hardly wait for the day when I can see some Yankee pilots coming over this area. The Colonel is due on the 21st of this month. His topic will be the American Revolution, which should be a bit unusual. I don't know which side he will take—he will probably run down both sides. At least it should be a little different viewpoint than the one we were taught in school.

ISLAND OF HOKKAIDO—MURORAN
Wednesday evening, January 17, 1945

This has been the coldest day yet. But we have just finished being parboiled in our community bath and so we are quite comfortable. Have just been talking to one of them who says that that this business is going very bad for them, and he expects it all to be over soon. He further stated that when the fighting finished in the Philippines, that was the death knell, well, this cheered me up no end. While we have had no news for about a week the plan must be progressing without a hitch, judging form his attitude. Did I mention that in each food parcel there were two packages of Wrigley's spearmint gum? Since I have no use of the Japanese cigarettes we purchase in the canteen each week, I have been swapping for gum. Some of the English soldiers with plates who don't or can't chew gum gave me theirs. My four American Corpsmen heard that I wanted gum, and Christmas morning as a present with quite an original card, I received a box full of gum, ten packages. Now I have a roomful—and the Shoko has just told us that there will be no food boxes returned to Hakodate which means that we will get almost two full boxes more. That carries us on to the end of February. Perhaps there will be another shipment in by then. Ah, bugle blaazen for supper. We have had onion soup 3 times a day every day for the past 16 days. When I get back to Fred's Steak house, I think I will take that Delmonico without onions.

ISLAND OF HOKKAIDO—MURORAN *Saturday, January 20, 1945*

Another acute attack of the *Let's-get-out-of-here Blues.* Really fed up. Have had a sudden spurt in the educational field, and have been doing quite a bit of physiology. But it is wearing off already. The Colonel is due tomorrow. Late flash from the Socho—not until the 25th—I was hoping he would break the monotony.

ISLAND OF HOKKAIDO—MURORAN *January 21, 1945*

I keep trying to realize this is 1945. Whenever I think of home of California, I visualize conditions as they were in '41. How much of a change is there? No new cars since Jan. '42—Army or Navy everywhere one turns. Do people still go to shows, nightclubs, dances, ballgames? I suppose they do. How about the big hospitals? Probably all women interns or medical students. And who attends the colleges and universities? Only the lame, sick and weary should be left. Are big Army bombers an every day sight? Probably no one even looks up when a flight of four motor jobs go over. I have been straining my eyes to see an American plane for three years now. I am sorry I ever came out. When and if this business ends I have some moral obligations in Manila that I must take care of.

We are having our monthly weighing and medical inspection of the troops yesterday and today, and we certainly can see the results of the Red Cross food. Some men have gained as much as eight kilos in one month and the average for the camp is an increase of about 3 kg.—that's almost 7 lbs. Along with this, the cookhouse issues has been the scantiest since I have been here. Onions and rice 3 times along with some dried fish at noon—If the men could get even one box a month I feel they would all come out of it alright. Even I gained two kilos and still have not finished my Red Cross food. We had one man discharged today from the dysentery ward who has gained seventeen kilos in four months. I think he is ready for discharge. Including the isolation there are only 12 patients altogether. None seriously ill. A year ago there were almost forty. But when I came here almost a year ago, we would go sometimes for 2 or 3 days without even aspirin. Now, with a room full of Red Cross drugs, it's a difficult problem to decide which drug to use.

ISLAND OF HOKKAIDO—MURORAN

8 P.M, *January 27, 1945*

And I have just finished some toast with butter and strawberry jam on it, and coffee with powdered milk and sugar. There aren't many POW's sitting down to an evening snack like that. We can thank the good old Red Cross for that. And in four days we get our fourth unit. While I am not quite ready for it, most of the men are. Our hospital figures were down to 8 yesterday but we put a man in last night who was passing a good deal of blood and mucous. A microscopic on his stool today revealed numerous very suspicious cysts mononuclear, along with some vegetative forms not too typical of histolysis. But on the clinical findings I think we will give him a course of emetine.

ISLAND OF HOKKAIDO—MURORAN *February 5, 1945*

A *Yasumay* Day, and just about the nastiest one yet—which is saying a good deal for this part of the world. The old dependable breeze from Siberia is whipping a snowstorm around so well that I managed to get quite well covered on my short trip to the cookhouse this AM At present, we should be quite elated about the general progress of things, but I have been way down in the valley and very hard to get along with. I think I have been extremely careful to keep this to myself but Major Murray has sort of let himself go. He started off by telling the two cadet Officers in our mess that he didn't like them shaving in our mess-room just because it had a stove. He mentioned that all the other Officers, 4, to wit, shaved in their rooms, and they could, too. Since these two men are Dutch, they were a bit upset that the Major should try to tell them anything. And in the midst of all this he further informed one that he should stop using an open five-gallon can for a urinal in his room at night, as it stunk up the baggage.

All through this I didn't open my mouth. The Major is a bit difficult to live with. He states his side of the situation quite positively, and as soon as anyone tries to put forth a different viewpoint he replies—Let's drop the matter—very difficult, very difficult. I think I have learned my lesson; I never disagree with him about anything if I can possibly avoid it. When I first came here I would go in the mess for breakfast or supper and find everyone reading—that looked a bit peculiar, and for awhile I tried to carry on a conversation with each one in turn, but soon I found myself doing the same thing there was just no one to talk to.

A brief note of pertinent parts of Bulletin for future reference

POW Information Bureau
Washington 25, D.C.
POW Information Bulletin
Revised April 1944.

1. General—Information is herein tendered to military personnel of the U.S. held as prisoners of war. Their requests, applications, and inquiries

are invited, as may become necessary and may be made in the manner described in Par. 13.

2. Pay and Allowance accounts
   a. Credits—During absence pay and allowance at rates in effect at time of capture continue to be credited to the accounts of POW There are also credited any increase in pay allowances accruing during absence by reason of legislation, new regulations, length of service completed or promotion.
   b. Debits—POW pay received from the holding power will not be charged against the pay accounts of the individuals.

4b. Normal allotments—may be made to individuals, insurers, banks, or for purchase of bonds. No special form or request is required but each request should state clearly the purpose, monthly amount, date of beginning, name, and address of the person or institution to receive payments, and the signature, rank, S. Army serial no. of the individual making allotment.

5. Purchase of Bonds—Bond allotments from pay and allowances for the purchase of Government, bonds may be in one of the following amounts or multiples thereof: $18.75, 37.50, 75.00, & 375.00. In 10 years mature to $25.00, 50.00, 100.00, & 500.00. These bonds are redeemable at any time after 60 days from date of purchase . . . Bonds may be left with the Treasury Dept. for safe keeping and receipt thereof will be sent to a designated person. Request for purchase must indicate the personal desire of the allotter and is acceptable in any form so long as the allotter's signature and essential information are presented.

8. Soldiers and Sailors Civil Relief Act.—Authorizes court to protect interests of persons in service by staying lawsuits setting aside judgments for indebtedness, recovery of property, etc. where the serviceman is prejudiced by inability to be present.

9. Taxes—No exemption from payment of income taxes—Legislation—automatically postpones for POW the payment of federal income taxes.

10. Power of Attorney—The instrument should be acknowledged by Notary Public or other official authorized to make acknowledgements and wit-

nessed by 2 witnesses.... Acknowledgements taken by Commissioned Officers should show the rank, serial number, and branch of service of the officer and the person making the acknowledgement. For further information write to Swiss Legation for War Dept. pamphlet. "Personal Affairs of Military Personnel and Aid for their Dependents."

11. Promotions
    a. *Officers*—The policy as to temporary promotions of officers allows action to be completed on recommendation in process when an officer is reported as missing in action or as a prisoner of war.
12. POW Information Bureau—Established in Washington in accord c Art. 77 of Geneva Convention. It receives cabled reports from Central agency of POW operated by the International Red Cross in Geneva, concerning American POW's, their wounds, hospitalizations and physical condition. Similar information is also received through the protecting power (Swiss). All such information together with mailing instructions and a general information circular containing excerpts from the bulletins promptly transmitted to each next of kin. An individual file for each POW is maintained and inquiries concerning POW are answered.
13. Communications: All official requests, applications, or inquiries from POW will be mailed to the POW Information Bureau, Washington 25, D.C. and will be transmitted to appropriate agencies for action. It is the War Department's policy to comply as far as practicable with the desires of POW on service matters communicated by them in personal correspondence to dependents who transmit them to the War Dept. Many allotments have been initiated or increased.

Quite a bit—and I have left out a good deal relating to E.M.

ISLAND OF HOKKAIDO—MURORAN *Saturday, February 10, 1945*

Right in the middle of another earthquake—the third in the last fifteen minutes. The brick chimneys in the cookhouse had a close call on the last one. This time not so bad—so far. Anything can happen in this country and frequently does. It appears that the people are being kept up pretty well on developments and getting conditioned to the inevitable future. I find it much easier to study and read medical books with the thought of getting home. All the Cabanatuan boys must be delirious with joy. But there's not much use in kidding myself about our getting gout of here in a month or two. We will be fortunate to be free by this Christmas. In fact I was more optimistic a year ago, I am sure.

Some of the Englishmen here who have been getting airmail cards from home dated Sept. 1944 tell me that their families haven't received any postcards from here dated later than 1943—that certainly was bad news. Now I fear that you don't even know I am in Japan, as I didn't write from here until March, 1944—and we have been sending a card every two weeks. I have just sent a message to the POW Information Bureau in Washington requesting them to increase your allotment from $80.00 to $120.00 and to take all my back pay plus the remainder of my monthly pay and buy liberty Government Bonds. It seems odd that the Japanese will permit us to buy Liberty Bonds with our pay. They probably don't realize what's going on.

ISLAND OF HOKKAIDO—MURORAN *February 16, 1945*

Many changes—Mast/Sgt.Socho and S/Sgt. Gunso have been relieved by two Gochos. The medical one is quite young and if reputed to speak English extremely well—I haven't seen him yet. And my old opponent in the cookhouse is supposed to be relieved in three or four days. From what I can gather on the last inspection his books didn't balance very well, and the local general goes so far as to hint strongly that my friend, Mr. Kudo has been doing a bit of pinchy-pinchy—About four days ago our rice ration was cut from 700 gms. a man to 570—quite a slump. Then, yesterday I was told that all men who worked in the factory would get an additional 135 grams each day they worked. And above this is the 200 gms. of beans for the kurabyasi and 600 gms. of beans for the night workers. At the present state, the night workers are skimming by on a bare 1305 gms. while the camp workers are putting away 570 per day without any trouble. I still have some Red Cross food so I haven't felt the pinch yet but some of the boys are taking in their belts another notch. Trying to put out the rice in the morning now is like a Chinese puzzle. No two groups are alike. A job in the new camp looks better to me every day.

ISLAND OF HOKKAIDO—MURORAN *Sunday, February 18, 1945*

Our two noncoms haven't gone yet, but it should happen any day now. The Medical Socho has come in and introduced himself as Sgt. Umiki. He then proceeded to tell us about himself. He is the artistic type, and has done some professional ballet work up to a year ago. Thinks classical music is lovely, and he loves to hear about any of the arts. He sketches, too, and this morning he was burning violet scented incense in his office next to ours. I suggested to him that he would fit in very well in a Greenwich Village Studio. Incidentally, he has seen duty in the Philippines following the capitulation, and was at Little Baguio, Corregidor, and other familiar places. We have already seen pictures of himself, his home and his sister. The last quite attractive. His English is extremely idiomatic.

ISLAND OF HOKKAIDO—MURORAN
Friday morning, March 9, 1945

Have been working on my model of a B-29 from various sources of information. Trying to do it to scale is a difficult job as I don't have very many of the dimensions. But I did have the span of 140 ft. and the area of 140 sq. meters. Computing the probably length of the fuselage at 96 feet, I worked on the scale of one inch to 11.66 feet giving me a wing span of 12 inches. My supply of material consisted of slabs from different Red Cross boxes and Dr. Lutter's penknife. The Camp Commandant has seen me working on it at various times and asked whether it was supposed to be a consolidated B-24. My reply was that it was a Boeing B-17.

While the weather is getting warmer the camp is getting colder. We were completely out of coal for 3 days and the cookhouse had to use empty crates for preparing the food. Coke was issued to the groups, but in microscopic quantities—7 kg. for a group and we received four for the Officers mess. Everyone is burning wood and where it comes from no one will say. There are quite a few empty billets and if any more wood is taken from these, they will certainly collapse. There should be a fair amount of excitement here when the local authorities finally stumble on to it. Yesterday the CO told the orderlies that all the stoves would be removed on the first of April—last year we had them until May 15ath and there were many cold days after that. As long as they can keep coal for the cookhouse we will manage to get along.

I have completely forgotten to describe the most serious event that has occurred in this camp since I have been here. The General from Tokyo came for his inspection with Col. Emoto, and he was very upset about the large number of people who were not doing their part for Die Nippon by working out at the factory. Second hand we received the information that he had the O.C. and the R.C. on the carpet because of the low working percentage. He mentioned that in the Tokyo camp 95% of the men were working while here we were below 80%—Which puts us on the bottom of the efficiency scale. He was also very upset when he saw the Colonel's policy up on the wall in English in all the groups and buildings. The story goes that this General was born in the States and speaks English flawlessly, but has taken a vow never to say a word of English. It seems he doesn't like the Americans at all.

ISLAND OF HOKKAIDO—MURORAN *Tuesday, March 20, 1945*

My plane is finished and now I can begin to catch up on many neglected duties and tasks. While I still have to work out some sort of a stand for it, I decided to give it a rest.

Big news for me yesterday. The medical gocho told me he saw a card for me in the office from my mother. I ran down to the interpreter to see if he would let me see it. We discussed it for 15 minutes, but after awhile he softened up and permitted me a quick glance. I was able to see your familiar hand with the date Nov. 6, 1944 mailed from Brookline, Mass. This makes it the most recent mail to come into this camp to date. My excitement got the better of me and the twenty-four words are not too clear in my mind. But it shouldn't take him more than 24 days to censor those 24 words. It was a great relief to me to find out that you were well as recently as four months ago, and as the card is addressed to Hakodate, you must know that I am in Japan. Now that mail has caught up with me again I hope that your letters will come regularly. It would be something to get my periodicals here such as the medical Journals and *Readers' Digest,* etc. but if it takes 24 days to censor 24 words I fear that they would never get through a single copy of the J.A.M.A.

ISLAND OF HOKKAIDO—MURORAN

Friday, March 23, 1945

Have just read *Kings Now* by Henry Bellarmann. I feel that I have read a condensed version of it sometime ago, but I can't quite place it. Probably in a Readers' Digest of long ago. But I enjoyed going over it again. The A.R.P. MEN and carpenters have been very busy this past two weeks altering the two shelters for the Japanese personnel. R.R. ties have been brought in for the framework, and then truckloads of cinders are being used to cover them over completely. I don't know what the recent news may have been, but the Shoko had all the Japanese office staff including himself and the POW Officers working in moving the cinders. He appeared to want the shelters finished right now. We have just received another card to write home and I went down to the office to see if it were permissible to mention your card. Michicawa San said it was all right, and showed me two more cards. One from you and one from Albert. Both dated Nov. 26, 1945. I really took my time looking them over this time. Albert mentioned that he gets home often which was glad to hear, and you asked me to send you a cablegram collect—that sounded quite humorous. There's no more chance of my getting close to a cable office than there is of my calling you long distance. We are completely isolated from civilization in the literal sense of the word. We have been sending out radiograms every so often and I have sent a couple I think. Do they get back to you? Just to make sure that I am not passing up anything I will ask the Camp Commandant about this cablegram business. He can't do more than say now.

ISLAND OF HOKKAIDO—MURORAN *Saturday, March 31, 1945*

Tomorrow morning I go back to the cookhouse for a month and I am not looking forward to it at all. In fact, it has kept me feeling depressed all day. While the news is as good as one can expect the days and months are going by and the finish is not yet here. One quarter of 1945 gone by and last June Al Brown was so convinced we would be out of this by Christmas.

A little more than a month ago, about Feb. 26, one of the men was brought back from the factory following a crushing injury to the right foot. Emergency Rx., consisting of a few holding stitches and two drains, was administered at the factory hospital, but when we examined him here, we were unable to determine whether the three small toes would have to be amputated or not. One deep laceration running between the fourth and fifth toe extended up the right side of the foot. Another laceration not so deep extended from the middle of the first metatarsal to the distal end of the middle phalanx. The Japanese doctor had put a drain in each one of these. Arterial bleeding was evident and not controlled.

We requested permission to take the man to the local general hospital so that we could use the surgical facilities if it were necessary to do an amputation. Surprisingly enough, we were told that if we brought all our own medications, gauze, and instruments it would be all right. And they had a small motorcycle truck to take us over—Major Murray, Sgt. Stevens, the Japanese medical *gocho,* and Asa Hei and myself, plus the patient on a stretcher. We were hanging on from all sides. We tried to carry the stretcher in the hall of the hospital but had to go back to take off our shoes. Of course we all had holes in our stockings. We planned on giving a spinal, but I had taken a can of ether along just in case. We also had gauze, roller bandage, masks, procaine, iodine, alcohol, syringes, bard Parker blades, and instruments. Everything I thought we could possibly need. All the staff was quite helpful, and extremely curious.

The head surgical nurse, an Ishycawa San, was quite the most helpful and had a great deal of poise, although she could understand no English. She saw to the sterilization of all our instruments, and assisted us in Surgery. It was necessary to take off our stockings, and try to wear small wooden block slippers. Major Murray couldn't manage them and stood on the wet tile floor in bare feet for an hour. The gowns were also constructed for smaller men than us. Mine wouldn't tie across the shoulders at all.—No gloves. We had quite an audience—4 or 5 doctors plus at least 9 nurses—in addition to the two nurses who were assisting us. Fortunately, the spinal went without a hitch, and then everyone waited with open mouths to see what the foreign doctors would do next. The worst part was the bleeding wound over the 5th metatarsal and small toe. The latter was hanging out at an angle, and the pereostium of the 4th phalanges was evident. Yet the circulation to the toes appeared adequate, as there was no evidence of cyanosis in the tissue. I decided not to amputate any of the toes temporarily, but to stop the arterial bleeding, approximate the tissue and get out. I had taken out the drains for more adequate explorations, and I was preparing to put a suture in the medial laceration, as there was no evidence of bleeding. It also connected across the dorsum under the skin with the lateral laceration. The needle holder was already in my hand, when one of the Japanese doctors became quite excited and gave out many *dame-dame's* (Bad Bad). The *gocho* explained that he didn't want me to close it up as the wound was dirty, and that was why he had put a drain in at the factory hospital.

Apparently he had been the doctor who had put in the sutures. I was getting a bit hot under the collar by this time, and while I realized he was probably right, I didn't appreciate his interference. I told the *gocho* that if the Japanese doctor wanted to go ahead and do the job it was all right with me, but if not then I would go ahead and do it the way I thought best. The doctor went out in a huff. It was necessary to extend the lateral wound to find the bleeding point, and as the tissue had been crushed and macerated under the skin, I had quite a time finding it. Finally, with everyone getting hungry, we finished up at one-thirty, and had to wait a half hour for the motorcycle to come back. The nurses wanted to keep the American facemasks and bandage for souvenirs, and Sgt. Stevens had four packages of chewing gum, which he gave to them. They were quite thrilled.

We started back, all packed in again, and as the driver was going quite fast, I told him to cut out the speedo—none of us had any kind of a hold, and the stretcher extended across the whole center. Not three minutes after my warning he took a corner without slowing down, we skidded over to the left side of the road, and ran into a four-foot canal, turning us all over. Major Murray landed on his head and was momentarily unconscious. The tray of instruments and medications flew every which way and were buried in the snow. The patient and litter slid over to one side pinning the Nip Asa Hei to the side of the truck. The rest of us were badly shaken up.

After checking up we found no one was seriously hurt, although I had to put two stitches in Major Murray's scalp when we returned to camp. With the help of at least fifty school children who had collected from all sides, w were able to pull the overturned motorcycle out of the trestle covering the canal, and get it back on the road, where it looked quite hors de combat, leaking gas and oil, with the front fender and headlight rolled up on a ball and the handlebars out of line. The driver calmly took out his tool kit, found a big hammer, and began knocking the fender back to its proper place. Meanwhile the rest of us, with the exception of the Major and the patient, tried to locate the instruments and medicines in the deep snow. At first we found very few, but gradually a new piece would come to light.

By the time the driver felt he was ready to try again, we had found everything, even to the small package of Bard Parker blades. A third time we piled on the back of the pickup, and away we went. There was no need to tell him to go slow, as the front wheel was rubbing against the frame, along with the clutch smoking. We never were so glad to get back to prison, where it was safe, at half past three, and we had left at ten. All of us were walking with a limp for the next few days. We were very fortunate with the man's foot. In 24 hours on changing the dressing, there was no evidence of gangrene or impaired circulation to the small toes, and no active bleeding. And after 72 hours I removed both drains as the wounds did not break down. I wish that Nip doctor could have seen the foot then. Of course, we were lucky that there wasn't any suppuration, but I wouldn't admit it to him. The Nip orderly took a drum of dressings to the hospital to be sterilized, and I gave him a piece of Camay soap that I had for the surgical nurse to show our appreciation for her help. When the orderly returned, he told me that she was very pleased with the soap, but the other nurse who helped us was quite hurt because she didn't get any. So when he went back, I sent her a piece of Red Cross soap. Now everyone is happy, for a while, at least.

ISLAND OF HOKKAIDO—MURORAN
Easter Sunday, 9:00 PM, April 1, 1945

My month in the cookhouse has begun.

ISLAND OF HOKKAIDO—MURORAN
6:50 AM, April 19, 1945

Three years ago today found me dragging my weary bones up the road from Marivelas toward Capas and then I managed that fortunate detour to Hospital No. 1. Those last 3 years seem like the biggest half of my life. But I know that it will fade into a pleasant subconscious as son as it is all over. And to us the biggest news is that we now get up at 5:30 AM, which makes another half hour to keep warm in. The coal issue for a billet of 30 men is now three kilos. With this they are supposed to have a fire in the group from 5:30 AM to 6:30 AM and from 5:00 PM to 8:30 PM at night. I don't think it lasts them an hour. But this camp is only half full now—407 men, and there are a group of 15 empty billets. The men have been burning everything but the four walls of these buildings, and I expect those to disappear at any time. Even the doors of the latrines have gone. This is a cold country and when the Siberian wind comes down, it is quite uncomfortable even with the sun shining.

ISLAND OF HOKKAIDO—MURORAN
Sunday–Friday, April 15, 1945

The 13th I heard that President Roosevelt had died. The news stunned me—the loss was too much to realize—F.D.R. gone—it couldn't be true. But it was true. I could read the confirmation on the faces of the Japanese staff, as they came back from listening to the radio. They were bursting to tell me about it, but didn't know whether they should give out the news. All evening I could not shake off the feeling of deep depression, and I went to bed immediately after *tenko,* at 7:30 PM Yesterday morning *Yasumay* day, the medical Gocho told me that President Roosevelt had died of a cerebral hemorrhage at Warm Springs, April 12, and the new President's name was Toruman—which could mean Torman, Trueman, or even Dorman. I told the four American Corpsmen that we would have a short service at 1:30 PM just for the five of us—and at that time said the following:

"Americans throughout the world today are pausing for a few moments to pay homage to the memory of a great American, the late President of the United States. To we five men, soldiers in the Army of the U.S., the death of this man is the death of our Commander in Chief, and I feel that we, though isolated from our fellow Americans in a prison camp in the North of Japan, should also pause for a few moments, to also pay homage. To me, Franklin Delano Roosevelt has been the greatest American ever to occupy the White House, and I am certain that future historians, who will more coolly evaluate his career, will bear this statement out. Indeed, the people of America, in reelecting him for the fourth term to serve as President of the U.S. give proof to the world of their esteem, their appreciation, and their trust in this man. Evidence that he has been a firm representative of our country, we have amply seen by the wholesome respect for his ability which the mention of his name brought forth wherever we have been these last ten years of turbulent times.

I, as an American citizen, and an Officer in the Army of the United States, have always taken a personal pride in having Franklin D. Roosevelt as my Commander in Chief, and the news of his death yesterday affected me, as would the loss of a close blood relation. I feel this is the greatest tribute I personally can make, and I make it sincerely. The father of our great family, the American People, has died, and while another man must take his place as the head of our nation, as the Commander in Chief of our Armed Forces, as the new occupant of the White House, no man can take his place in our feelings and sentiments."

Four or five times, while I was reading this, it was necessary to stop, as my voice cracked. I didn't think I would be able to finish. In fact, I haven't been so moved, emotionally for many, many years. After the service I felt a great deal better somehow. I attended the services of the Church of England and appreciated the fine tribute the British troops made to Roosevelt by the wearing of black.

ISLAND OF HOKKAIDO—MURORAN *8:00 PM, April 24, 1945*

Blackout tonight, and 20 military guards have moved into camp today. Planes are droning overhead now, but I am afraid they still sport the rising sun. The past week has developed a full fledged rumor that we are going to be moved to a new camp and numerous incidents have occurred these past seven days to bear this out. The Shoko has been to Hakodate.

Our move to a new location seems to be still in the wind. The Shoko was checking up on equipment and asked me how many boxes I would have of Red Cross drugs. When I told him twelve, he thought it was too much. Yet they haven't finished packing their drugs, and have used 26 containers of all sizes. Yesterday I began packing some of our vacoliters and sulfa drugs in deep straw to be sure that they would not break—and this morning I found my back giving me my same old trouble in the same place. Do you remember my having x-rays taken while I was in my last year of medical school? It's not too bad I thought, and I am expecting it to clear up if we leave here.

Well, we have had another little set to with Capt. Borski. About two months ago the Shoko issued a list of non-smokers and included my name. So I went down to see him and explained that I did smoke occasionally, and I used the rest of my cigarettes to give the men for washing my clothes and cutting my hair. The Shoko replied that cigarettes were very scarce and told me to give the men money. So I had to tell him that these men had plenty of money and no means of spending it. He said that whenever I wished to get cigarettes in the canteen, to order them through Capt. Borski, our canteen officer. I ordered 30 on the 7th of April and the 14th of April, but forgot, to tell him to get them for me on the 21st, so I didn't expect them. Then on the 24th. By accident, I found out that the good Capt. had ordered cigarettes in my name, and also Dr. Lutter's, and hadn't given them to us. Major Murray asked him how many cigarettes he ordered for the Officers' Canteen on the 21st and he said 120, which he gave to the four smokers, Major Murray, himself, and the two *vandrigs* (cadets). That afternoon the Major and I found out that he had actually received 180 cigarettes. So that evening the Major confronted him with these facts, and he admitted that he had lied about the figures in the morning, and had received the 180, but he had kept these for a reserve in case the men's canteen was short. Major Murray told him he didn't believe a word of it, and we told the other Officers in the mess that night that we didn't think that Capt. Borski was to be considered as an officer and gentleman under the circumstances and we didn't want him to have anything further to do with the Officers' Canteen. As a result of this Dr. Lutter is now our Canteen Officer. Recently one of the Dutch troops told me a bit of Capt. Borski's history, and his recent behavior can be more easily understood in this new light. He had served as an enlisted man in the last war and was pensioned off as a second lieutenant. On the occasion of the invasion of Holland he was recalled to active duty and promoted. From now on I will treat him as he deserves—ignore him completely and watch him quite carefully if it is necessary for me to have any dealings with him. And I will go my best to see that he has nothing to do with any future Red Cross supplies that may come to this camp.

Rec'd 60 cig—4/28/45 30 cig. 5/5/45

ISLAND OF HOKKAIDO—MURORAN *Friday, May 11, 1945*

Surprise of surprises—Colonel Emoto has paid us another visit. We never expected to see him back here after his last visit with the Tokyo General. And I am quite sure that the Camp Commander and his staff didn't think he would come either, as they were gradually slipping back into pre-Emoto customs. The new military guard was beginning to **hit** the boys, and ordered the POW Officers to salute the guardroom. Capt. Borski wrote a letter to the Shoko quoting the old standing orders that Officers would not salute anyone of inferior rank. He received no reply to this. The next night, in the hallway, one of the guards stopped Borski again and ordered him to salute. He tried to explain that POW Officers did not have to salute. Without more ado the guard slapped him. This upset the good Capt. quite a bit and he came back and wrote another letter of complain in French to Lt. Hirati stating what happened. Still no answer.

The next morning, it was necessary for me to go by the guardroom to the office and I decided to walk right by and see what happened. I figured that the guard who sits in the window could only yell at me if I didn't salute.

I passed him and nothing happened. On my way back to the hospital I could see the guard waiting for me to salute, but he didn't say anything. A half hour later the Shoko sent for Major Murray, and when he went down he had to salute both ways. So I decided to keep away from the guardroom as much as possible. About five days after Capt. Borski was slapped we witnessed the familiar hustle bustle of cleaning the camp up which used to announce the impending arrival of the High Commander. We could hardly believe that he was actually coming again. He arrived and began interviewing the troops as of old, along with a talk on the Boer War. He saw the Dutch troops on the 8th, all the British on the 9th, and he was scheduled to see the Officers on the morning of the 10th. We were sure that Capt. Borski would tell the Colonel about his getting hit by the guard and that his standing order was not being enforced. But he said that even thought the Shoko had not answered his letter, he (Capt. Borski) was sure that the Shoko had spoken to the guard and everything was all right. Therefore it wasn't necessary for him to report this to the Colonel.

In all the time the Colonel has been here Capt. Borski has never made a complaint. But he orders one of his men to do it. This time it backfired. He told his men to complain that the fish was bad before we received it; and he caused an upheaval. We have been getting a great deal of fish this past month, sometimes twice a day, and actually it has been quite good. The camp staff was quite upset over it, and the Shoko began an investigation, which I think will end up with the ever-present Capt. B. Major Murray had decided to bring the guard business up to the Colonel so we would have the situation cleared up, one way or another, but the evening of the 9th, the night before our interview, the Shoko called Capt. Borski down, and said that the POW Officers would not salute the military guards in the camp either in the guardroom or around the grounds.

We have very few sick in the camp with only 4 chronic cases in the hospital. When the Colonel asked if we had any requests, after everyone else had finished, I stood up and asked if I could be sent to another camp where there was more need of a medical officer. I said that there were two very capable Dutch and British CO's to take care of their own troops, and they had no need of me. I also said my quarters here was quite good, and

I personally was quite comfortable, but that I would prefer to go where there was more medical work to do. His reply surprised me. He said that other camps had more medical Officers than this one, but he appreciated my noble (?) intentions and feelings. If he found a camp where they were in need of a good (?) Medical Officer, he could arrange it with the war minister. That was yesterday—I didn't make up my mind to ask him this until the last minute, but I am getting fed up with this whole setup. I need to get back with a group of Americans—we have our faults, but at least they or we all speak the same language and have the same relative standards for evaluation of every day happenings. In our mess, most of the time I feel that I am alone in a foreign country, and not Japan either.

The Colonels' explanation of Japan's preparedness included the fact that each pilot is trained to body crash his ship into an enemy objective.... In the past month, the Japanese claim to have sunk 520 American war ships out of a fleet of 1400—including 19 battleships, all our fastest aircraft carriers. **The men expect the war to end any day now,** since the Colonel told the men that we could have plenty of coal and food where we were going in a few days. Some of the men figure they will be going home then.

My typewriter seems to write in fits and starts. I will have to quit for now .

ISLAND OF HOKKAIDO—MURORAN *May 14, 1945*

I will try again and see if it works better this time. Yesterday all the medical books and library books were called in which we are sure there is another step. During the Colonel's interview the Major asked him why the Red Cross personnel had to work outside for half a day. He replied the Emperor had not signed the International agreement at Geneva and so were not bound by it. Then he told how everyone in England and America were working and he felt these men should do something, and also if they worked he would be able to give them more rice. All in all, he wasn't very happy in having to admit that he was forced to make them work. The Major then gave the Colonel the numbers of the three British orderlies, and said they were very keen to work all day outside. So much the better, said the

Colonel, and he stated he would arrange it. The Major told me the reason the three Br. orderlies wanted to go outside was because they were tired of being *"Buggered around"* or heckled by the Japanese Asa Hei. I suggested that I didn't think it right for all 3 Br. orderlies to be outside, and the Major replied that I wasn't being *"buggered around"* and he was going to get them out of the hospital if he could, because he couldn't' stand seeing it. Well, I said no more. My point is that two thirds of the troops in this camp are British, yet all the British orderlies are willing to leave the corpsman duties to two American orderlies and 3 Dutch. It isn't that there aren't plenty of orderlies left, but I think that the British orderlies are here for the purpose of taking care of the British personnel.

ISLAND OF HOKKAIDO—MURORAN *May 20, 1945*

~ Yesterday has been a red-letter day for the camp. We now have a full-blown case of smallpox among us. At least he is still in the confines of the camp although they have put him in the furthermost corner in an empty billet. It all began about five weeks ago. A man from group 11 was struck in the eye and examination revealed an iridialysis of the rt. eye with complete loss of visual acuity associated with much pain. He was hospitalized and atropine ointment applied. Gradually his vision returned and he was discharged from the hospital on the 11th of this month, feeling quite fit. The next morning he came on the sick parade complaining of a severe attack of "flu", with headache, backache, etc. and a temp. of 101. Previous to this he has had repeated attacks of undiagnosed fever and malaise, not responding to quinine, sulfa drugs, codeine and asa, or atabrine. I gave him some Cod. and asa to make him more comfortable but next morning his temperature was 101.6 although he had had a good sweat the previous night. Major Murray saw him as I was busy packing the Red Cross drugs. He repeated the Cod. and asa. T.I.D. as there were no physical findings with the exception of a questionable spleen. But on the morning of the 14th, his temp. was 103.6 so we whipped him into the hospital and I suggested we try him on a course of sulfathiozole as he previously had had diazine.

The next morning his temp. was down to 99.6 and he felt better. He had had a complete sponge bath, and a change of blankets. The orderly who gave him the bath reported that he saw a rash on the pts. chest, which he thought, was a heat rash. Exam. revealed about 10 discrete maculo-papular lesions, about 5 mm. in diameter irregularly spread over the abdomen and thorax, with a few on the thighs, arms, and neck. No itching then. The Major asked me if I had ever seen a rash like that and I replied that I wasn't sure. While a few had vesicles, the majority was in the same stage. The next morning the pt's. temp. was normal but his rash had developed into a blanket of erethemetous papules from his scalp to his toes, including his eyelids—almost confluent. I couldn't remember which it was, chickenpox or smallpox. That was monomorphous, but I was certain that whichever it was that had this characteristic, we had a case of it. The Major said that there was no question about it being chickenpox, and that was good enough for me. I decided vancelle or chicken pox was the monomorphous type. The Major changed the admission diagnosis from malaria to chicken pox, and notified the Japanese medical Socho. He immediately called the nearby Japanese 2nd Lt. Medic to come over and see the case. Incidentally, we found out that he had never seen a case of smallpox.

I was still packing when he arrived, and so he and Major Murray went over to see the man. The Kip doctor looked at the man from all angles and finally agreed with the Major that it was chickenpox, and that he should be moved over to isolation. When we made rounds in isolation the next morning the pt. was a horrible state. The number of papules had increased if possible and there was no area of skin free from them. He even had lesions on his tongue. His scalp and neck, ears and face were covered along with a cervical adenitis. He had not had any sleep and his skin was extremely itchy. The Major asked me if I thought the foot powder would help him. I replied that I didn't think the salicylic acid powder would do him any good, but he decided to try it. His course of sulfathiazole had just finished. All his lesions were of the vesicle stage with a raised erythematous base. He appeared fairly ill although his temp. was only 99.4.—this was the 18th.

The next morning he was a little more advanced and was having difficulty in swallowing, being able to eat nothing except milk. After I helped him pull back his blankets and got a good look at his skin, I decided to wash my hands well in cresol. As we were walking back from the isolation ward I said that if that was chickenpox it was certainly the most severe case that I had ever seen. The Major then said that he hoped it wasn't smallpox. When I heard this I decided to clear up one thing in my mind right away. Which of the two diseases was monomorphous in its lesions? If smallpox was, so then there was no question that the man had smallpox. If chickenpox was, such then he had the latter. The Major told me that he knew that variola, or smallpox was the monomorphous type and he had suspected smallpox the day before but hadn't said anything. That was enough for me. The next thing was to go down and unpack Cecil and see what he had to say about it.

Fifteen minutes later I returned with the textbook and told the Major, there was no question in my mind that the man had a full-blown case of smallpox. He told the Japanese, and from that moment things began to happen. The same Japanese doctor returned that afternoon, and he wouldn't even touch the pt. And we had to spray him from head to foot with phenol after he left the room. That called off the move in no uncertain terms and also resulted in a quarantine of the camp. None of the men could go out to work, which was the worst result as far as the Asa hei was concerned. He just couldn't stand the thought of POW's not working. Dr. Okamura arrived from Hakodate the following morning and we vaccinated everyone on the 21st. He wanted every man's temperature checked and all men examined every day for a week. He said no one would work for fourteen days and the pt. would be removed to a Japanese military hospital the following day. We began that morning and for seven days not a man had a temp. above normal. He wanted the reactions recorded the 4th, 5th, and 6th day, which was a bit early, but we did it. We had all sorts of quarantines inside the quarantines. The orderlies that took care of the pt. were quarantined in the far corner of the camp. The other orderlies moved into the hospital and were quarantined there with the patients. The men in group 11, where the pt. stayed for two days when he first became sick were in a separate quarantine. Yet, 6 men, transferred to group 15 from 11, who were in 11 at the same time as the pt. (in fact, Fitch, the American corpsman took care of him for one whole day) were not isolated at all.

We can thank the good Lord that we didn't get a good solid epidemic here. Many of the English troops were never vaccinated as a child, and their routine Army did "not take". But they all took here. The 2nd day of the quarantine the order came out for 1/2 hr. plus training physical training from 5:30 AM and at 1:00 PM. And after 5 days of quarantine the Nips couldn't stand it any longer, and said that all the men except group 11 would go out to work after only one week of quarantine. Dr. Okamura asked me if I thought it was all right. I replied that it wouldn't make any difference to the POW's if the quarantine was broken, but it might affect the people they came in contact with out at the factory. So out they went—the Doctor also told us that Colonel Emoto was going to be changed in a few days, and a full Colonel would take his place. This was bad news for us. Another thing he said was that the Japanese would take over control of the Red Cross drugs. When we protested he told Major Murray that he had to keep a record of what we used, but we could get the drugs whenever we wanted to use them, and that I would still keep the books. The Asa hei had already seen me and told me not to use any more American B1, but to use Japanese vitamin powder, which I think is made up mostly of rice flour. He is already planning what he is going to do with these medicines after the war. I saw Umeki Socho and asked him if he himself would handle our medicines so that the Asa hei would have nothing to do with them, and he said that he would. I hope so. Fortunately, we still have the three medical kits made up which have all the essential drugs in them.

ISLAND OF HOKKAIDO—MURORAN

Memorial Day, May 30, 1945

And latest word is we will move on the night of the 2nd of June. Tomorrow morning our new High Commander, Colonel Noboi will look us over. We were all ordered on parade where he delivered his farewell address. He had been ordered to duty with the northern army and it came to him like a bolt from the blue—that the pawn should not question the hand of the player when he is moved from one square to another. He hoped to meet us all when the war was over as gentlemen one to another and he had made some very good plans for us in the new camp, and he regretted that he would be unable to share them with us. The whole tone gave one the impression of a principal of a boy's school saying goodbye. Just to start things off right for the new HC, some of the boys were caught stealing a case of tinned salmon from a truck they were unloading outside. Four are in the guardroom so far, and we don't know what is going to happen to them. I think they have a good chance of being sent to a civilian prison. These past five days have seen us stove-less and the weather has been truly miserable. Rain and wind every day—the temperature in the mess room 8 degrees C.—not very comfortable. A stove remained in the C.I. room and that is where I have been spending most of my time. If our camp is joined to that of Hakodate I believe it will be more pleasant. With more officers, there will be less need for our present close associations. Although with the stove out of the mess, we have very little contact with each other.

ISLAND OF HOKKAIDO—MURORAN *June 1, 1945*

The end of the Chapter a la Galsworthy.

NEW CAMP *June 9, 1945*

Located in the new camp and not yet sure that we have been shaken down properly. Our move began very badly on the 3rd of June when two of the British troops were killed at a railroad crossing while loading up the boxcars. The men were waiting for a train to pass one way and they were hit, and knocked into a slew about 40 yards down the line. One man was found dieing at the edge and brought in to me with a compound depressed fracture of the left frontal region along with a crushing injury of the left chest wall and multiple fractures of the right arm and left thigh. He was given some caffeine but his circulation had already ceased. The other man was not found for almost an hour, and after the bottom of the slew was dragged repeatedly, he was found with his head torn completely off—a nasty business.

NEW CAMP *June 24*

One thing for me, every time I have anything to do with a new camp the time passes quickly—It was quite the same at O'Donnell, and at Camp III—Here there were many problems with no one to take care of them. When we arrived here on the fourth of June we found 86 men from the Cemento Camp along with six hospital patients. And as the hospital people from Auroran were with the first party, we had to set up right away. Of course, the camp wasn't finished by half, and the patients were put in two small rooms next to the central door, and one room was assigned for all the Officers. And I thought we would not be thrown so closely together in the new camp. The worst thing I found right quick was there was no water in the camp or out that was potable. And in the camp was a single small well that would pump dry in 10 minutes. The main water supply had to come from a small stream about 150 yards from the front gate in soup tubs. Enough water for cooking, drinking and washing. There was no evidence of a bath at all. We started a water detail for the cookhouse of 30 men and it took them over an hour to carry enough water for one meal. The cookhouse had only four large cauldrons, and was one-sixth the size of our old one. To make things a bit more difficult, the Japanese cookhouse man didn't come up here with us, and the new one had no idea what the daily issue was supposed to be. What made it worse was that he was quite ignorant and could not do the simple set multiplication or division. As a result, when I gave him the ration scale for one man, he couldn't figure out the amount for 507 men. And he wouldn't let me show him either.

After 3 days, I gave up, and told the Nip in the office that he was worse than useless and we couldn't run the kitchen properly with him in there. It surprised me, but he was relieved, and now it is pretty well left up to me. The office man, Igarashi, comes over once each morning, and I tell him what we should have for the next 24 hours, he gives me the keys to the stores—we draw the supplies, I sign for them, and then I don't see him for the rest of the day. Sometimes, when he is busy in the office, he just gives me the keys and doesn't come over at all. He leaves them with me in case I need anything before he arrives in the morning. A peculiar business! I think the reason why he doesn't worry about me, is that when we first arrived all our food supplies over 200 sacks of rice, 100 sacks of barley, beans, fish, flour, soya niso and vegetables were thrown in one big pile in the stores, and for four days I worked in there with ten men and made a detailed inventory of all the supplies. It certainly reminded one of O'Donnell. The trouble was that many of the sacks were in bad condition, and a great deal of rice, barley, and other foods was lost, strayed, or stolen along the way. I saw one boxcar when it arrived, and the rice and beans spilled on the floor was more than six inches deep.

NEW CAMP *July 6, 1945*

A full two weeks—the biggest event was the sudden loss of Major Murray. At 11:00 AM on 6/24/45 the Shoko told Major Murray that he was ordered to a new camp and would leave in an hour. I went over and asked the Shoko to send me instead of him because these were his troops here, but he said the order had been issued and nothing could be done about it. The Major asked me to take over the command of all the British troops and when I agreed to this he gave me a written order to whom it may concern—"On leaving this camp, I have left Lt. M.M. Andler medical Corps, U.S. Army, in command of all British troops. (349 n.c.o.'s and men.)"

F.J. Murray
Major of R.A.M.C.
O.C. British troops and
S.M.O. Camp

He also informed Capt. Borski of this and I haven't had an easy day since.

NEW CAMP *July 9, 1945*

After getting ready to give up because of the complete blockage of paper supply from Die Nippon, I have discovered a new source of supply. The backs of these typed sheets. Of course, one will need a road map to follow the continuity, but the Nips will probably burn the whole business one of these days, so it won't make much difference. I find this was first begun almost three years ago, and it is noticeable that events occurring during our prison camp existence have remained extremely vivid. It has been only two weeks since Major Murray was ordered to a new camp, and it seems months. It's a good thing that I finished my duty in the mess so that there was more time to take over my new responsibilities. Even so, the British honchos come to me and complain about their rations, while Dr. Lutter does not want to listen to complaints any more than I do. We tried to split up the British sick parade between us, because I didn't have time to see them all after dinner, but it didn't work, as the scroungers would get in Dr. Lutter's line, because he didn't know them as well as I did, and they would manage to get off work when they weren't sick. Now I am splitting up the parade so that I see one half before dinner, and the rest after the evening meal. Since the men work in three shifts, it works out fairly well.

The past two days have been relatively pleasant, as the medical *gocho* and *asahei* (medical orderly) have been away and aren't due back for another two days. But to counterbalance this period of quiet I have had another run-in with our little friend the Shoko. The day after Major Murray left, he called me in and wanted the names of ten men for a new working group to begin the following morning. I checked over all the British troops and reported there were only eight men not working who were fit to go out. He replied that they would be sufficient and issued orders for these men to report at the work parade the following morning. That same evening the sick parade was extremely heavy and Dr. Lutter and I had a large number of men stay in. Everything was quiet until we got down to lunch the following day when Capt. Borski told us that the Shoko wanted to see us right away. When we went over to his office, he was studying the work figures. He told me the day before there had been 368 workers. After he ordered 8 more men to work last night, there should have been at least 375 or 376 workers go out and instead there were only 353 men working. I tried to explain that the long walk of 6 km to and from work was too much for these men on the present ration and instead of more workers I expected more sick men every day. Many men were complaining of faintness and dizziness when they stood up suddenly.

After I spent fifteen minutes explaining all this, he called the Japanese orderly in and told him that from that evening on he would decide who would go out to work and who would stay in. In spite of my protests he sent the majority of the sick parade out the next morning and the working figures increased to 385 men, which made him very happy. The next evening he was worse, sending out men with hernias and fevers. That was about as much as I could stand. Before the men were supposed to leave the following morning, I went to see the *Gocho* and told him that I wanted to see the CO about the Japanese *Asahei* and the sick parades. If he was going to continue his present course there was no need for us to see the men at all, as he completely disregarded our opinions about the men. I gave him the names of three men who shouldn't go out that morning. He told me there was not any need of my seeing the Shoko, that the three men could stay in, and from then on he himself would take the sick parade. This made a great deal of difference. He didn't send out a single man we asked him to keep in, and still there were the same number of workers as the day before. Since then he has been coming each night.

We are only worried now that very soon he will get tired of it and let the *asahei* do it again. When they left he gave me 35 sick tickets and told me not to have any more than that in. Dr. Lutter and I have managed very nicely with this. While a number of the men complain now of general weakness while working, the actual sick number is not very high. Many are being troubled with hemorrhoids, coming down with this long hike. Incidentally, Dr. Lutter and I made the walk to the station with Major Murray and I carried his suitcase halfway. By the time we returned to camp we were both well tuckered out, and hadn't even done any work, which puts me in a better position to appreciate the complaints of the men about the long walk twice a day. July 10, 5:00 PM Just about ready for the sick parade . . . the first half of the British troops. Then at 6:30 PM I go over the second half. After that I go over the whole list with Dr. Lutter and we decide which 35 men will stay in for next day. Quite a procedure. The British are not in as good shape as the Dutch, and so I have many more stay in than Dr. Lutter. He is quite decent about it. But this should be our last day of grace before our Nippy friends return from the city and take over.

NEW CAMP *3:00 PM, **July 15, 2004***

We are in a state of perpetual air raid alarm, for the present at least. No one is sure of anything, but it appears this island is beginning to experience daily visits from the U.S. Army Air Force, and they don't relish it. The work hanchos told the boys at the factory yesterday that Sapporo and Hakodate were bombed by 150 carrier-based planes. We heard what sounds like bombing about ten in the morning but it was quite distant. That means there are infantry stationed in the vicinity. But the ceiling was extremely low and we were unable to see anything. Sgt. Matuozzi, my American corpsman said suddenly, "If that's an American plane, the pilot has probably struggled thru ham and eggs for breakfast and when he lands back on his carrier, he'll have only one hour to wait before he sits down to a regular Sunday dinner of fried chicken and all the trimmings. Well, that started a train of thought that has been going around round and round and hasn't stopped yet. We discussed in detail just what his routine would be after he reached the wardroom and had his homecoming cup of java. I mentally strayed down to Fred's Steakhouse on 6th St. for a Delmonico Steak. You know, this mulberry leaves stew we have been getting for the past two months leaves much to be desired in a well-rounded diet, and no pun was intended. Corp. Jackson, a Singapore volunteer who was Firestone Tire representative in the Far East, and had been in L.A. in 1938 asked me if I had ever been to Carl's Drive-in? That set me off anew. We visited the Brown Derby, Beverly Hills Hotel, Santa Monica and all points south. Each place brought to mind another. We finally wound up this mental gastronomic debacle by having a piece of dried fish and boiled rice for lunch. That brought us back to terra firma in no uncertain terms. But we can see the picture changing, with 2900 planes reported over the island in one day. Let em come, God bless them.

NEW CAMP *8:00 AM, **July 18, 1945***

Since we begin the day at five AM it seems like a long time since last we ate. The Shoko returned yesterday from Sapphoro in a foul humor. A good sign of the times. During the three days he was gone I had arranged for 3 men who couldn't walk the five miles to the factory to join a work group out in front of the camp where they could work, but wouldn't have to do any walking. One of the men has a poor reduction of a fracture of the os calcis and the other two are handicapped with bad feet and bronchitis. *Abbe gunso,* the *shuban kashkan* (orderly sergeant) ordered the men to work, on my recommendation, as this permitted me 3 more places on the sick parade to keep men in that were acutely ill. The old shoko really let himself go on this one. He called in Capt. Borski, the Dutch CO and me, and demanded to know by whose order these men had gone out. I tried to explain that since he hadn't been here it was necessary to ask the Japanese N.C.O. about orders. All he could say was, "It was not my order."

He then proceeded to line the 3 men up and said, "For the next 30 days you must work every day with your own group." That's all there was to that. The 3 men have hobbled out the gate this morning, but they can't possibly keep up with the column. I tried to see the Shoko about it again last night, but he wouldn't even talk to me. The boys at the factory report that the Nip civilians are feverishly digging air raid trenches and shelters in every available spot. War work in the plant is completely neglected. Yesterday they were even trying to camouflage the horses. The desire to see one of our planes has been like a deep ache, but probably after I experience one flight doing its business I won't wait to see any more of them. The thought that our carriers are so close, makes one contemplate the possibilities of escape again, but even if the chance developed, I couldn't take it now that I am saddled with 350 British troops to mother. Some of these limeys are trying to put one over on me. One chap came on the sick parade complaining of diarrhea with nine trips to the latrine and feeling so weak he could hardly stand. He put on a pretty good show, and I had him come on the Japanese sick parade that evening and get a ticket to stay in for the next day.

Afterwards, I began checking up on him with some of the boys. They saw him at the latrine no more than once that day. Also on the way back from the factory one man saw him pick up a piece of dirty dried fish and eat it. That was enough for me. I had given strict orders for nothing to be eaten outside of our camp to try and control the dysentery. I whipped him back to the M.I. room and told him I didn't believe a word he had told me. Also that he would be going out to work the next morning, and took away his ticket. A very difficult business, especially with the sick parade as tight as it is. If the medical *gocho* decides only 18 men will stay in, it doesn't make any difference if fifty are too sick to go out. Only 18 stay in, unless I can manage to get around the rascal some way or other. There's some shenanigans going on about the Red Cross medicines, but I can't figure out what it is. Yesterday the *Gocho* told me the Japanese Doctor wanted a list of our drugs, but that I should only make a list of two thirds of our supply so that the main camp wouldn't think we had too much and try to take some away. I asked him what would happen if the Dr. came here to check up on the list, but he replied that he would explain things if it were necessary. We shall see what develops.

NEW CAMP *July 19th, 1945*

Time for another sick parade. It seems I am just getting over one or ready for another. Managed to convince the *Gocho* that we should use some American thiamin and we have 115 men on a ten-day course, ranging from 25 mgm to 1 mgm a day. But I don't expect much improvement. What these men need is large doses of good American chow. They have been eating mulberry leaves for more than two months now, and they just don't do the trick.

NEW CAMP *July 20, 1945*

Last night the men from the factory brought back the story that a large-scale landing had taken place around Nagasaki, with heavy equipment and supplies. All this, according to one of the hanchos. Naturally the men were extremely elated, but I fear that it hasn't convinced me. We shouldn't be ready to invade the mainland yet. Basing their course on the procedure followed with Saipan and Okinawa, they should utilize at least another 60 days and nights in concentrated bombing and strafing of all enemy fields, supply depots, communications and transportation centers, laving mines and crippling shipping. It would be wonderful if I was wrong and this was all true.

NEW CAMP *July 26, 1945*

Almost lunchtime. Nothing like a spot of rice to break the monotony. As long as the spot is big enough. We have been eating that stuff for almost 3-1Đ2 years now, and we never get enough. An unusual food. The front office in a hustle and bustle. Another inspection coming up, this time a General. And these boys really jump for a General. We have to worry about them too, because if something upsets them, repercussions hit the camp. Day before yesterday, about one half hour after the ARP siren cut loose, we saw a plane fly overhead much too high to distinguish any markings or type of aircraft, but with an air raid on, the chance that it was one of ours was quite good. I think I strained my eyes but to not avail.

For the past three days, after the morning routine is finished, I have been going out on the road for an hour to do a bit of scooping with the men. I found that while I was losing weight, the flesh I still had was extremely soft, and if one wished to be just the least bit vulgar one could call it flabby. Well, today, as I started out the front gate past the guardroom, the guard commander said *dame, dame* (no good!), and led me to understand that *furio shokos* (POW Officers) could not leave the camp. I traipsed off into the Shoko's office and informed him that I wanted to do some constructive labor on the camp road, but the local lads wouldn't let me out. He had been having a great deal of trouble trying to get Capt. Borski, the Dutch CO to any kind of manual work, and as soon as he hears that I wanted to, he jumped out of his chair and personally took me past the guardhouse. He is a great believer in everyone working. That's my big trouble in handling the work parade.

NEW CAMP *August 3, 1945*

A *yasumy* day (rest day) for the camp and a busy one for me. This month I am back in the cookhouse along with my other duties. We had a parade two nights ago by the Shoko and he read a stern warning from the high commander. Two men attempted to escape from the main camp on the 18th of last month and they weren't picked up for eight days. One was a Warrant Officer, and the other a cadet, both British, and supposed to be pretty levelheaded fellows. These men must have had some good contacts or they wouldn't have tried it. Perhaps the boys are a lot closer than we realize. These Nips don't use their heads at all. I am sure they have sown a seed in some of these fertile brains, who hadn't thought about escaping for many a moon. After the parade the Shoko called Borski and me into his office, and told us it would be very bad for the camp if one of our men attempted to escape. He wanted our cooperation. We solemnly agreed that it would be very bad for the camp, and could hardly wait to get out and try to figure out what it all meant. As a sequel lie, at dinnertime last night, the guards and staff drove all the men out of the groups from eleven to 16, one half of the camp, and searched the billets from ceiling to floor. They confiscated any canned Red Cross food that could be used in an escape, as well as pieces of rope, knives, straight razors, plus any knickknacks that took their fancy. The men all came running to me that the guards had taken their razor blades, rocket knives, and other personal things, but when I in turn protested to the Shoko, all he would say was *"mati, mati,"* which means wait.

NEW CAMP *August 5, 1945*

Things have really been happening. Last evening, while the Nip staff was indulging in a sake-drinking orgy, someone broke into the supply building. Among other things, some Jap. winter woolen underwear was missing. The supply sergeant, Abbe just about went mad. Every single man in the camp was rounded up outside, while the guards and staff literally tore the barracks to pieces. The floors and walls were torn up, and even the partitions of the ceiling were removed. There they struck gold. First they found about two dozen pairs of new socks over one Dutchman's bunk. They dragged him out in front of the guardroom, and systematically began to beat him up. Just about this time Dr. Lutter told me that this fellow hadn't had anything to do with it, but one of the other men had put the stuff over his bed. Of course the Nips wouldn't believe him. As I finally pieced the story together this sort of thing had been going on for quite awhile be a group of about six Dutchmen who have been stealing socks, underwear, towels, and anything else they could find, taking these articles to work with them under their clothes, and then trading it to the civilians at the factory for food. Finding this stuff on the roof of one barracks gave them a good lead, and they searched the entire ceiling. The articles that were found seemed unbelievable.

One British soldier had put five diary notebooks up there telling in detail all his black market tradings on the outside. In addition, he had copied verbatim all the news bulletins that Jongsma had been translating from the Nip papers that had been smuggled into camp. This really blew the lid off. The Shoko hustled him into the iso, incommunicado with orders for nothing to eat or drink until he confessed to how he was able to get this news. The soldier's story was that he had picked up the news form the Koreans with whom they had been scooping. The Shoko called Dr. Lutter in as interpreter and said that was ridiculous. He showed Lutter where the account in Allen's notebook was an exact translation of the newspaper account. More clothes from the supply building were found today, and five more Dutchmen are in the process of being starved and beaten up. In addition, the Nip civilians at the factory have been searched as well as their homes, and much of the traded stuff has been found. Their position is not too tenable either. We are all a bit perturbed, as we don't know what else Allen has put in his notebook. His roommates say that he has been keeping these in minute detail, recording all the atrocities as well as all the workings of the camp underground. Mr. Johngsma is getting a bit warm under the collar, and is trying to decide whether it would be better to go and tell the Shoko that he has been translating the papers, or whether it might be wise to wait and see what develops.

NEW CAMP *August 8, 1945*

These past three days have been a nightmare. A sack made out of the pant leg of a British uniform was found over the washroom between the Dutch and British barracks, filled with about three kilos of rice. The Shoko had every British troop line up in front of the barracks after they returned from work, and said they would stand there at attention all night until someone came forward and claimed the sack of rice. Some men from the sick parade were too ill for this, and I tried to explain this to Hirati. He condescended to let them sit on the ground, but wouldn't let them go back in the barracks. I took Dr. Lutter in to his office to explain that the Dutch troops had British trousers and had made sacks in the same manner, and therefore anyone in the camp could have put the rice up there.

Well, the Shoko has always favored the Dutch troops, and he said that I could take the sack around to the Dutch billets and show it to them, and if any of them claimed it, then he would dismiss the British troops, but if they didn't then my men would have to stay out there. Of course none of the Dutchmen had ever seen it, and there we were. I knew pretty well who our rogues were, and I tried to appeal to them to take their medicine and not make the whole group suffer for their actions. But no response. At midnight, the Shoko finally permitted the men to turn in, but said that all the men would go to work at five AM as usual, and would return to the lineup the following evening as soon as they had returned from the factory and the mines. The only reason why he was allowing them to quit was so that they would be able to go to work in the morning. This procedure has continued for three days and nights now, and we are no nearer the solution. The sick parades are brutal. Some of the men can hardly stand on their feet. And little can be done for them.

Fortunately our demon, Terabyashi has been ordered to another post, and his replacement has not yet learned the ropes. In fact the sake party last week was to see the menace off. About eleven o'clock that night, Terabyashi staggered down to our quarters, wearing only a g string, and so drunk he could hardly walk. He tried to jump on me, while he was cursing out the Americans for what they were doing to Die Nippon. A couple of the Nips were trying to hush him up and drag him away, but he struggled like a tiger, breaking away and jumping on me. I had been sleeping on the floor, but I jumped up and tried to ward him off without hurting him. It was sort of a ticklish situation for a while, but they finally were able to drag him away, still screaming like a banshee. I could understand how he felt, especially when he had just been ordered to join combat troops.

Today I was asked to go over to the Nip civilian area close by where the civilian employees of the camp and the families of the guards lived. The wife of one of the men had an infected toe, and as a result her whole foot was red, swollen and tender. The temperature was 101.4. There was a small local pocket of pus by the nail, and so I went ahead and opened it up. Then I told them to use hot compresses. I even gave them some of our precious sulfa diozene. I found out later that the Shoko and the medical *gocho* were quite upset because I didn't use any anesthetic. That was enough for me. Dr. Lutter could take care of the rest of them, which was just as well. A few days later, they called Lutter over to see an infant, who was already moribund. Of course it was too late to do anything, and so he was on their list too.

In spite of the tenseness of the camp, it was necessary to see the Shoko again about the three sick men whom he had sent out to work for thirty days without rest as punishment. I no sooner began my story than he flew into a rage about everything in general. He finally concluded by shooing me out of the office. I think my feelings were more hurt than if he had actually struck me. One would think that by this time my pride would have been pretty badly battered, but actually my dealings with the Nips had almost invariably been on a fairly satisfactory plane. Of course I am discounting the time spent as a coolie on the farm at Cabanatuan. There the guards recognized no one's rank, and treated all alike, simply a labor unit. Anyway, I vowed to myself, he shouldn't have many more opportunities to act that way.

NEW CAMP *August 15, 1945*

Something momentous has occurred today. What it is, we don't know, but it must be disastrous to the Nips. Today began like any previous day, with the men tense and anxious because of the investigating going on. About noon one of the camp workers called me to the front window facing the Nip headquarters, and pointed out the whole Nip staff standing at attention facing the radio in one corner of the office. As we watched the speech was apparently concluded. They bowed and then quietly left the room. Later, one of the men who had been working near the office said he saw one of the Nip guards crying. To climax this, at 3 PM, just as the night shift was getting ready to leave for the mines, the *gocho* told me that work had been cancelled. He gave no reason. For the Nips to cancel work was really something. You can imagine how the rumors flew.

We could hardly wait for the men to come back from the factory at Nisi Asibetsu to compare notes. And they in turn, hardly entered the gate before we were inundated with all manner of fantastic tales, ranging from the death of the Emperor, a commando attack on the island of Hokkaido, the landing of the Russians from the Quirik Isles, to the actual ending of the war.

I neglected to mention that about two months ago the men reported that a new camp was being built near the factory at Nisi Asibetsu, and within the week they saw approximately 100 POW's moved in. The Nips were very careful to see that our men were not permitted to speak to any of them, but this only stimulated the boys to demonstrate their ingenuity, and it wasn't long before we had a two-way mail service going. A note was tossed over the fence telling the new arrivals that a slab of rock at the hedge of the garden where they worked would cover all future communications. The next day, an answer found under the rock was brought back to us in camp, which revealed that our new neighbors were part of the group of POW's recently brought over from Shanghai. They included 35 Americans, 3 British, 45 Australian officers plus 3 American hospital corpsmen. Most of the Americans were Marines from the American Embassy. We in turn sent them the list of our personnel. About a week ago a note from the "Town Boys" told us they had heard that "Uncle Joe" had joined the fray. We confirmed this with a Nip paper the next day. So of course our rumors had to include the exploits of the Red Army.

While we were eating dinner, one of the Dutchmen slipped in to tell us that one of the Nip guards with whom he had become friendly in Ag trading said that there was Senco War (war finished). I wouldn't let myself be shoved into anything. I hadn't forgotten those hard working days in Bataan when we had gone overboard for each new story. I did feel that something momentous had taken place; most likely some big Nip had been killed or died. That would be the only reason for the no work order. Even if the Allies had made a landing on the Jap mainland. I can't see why they would have the men stop working nor go out to work in the morning? The men just won't go to sleep tonight. We had a copy of this morning's paper. Of course there was nothing of the day's happenings in it. There was mention that the Russians had taken the island of Sashun, which was expected.

NEW CAMP *August 17, 1945*

It's true—I cannot believe it, but it's true. My mind can't grasp the fact that the war is over. Japan has surrendered. For the rest of the world the war was over August 14th, but for us today, August 17th, marks the beginning of our freedom. Let us go back to 5:30 AM on the 16th. The cooks prepared the rice boxes for the men to go out, and after waiting an hour with no word from the headquarters, I went over to see the *gocho*. I asked him if the men were going out as usual. He told me the men would not work for the next three days for there was a holiday Shinto feasts. Don't think this didn't set the men off again with another thousand rumors.

All day yesterday and today no men were allowed to leave the camp. The camp workers kept working, and while the midnight check of the guards were made in the barracks last night as usual, the men remarked that instead of blustering and in waking the heavy sleepers with the butt end of their rifles as was their wont, the guards meekly crept through and counted heads. To men, ever watchful to interpret the slightest change of mood of their captors, this was momentous. By this time even I was permitting myself to toy with the possibility of the whole business being finished. I couldn't help it. One could feel it pulsing through the camp. Throughout the day, men would come into the dispensary or the cookhouse with what they thought was an additional bit of information confirming the end of the war.

The *coup d'etat* was one of the boys filching the daily paper from the office this evening. Just a few minutes ago Jongsma translated the feature article on the front page, an imperial rescript from the Emperor. To prevent the total annihilation of the Nippon people and the homeland by the ruthless and indiscriminate bombings of the Allies, he had graciously agreed to end hostilities. This proclamation in the paper was the first hint that the people had had of any negotiations or feelers for peace. We knew, as someone had managed to smuggle in a paper almost every day, and we followed these news reports religiously. We simply can't comprehend what this means. My mind has been barricaded too long. I am certain it will take many days for me to realize that very soon I will be going back to America, I won't be eating rice three times a day, or even once a day. Now that's a good example of just how narrow we have become. Here, after three and a half years, I am a free man, with the world before me, and the first thing I think about is that I won't have to eat rice. But I will get used to it.

I have just had a short conference with Borski, and we plan to see the Shoko the first thing in the morning and tell him that we know the war is over and the first thing we want is more food for the men. Last night, I visited each one of the British barracks and gave them some instructions. The gist of it was this:

"Something of great import has happened, what it is no one actually knows. It may even be the end of the war. If we find this to be so, then I want each and every man to have the following information. By International Law, it is the responsibility of the Japanese Army to see that we, as former prisoners of war are safely returned to our own forces. Until this is accomplished, it is their duty to guard and protect us from hostile civilians, and to see that we are properly fed and clothed. If one of us attempted to escape from this camp to pillage the countryside or return to freedom on his own, a guard would be justified in preventing this by shooting him if necessary. Another thing, there are only 20 guards here with rifles, and we have over 500 men, so we can expect the Nips to be a bit jumpy and jittery. They are liable to get panicky and shoot if you startle them. Now you men have been POW's for more than three years. This may well be what we have been longing for. If it is, don't jeopardize your life by being too impatient. You are all soldiers in the British Army. As your present commanding Officer, I expect you never to forget it for a moment. We are making every effort to find out exactly what has happened, and I will see that you are informed as we do".

I don't know anything about International Law, but I could visualize disastrous results if our 500 odd men began breaking into the stores, and roaming the countryside. Surprisingly enough, the men have been extremely well behaved and quiet under the circumstances. I have just made a round of the 12 British groups to officially give them the news, and they were unbelievably restrained. I explained that we weren't going to let the Nips know we had the news until morning, so that we could approach the Shoko with our wants, and the men didn't. I really toed the line. While each group is a beehive, with everyone talking at once, the camp is quiet. The boys are making plans faster than they can think. One point I repeated. No man was to leave the compound under any circumstances. How can I sit and scribble at a time like this? I am doing it because I want to keep my mind from running away with me. I am actually afraid to release the brake. This keeps my feet close to the ground. Worrying about the men is good for me. The days to follow will keep me occupied, I am sure, and this may well be the last line for many a day. My chances of getting this home now have improved no end.

NEW CAMP *August 20, 1945*

~ We have come a long way in the past three days. Early Monday morning the 18th, Borski and I went in to see the Shoko. I did the talking as usual. He sat behind his desk, and made notes of everything I said without a change of expression. I too tried to show no emotion. "We know the war is over," I said. "As do the men. No one knows what will happen, or how much longer we will be here before we are able to return to our own people. Captain Borski and I have already explained to the men that you, as commanding officer of this prison camp, are still responsible for our welfare and safety and therefore must continue to give the orders. We will do our best to see that the men continue to carry out your orders. The only request that we not have for the troops is that you increase the rice ration so that the men can get enough to eat." Hirati sat there for a moment without saying anything. Then, ignoring our statement that we knew the war was over, he explained that the high commander controlled the food ration and he would have to get his authority before any change in the rations could be made. This he would attempt to do immediately, but it might take two or three days. You see, he too couldn't quite realize that it was all over. I explained that our men wanted to break into the storeroom immediately and take all the food; we had managed to convince them that the food could be obtained in an orderly military fashion. The quickest way for the Shoko to start a riot was to refuse this request. I reminded him that these 500 men had been starved for more than three years, and advised him to take the responsibility of increasing the food or Captain Boski and I could no longer be responsible for the actions of the men. This potent argument convinced him, he told me to use whatever amounts of rice I thought necessary, and keep a record of them. Does it seem strange that the universal demands of half a thousand men, free after being prisoners so long, should be for more rice?

All this time, the Shoko didn't mention or admit that the war was over. Borski and I returned and told the men the result of our meeting, I hadn't been back fifteen minutes before the *shuban kashkan* (Orderly Sergeant) came to me and said the *gunso* wanted the 10-man Nip water detail to carry water for the Nip bath, and naturally the men didn't want to go. I think I have already explained that all the camp water for drinking, cooking, washing, and bathing had to be carried from a stream about a quarter of a mile from the camp. It had always been necessary to keep 10 men carrying water every day to take care of the needs of the Japanese Headquarters. With someone else carrying the water they had become quite wrapped up in their washing and bathing. Every Nip has to have his daily hot soak. These jokers just couldn't realize that the party was over. It wouldn't sink in that the prisoners were no longer prisoners. Back I went to Hirati's office and I tried to explain to him why he couldn't expect our men to do any more coolie labor for them. For more than three years they had been pushed and shoved around, beaten up many times for no apparent reason, with high ranking British and Dutch troops doing menial tasks for the lowest Japanese soldier, cleaning his shoes, washing his clothes, taking care of his room and doing the kitchen grunt work, even carrying his water and keeping the latrine clean. Now, when they at last found out the war was over and their countries were the victors, his soldiers still expected the men to carry on as of the old regime. I advised him to explain the situation to his garrison, and that they should feel fortunate that our men hadn't demanded that his soldiers start carrying water for us. Hirati replied that he would speak to his noncoms and see to it that the Nip soldiers would not bother our men any more. Now this is hard to believe.

Not an hour after I had returned to the dispensary, the Shoko sent for me. He had talked with the *shuban kashkan,* and as a result asked me if I couldn't persuade the water detail only to keep working. His reason, that there were so few Japanese in the camp. They just didn't have enough men to carry on the office work, maintain the camp guard and carry water too. And he wanted me to use my influence with the men to carry water. In fact, he ordered me to order the water detail to report for work. By this time I was beginning to fester a bit.

"Hirati," I said, "don't you know that the war is over. Japan has lost the war. These 500 men know it. They don't care if your men ever have water. If you still insist, the water detail will be ordered to carry water for your kitchen and bath, but I can promise you, it will stir up a tempest that no one will be able to control. Why the men haven't already torn the camp to pieces is beyond my understanding. It won't take much for these half starved overworked men to become a wild unruly mob. As CO of this camp you are responsible for the safety and protection of these men until they are turned over to their respective Armies. I advise you very strongly not to insist on this order. Otherwise I am certain there will be much trouble." Hirati was quite subdued and repeated, "You don't think I should give this order?" When I assured it that would be the best course for him not to, he meekly agreed. Apparently Hirati had no problem understanding my English now.

Early Monday evening. Still the 18th. In the midst of all the hubbub one of the boys working in the cook house come puffing up to tell me that two of the Nip civilians were loading a cart with sacks of rice, beans, flour, sugar and soy sauce from the supply room. They were getting ready to take it out of camp. Back I went to the Shoko, each time gaining more confidence, and realizing more that the war was actually over and we were finally in the driver's seat.

I explained what the men were doing. I further stated that as far as I was concerned the food supplies in the compound were sent there for all concerned. Since we didn't know how long it might be before we were actually liberated, no food should be removed from camp. This was an opportune time to clear up another matter in the issue of rations. It had been the custom of the nip supply men to keep no record of the amount of food used by the Nip kitchen. They drew whatever they wanted from the camp stores and it was included as a part of the POW rations. They used a quarter of a sack of sugar for twenty odd men while we used the same amount for more than five hundred. This same proportion applied to meat, fish, or any other food of value. Of course they had a special store of white polished rice reserved for themselves. This we didn't mind so much as we wanted the benefit of the whole rice. The rest of the food was a different matter.

The best thing for everyone was for me to take over the supplies. The same ration per man would be issued to everyone in the camp. If the *furio* cook house used 30 gms. of sugar per person then the same proportionate amount should be sent to the Nip cookhouse. I would keep the keys to the stores—and from now on no one could draw any supplies for either kitchen without my approval. Without a word of argument Hirati agreed. He only

Medical staff, Nisi Asibetsu Camp: (left to right) Ensign Jonker (Dutch Army), Lieut. Lutter (Dutch), Lieut. Andler (U.S. Army), Capt. Borski (Dutch), Ensign Jongsma (Dutch).

cautioned me that we might be there more than a month and he didn't think we would get any more supplies. It was all like a wonderful dream. Back went the supplies to the storeroom and the Nip supply sergeant gave me the keys.

NEW CAMP *Sunday, August 24, 1945*

This is the day—yes it finally happened. I am not too sure about the details but the Americans arrived. They didn't stay but at last we got to wave at them. It was just before noon. We heard planes and out of nowhere a carrier based Navy torpedo bomber came, dipping and waving over the compound not more than 200 feet from the ground. In short order three more were banking down the gully above the compound to buzz the area. The men swarmed out of the barracks like bees to honey, and when I saw that short cropped, blond headed sailor grinning out of the rear of the gunners pit—I cried—I couldn't help it. It felt so good to see an American again I just flowed over. The men were all screeching and shouting but I couldn't say anything. I just beamed.

The four planes circled the camp a second time then three of the planes came over with their bomb bays open and as they reached the open compound each one pulled up in a stall not a hundred feet above the ground and each dropped four sea bags from their bomb racks. The last plane I felt sure would crash he dropped so low, but the pilot gave it the gun, waved a last time and zoomed away.

One of the planes dropped a bit short and a detail of men went out into the hills to locate the valuable sea bags. All the bags were brought into the dispensary and opened there. A note in the top of one explained that the planes were from a U.S. Aircraft Carrier. Some of the boys by Sunday Morning, decided to see if they could locate any of the prison camps in the area. They filled their sea bags with cigarettes, e-rations, Hershey Bars, Chewing Gum, hometown news and magazines from the wardroom. They then set them up in the bomb bay and took off. They certainly found us without much trouble.

Even though we didn't have enough of each article to go around I decided to divide everything up right there and distribute it to the group so that they could have it for lunch. It included 229 packages of cigarettes and about 300 K-rations but the men enjoyed even a taste and the news found in the late overseas issue of *Time* and *Life* were read and re-read.

The planes were beautiful after watching those Nip kites flounder around. The sleek black devils looked like something from "Flash Gordon". The U.S. insignia on the wing and the fuselage looked better than anything I had seen in many a moon. American planes again—what a wonderful world. I had been looking for those planes from the day the war began. Never again I am sure will there be, in my life, a moment so emotionally overwhelming. Actually tears come to my eyes as I re-picture this morning's mad doings—does this sound a bit slushy? I can't help it, the war is over, the marines have landed, and the situation is well in hand. I am surprised I can even write—think of it, just a few hours ago American dive-bombers were here in Nisi Asibetsu. They are coming back and we are going home. Say, I had better watch myself or I will be a candidate for a psychiatrist.

Just the same Mom, Uncle Sam and the boys came over the hill this morning and I will never forget it. The August 13th, overseas issue of *Time* came and gave us our first knowledge of the Atom Bomb and Hiroshima. The Nip papers hadn't let a word slip out. The American papers were fascinating—*Life* had a big spread on the atrocities of German Concentration Camps. They showed boxcar loads of human skeletons and told stories of lampshades made from human skins—thousands killed in gas chambers and in medical experiments. The Nips had never done anything like that. Our ill treatment had been mostly the result of neglect and lack of food and supplies. There was no premeditated cruel treatment except in the combat zone.

I had quite a thrill yesterday. The Senior British Warrant Officer, Sergeant Major Bancroft, told me that the British troops were going to have a formal parade at retreat, and they wished me to attend. To hear a British Sergeant Major handle a formal parade is quite an event. I brought out my only clean shirt and transferred my worn collar and shoulder insignia and out I went. Helmer, my clerk, had warned me in advance that the troops were presenting me with a scroll so I had a chance to throw together a short bit of rebuttal. Bancroft was about 6 ft. 5" and had a voice down in the cellar. With the men at attention Bancroft unrolled the scroll—2 feet square and began to read. Then—As he finished he handed me the scroll, saluted and fell back in formation. Every British troop had signed his name and organization on the back. Considering what the men had to work with, someone had done a really fine job. I found out later that the artist was one of the British cooks whom I had relieved from duty in the kitchen the week before. He had used some abusive language to the man in charge. I was glad to hear that he still went ahead and made the scroll.

In reply to their very gracious message I said the following:

> "I am quite sure that very few officers have ever been honored in such a manner and certainly never under such circumstances as

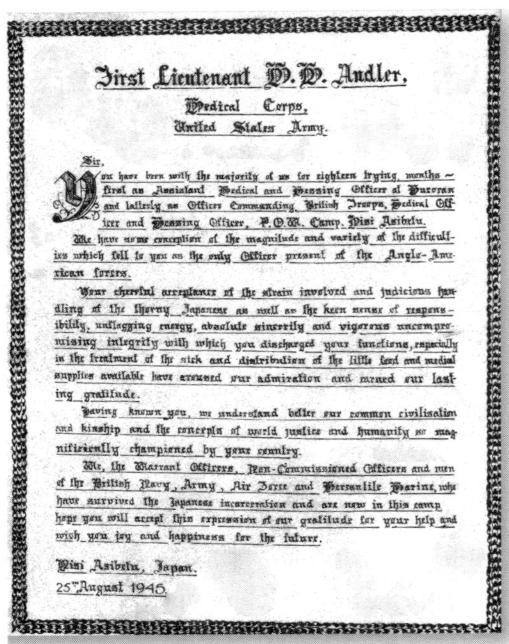

First Lieutenant M. M. Andler,
Medical Corps,
United States Army.

Sir,

You have been with the majority of us for eighteen trying months — first as Assistant Medical and Messing Officer at Muroran and latterly as Officer Commanding, British Troops, Medical Officer and Messing Officer, P.O.W. Camp, Nisi Asibetu.

We have some conception of the magnitude and variety of the difficulties which fell to you as the only Officer present of the Anglo-American forces.

Your cheerful acceptance of the strain involved and judicious handling of the thorny Japanese as well as the keen sense of responsibility, unflagging energy, absolute sincerity and vigorous uncompromising integrity with which you discharged your functions, especially in the treatment of the sick and distribution of the little food and medical supplies available have aroused our admiration and earned our lasting gratitude.

Having known you, we understand better our common civilisation and kinship and the concepts of world justice and humanity so magnificently championed by your country.

We, the Warrant Officers, Non-Commissioned Officers and men of the British Navy, Army, Air Force and Mercantile Marine, who have survived the Japanese incarceration and are now in this camp hope you will accept this expression of our gratitude for your help and wish you joy and happiness for the future.

Nisi Asibetu, Japan.
25th August 1945.

Scroll, Nisi Asibetsu, Japan, August 25, 1945.

these. I am equally sure that I am not deserving of such a tribute. Nevertheless, this does not lessen the pleasure and a satisfaction, which the receipt of this testimonial gives me. You have all made me feel that I am your officer, regardless of my nationality, and your officer I am very proud to be. My only hope is that I have in some degree fulfilled and can continue to fulfill the obligations that, with the departure of Major Murray, have fallen to me. I have good reason to believe that within a very few days, I will have the happy taste of returning you to his care when we meet with him at Hadokate. I will take great pleasure in telling that these past two months and especially these past two weeks, as Officer Commanding British and American troops in this camp, have given me one of the greatest experiences of my life. While I take formal farewell of you at this time, I believe that we will travel together at least to Manila. On this assumption I am inviting all of you to have dinner there with me to properly celebrate our return to Allied Hands.

MAY GOD BLESS YOU ALL AND KEEP YOU IN GOOD HEALTH AND HAPPINESS."

GOING HOME *August 26, 1945*

I told the Shoko that from now on we would hold our own *tenko*. The Dutch and British NCO's could check their respective troops and the Nip guards with Shuban Kashan could go along with them so they could keep track of the men—by now his agreement was automatic. At the next formation of the British troops I gave them another short sermon. From now on they could hold their own parades. They were to look like a British Army should look. Each man would wear his most presentable uniform. They would report on time to the British Bugle Calls and handle themselves like any British Troops should. At this stage of the game we were giving the men bulletins about every 20 minutes, but they were taking it pretty well. The important thing was to make them realize that they were once again British Troops.

The Dutch Perimeter Guards reported that 2 British soldiers from the Cemento Group had gone over the fence early this morning. They had taken some cucumbers and tomatoes from the camp farm. This was strictly forbidden and against orders that I had issued the day before that no man was to leave the camp area without permission. One of the British boys confirmed this. If our discipline was not established we were lost and if these men were not punished the camp, would fall apart. I arranged with the Shoko for the British MP's to take over the Iso. I explained to him that some British soldiers had to be punished and it was best that I did it. He thought this was an excellent idea, as by this time, his guards were afraid to say anything to the men. Sergeant Moffit, who had been in the British MP's, was put in charge and I gave him the keys. We both went down to the Cemento Group and had Bancroft call out the 2 men. They both admitted they had left the compound without permission. In front of all the men in all the camp I ordered Sergeant Moffit to place them under arrest, lock them in the guardroom, and put them on half rations. One of the men protested in the British Army. He said, a man could not be sentenced without a trial. It was necessary to explain to him and the rest of the men that under the circumstances I would have to modify the regulations as I saw fit. Sergeant Moffit took them away without any difficulty.

At lunch they refused the rice ball that was sent in for each of them, but by dinner they decided it was better to eat what they could get and protest later. AT 9:00 PM that night Sergeant Moffit released the men and brought them to me. With the men at attention and in my most judicial tone I repeated the same story—they were British Troops and as long as I was their commanding officer, they were to obey my orders. If they understood that they could report back to their barracks, if not Sergeant Moffit would escort them back to the guardroom. Both the men signified they understood and that incident was finished. It is a ticklish job for an American Medical Officer to discipline British Troops in a Jap prison camp but there was not any choice. In sounding out the rest of the troops I was convinced they approved of the need of discipline.

A unit of British MP's had been captured amongst those troops taken in Singapore, and since Moffat was as senior of that group, I ordered him to pick ten men and form the first detail. There were a few men in that unit who hadn't stood the strain too well. We decided not to include them. A short while later, however, one of them came to me and was quite indignant that he had not been assigned to duty. I simply recited three or four reasons why, in my opinion, he wasn't qualified. (1) He had been in the sick bay most of the time. (2) He developed strange fainting spells when the work was **hard** (3) He head been trading his rice for Jap cigarettes against specific orders. In short, he wasn't the man the troops would be inclined to obey.

The British MP service was made up of the tallest troops available, all over 6 feet 2 inches. At a time like this, such a qualification was a great help. The men took to the idea exceedingly well. They were getting the feel of being free troops again and appreciated the evidences of their own discipline.

The boys were just planning for a treat or a *tenco* before dinner. Bancroft hadn't yet started his routine, and the Dutch were still milling about the upper end of the compound. One of the men sighted the silhouette of a plane far out over the west ridge of mountains in the direction of Capfowa. We had been expecting the B-29s with relief supplies for days after hearing the repeated news bulletins. Someone came running in for me to see if I could identify it as a B-29. I had to admit I had never even seen a picture of a super-fortress—much less the plane, but that didn't stop me from tearing out after them to take a look. It was so far away the plane appeared to be hardly moving across the skies. It had the long nose we had read about in the newspapers, but it didn't look big enough. After hearing the Nips talk about the *B ge ques* for so many months, we expected to see a plane as big as a hangar fly over. The retreat bay was forgotten as everyone speculated on the identity and purpose of the plane. Finally it circled around and headed down the northwest gulley, as had the Navy dive-bombers. This brought it well over our heads and flying fairly low, but not low enough to recognize the crew as before. As it came overhead, we saw printed on the underside of the wings in enormous black letters P.W. Supplies. That really set the men up. Everyone ran every which way. After Sunday's episode with one dropping out on the hills, we sent all the MP's out to surround the camp to spot the bag as it came down in case some of it missed the camp area. The pilot circled around by the river and lined up the second run down the valley.

He flew considerably higher than the dive-bombers had been. The lines of the ship were beautiful. We could see the gigantic bomb bays opening and while it was still quite a distance from us we saw many small specks dropping out and come flying toward us. In just a moment there were a dozen different colored parachutes floating down, but only for a moment. Whatever was attached to the parachutes broke loose and it sounded like old times the way they whistled. The men started looking around for fox-holes. Before we could move, 55-gallon drums came hurdling down. I think there were six altogether, but only two lit in camp. The others, two—double drums welded—together buried themselves outside, one tearing down a section of wall.

In addition, there were half a dozen mattress covers filled with clothes, and they also broke loose. A sack full of shoes hit the South Dutch barracks and went through both decks down to the ground. While some of the men were collecting the spoils, we checked noses and found that miraculously no one had been hurt. It would have been a tragedy to have the men injured or killed at this stage of the game, with relief supplies.

Now to the supplies. Some of the drums had folded up making a fine mixture of canned peaches, K rations, pipe tobacco, chewing gum, tomato soup, cocoa, sugar, and canned milk. Others had held up quite well with many cans and boxes remaining intact. Again we had the men bring everything into the dispensary where we cataloged and divided them. All broken cans went directly to the cookhouse to be used before it spoiled. Chow was late that night, but no one complained. On the top of one gasoline drum was a little note, which was posted on the bulletin board. "Insert from the 500th bomb group of Saipan."

Don't think that didn't bring tears to my eyes. Here the war was over and I was crying more than I was laughing.

Three B-29's this time. They circled twice. We learned fast and we had prepared for this by laying out a circular target about a half-mile north of the compound to give the bombardier something to shoot at. Even so, we had everyone including the patients leave the barracks to avoid casualties. The planes too had learned by experience. Light square wooden latticed frames had been substituted for the heavy oil drums. The neatly stacked cases of food and supplies came floating down without any trouble, except for a crosswind that blew some of the parcels across the root end of a tree on the opposite bank. We received two loads this time, and there must have been at least a score of parcels. Everyone was more than willing to get the supplies back to camp.

Our storeroom was beginning to bulge with good honest American chow, and the Nip supplies were practically ignored. We started serving hot cocoa and cookies about nine o'clock at night along with Japanese canned tangerines, beer and sausage, which the Nips had brought in. MacArthur's Headquarters had issued a directive to the Japanese. All Allied POW's should be fed at least the equivalent of the best Japanese rations in the area. If this were not done, the individual Japanese commanding officer would be held responsible directly to General MacArthur. Just like that. Well, the *tumadachies* were taking no chances. Two army trucks are on the go all day long bringing in food drink, and whatever else they can get. Barrels of saki, truckloads of squash, potatoes, beef, pork, cooking oil. Where formerly we had issued four boxes of fish for 500 men, now there was one load of 56 boxes of fresh herring. The men had fried herring for breakfast, herring patties for lunch and herring chowder for supper. That did it. No more herring.

Yuntznow began screaming for the Nip radio as soon as we got the news the war was over. I confess this was one time I agreed with Yuntznow. The Shoko wasn't too happy about losing his radio, but across the compound it came to our quarters. Yuntznow and Yaks went to work on it immediately. That last night we heard KGEI for the first time. In addition, we were getting broadcasts from Australia and Manila. Yuntznow stayed up practically all night taking down the news broadcasts.

After hours of unsuccessful attempt, I finally got Camp Fore on the phone. Major Barron, of the U.S. Marine Corps, the executive Allied officer, spoke to me. They had no radio there, and the first run of B-29's had not brought anything because of the difficulty of the terrain. I told Barron about everything we had received, and had it send down to their camp. As we were now getting news (as long as reception was okay), I was also arranged to send them down a daily bulletin. When I told Major Barron that one of the dropped packages contained some chewing tobacco along with the cigarettes, he said that his some of his troops were old tobacco chewers had more use for the chewing tobacco, and we were more than glad to send it down to them. We also made arrangements for our men to visit their camp, and some of the officers to come up and see us.

Orders were coming thru to the Nips from MacArthur's headquarters pretty regularly now. Terraki came to me for help. He had just received orders to construct a sign with a black background and yellow letters 15 feet high of P.W. Far be it from me to argue with him, so a truck driver was dispatched to one of the neighboring towns, and he finally brought back yellow paint to fix the letters. The men were more than glad to do this type of work, and we constructed this large sign on a slope just in front of the camp gates facing north and south, with the north end slightly raised. The men didn't want to take any chances on the camp being missed, and climbed up on the roof where they painted large P.W. signs also. At first I was worried that the men, unaccustomed to such rich food might get sick from overeating, but the men ate all day long and nobody turned a hair. One thing was odd. In spite of the large amount of canned meat, soup, fruit, and vegetables that we were issuing, and the men were eating, they still wanted rice with their meals. They had become so used to the bulk of this type of diet, that they still had to eat it to feel filled. Gradually, as the days passed the men ate less and less rice.

There seemed to be a thousand things to take care of. Japanese headquarters had something new practically every hour of the day, and still supervising the meals as well as the issue of all foods. Captain Grosby has agreed that the clothes being dropped are not Red Cross clothes, but are from the American Armed Forces, and therefore I should be the one to issue them. I felt it is criminal to waste any of the food the Japanese had been pouring in, and so I am trying to dovetail that in between our issue of American supplies. Our menus are becoming six and seven course meals. The men are finally beginning to talk about something else than food, which is the best sign of all that they are returning to normal.

At this point the diary stops.

ADDENDUM TO MAX'S DIARY

The prison camp was liberated on September 14th. Max was taken by train to Tokyo. He was then taken to a replacement depot in the Philippines, (where they were deloused, cleaned up, given new uniforms and accessories). One note: before Max arrived here, one plane load of men, eager to return home were loaded into a bomber for the trip home. On the way, the bomb doors accidentally opened and the men were lost. On hearing this, other groups elected to wait for regular planes, no matter if it took longer.

From this depot, 10 officers and 50 men were chosen to be representatives of all the recovered American Military personnel. It was planned that they would be taken to Hawaii first, to be welcomed by the governor of Hawaii with a banquet and tour of the local sights. They were then to travel to San Francisco where they were to be greeted by the highest-ranking officers. Their families were to be at the ceremony in San Francisco. They were then to tour the rest of the United States as representatives of all the military branches, and were scheduled to end the tour in Washington D.C. where they would be greeted by President Truman at the White House. Max was one of the officers chosen, as was one of his friends, Dr. Marvin Pizer, another doctor from Los Angeles.

As planned, the men were flown to Hawaii and the officers were each assigned a convertible car with driver and a beautiful girl to accompany them. There was a big parade through Honolulu and a banquet in their honor. Of course there was much food and liquor. The officers were given all the liquor and cigarettes they wanted and they partied for a week. Then they were put on a plane to San Francisco. On arrival there, at a grand reception with all families present that were able to travel, the commanding General greeted them on behalf of the President. After the ceremony, the general assessed the condition of the men and sent them all to Letterman General Hospital to recuperate. Max did not remember too much of the Honolulu parties except that he had cigarette burns in his new uniform, and up until that time he had never smoked. The men were given silver ID bracelets with R.A.M.P. (Recovered American Military Personnel) engraved on one side and their name and serial number on the other. When Max was released from the hospital, he went home to Boston. He was granted 3 months of leave to recuperate. He and his stepfather went to Havana Cuba at government expense as a part of his R&R.

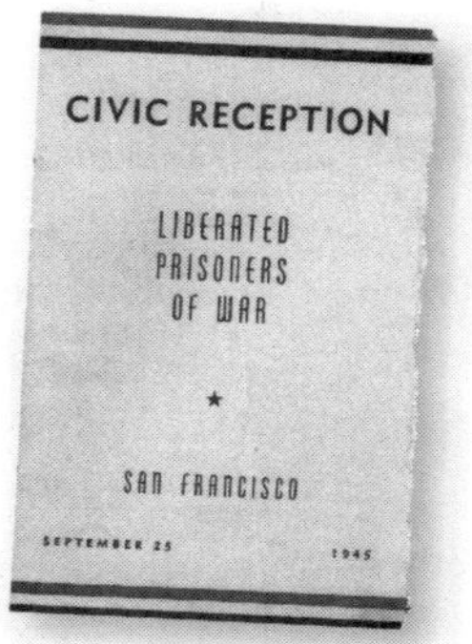

In March of 1946, Max returned to the Los Angeles County Hospital to resume his residency in neurosurgery. The county of Los Angeles had mandated that any personnel that were drafted or volunteered for military service would have their jobs waiting when they returned.

Max shaking hands with Lt. General Robert C. Richardson.

THE UNITED STATES OF AMERICA

TO ALL WHO SHALL SEE THESE PRESENTS, GREETING:

THIS IS TO CERTIFY THAT
THE PRESIDENT OF THE UNITED STATES OF AMERICA
AUTHORIZED BY EXECUTIVE ORDER, AUGUST 24, 1962
HAS AWARDED

THE BRONZE STAR MEDAL

TO

CAPTAIN MAXWELL M. ANDLER, JR

FOR

MERITORIOUS ACHIEVEMENT
7 DECEMBER 1941 TO 10 MAY 1942

GIVEN UNDER MY HAND IN THE CITY OF WASHINGTON
THIS 13TH DAY OF AUGUST 1985

CHIEF OF STAFF

SECRETARY OF THE AIR FORCE

AF FORM 2257, JUL 70

CITATION TO ACCOMPANY THE AWARD OF

THE BRONZE STAR MEDAL

TO

MAXWELL M. ANDLER, JR.

Captain Maxwell M Andler, Jr. distinguished himself by meritorious achievement during combat while serving in the Southwest Pacific Theater of Operations between 7 December 1941 to 10 May 1942. The actions of Captain Andler were in keeping with the highest traditions of the military service and reflect distinctive credit upon himself, his unit, and the United States Air Force.

THE WHITE HOUSE
WASHINGTON

25 September 1945

1st Lieutenant Maxwell W. Andler, 0381336,
Medical Corps

Dear Lieutenant Andler:

It gives me special pleasure to welcome you back to your native shores, and to express, on behalf of the people of the United States, the joy we feel at your deliverance from the hands of the enemy. It is a source of profound satisfaction that our efforts to accomplish your return have been successful.

You have served valiantly in foreign lands and have suffered greatly. As your Commander in Chief, I take pride in your past achievements and express the thanks of a grateful Nation for your services in combat and your steadfastness while a prisoner of war.

May God grant each of you happiness and an early return to health.

Harry Truman

Wednesday 3/27/46

Dear Mom—

It is 6 30 Am and I am already dressed in my new white uniforms and ready to go to work – I will go down and have breakfast first and then go up to the fifth floor and meet the staff. Yesterday I spent most of the day meeting old friends. It's surprising how many have come back to the hospital again.

You sounded quite well on the telephone last night and you must keep up the good work – Let me know what they tell you at the Deaconess Hospital when you go there.

I have a very lovely furnished room all to myself on the 17th floor and a really comfortable bed. I was very pleasantly surprised when they told me

Page 2

that since I was one of the permanent residents from before the war my pay had increased to $143.50 per month, and $40 was deducted for meals, room, uniforms and laundry. I am quite certain that it would be impossible to live outside on the same amount. I received six new uniforms and I have all my personal laundry done here also. With four meals a day available I don't think $40 a month is too much – And I still get my Army pay until September then I am entitled to $65 a month from the G.I. bill of rights, and $75 a year to buy medical books – It should help quite a bit. –

Last night I went over to Nultons for dinner but he was so busy that he didn't even get home – I am going

to call the rest of the family today, but I don't think that I will get over to see them for awhile.

I am sorry that I missed Don and Deidre. I was in New York only for an hour and tried to find them thru the Wilson Co. but was not successful – I was very lucky to get a ride so soon – I left New York at 11 00 Am and we went to Columbus, Ohio – from there the plane went directly to Kansas, and didn't even stop in Chicago – I was disappointed in not getting my suit, but they can mail it to me. From there we went to Amarillo Texas at midnight and it was much colder than Boston. I arrived in Phoenix, Ariz. at 4 30 Am yesterday morning and then I had to get off the

plane as they wanted to put on a lot of gasoline – but I only had to wait two hours before a plane took me right to Long Beach, Calif. about 25 miles from the hospital – and a fellow drove me right to the door. And from the time I left the Boston field I spent only 25 cents – that's not a bad way to travel from Boston to Los Angeles. The Red Cross had meals for us all along the way –

Well Mommie, its time I got started – my cold is just about all gone and I feel fine. Give my love to all the family and explain that if I don't write for awhile, its because I am just getting started –

All my love, Mommie and write me a long letter tonight.

Love [illegible]

Mom – I am enclosing a check for the long distance calls from Chicago and Los Angeles. They should come to about $10.00. Please give to your husband when the bill comes

The original letters home saved by his mother.

HAKODATE #1
NISI ASIBETSU POW CAMP

Hakodate #1B Main Home Main Camp List

American Roster

Andler, Maxwell m, 1st Lt, O & 381336, USAAC
Cox, Walter J., Cpl. 38002584, USA (Inf)
Fitch, Malcolm C., Pvt, 19015292, USA (MD)
Matuozzi, Robert E.,TSgt, 6910392, USA (CE)
Stevens, Lyle W., 1st Sgt, 6826019, USA (CAC)

(Note: ON NARA Data Base both #1 and #1B are considered "Main Camp")

Christmas card from American Medical Corpsmen. Right to left: Pvt. 1st Class W.D. Cox, 1st Sarg. L.W. Stevens, Staff Sarg. R.E. Matuozzi, Pvt. M.C. Fitch.

Max, medical school, USC.

Max, prisoner of war.

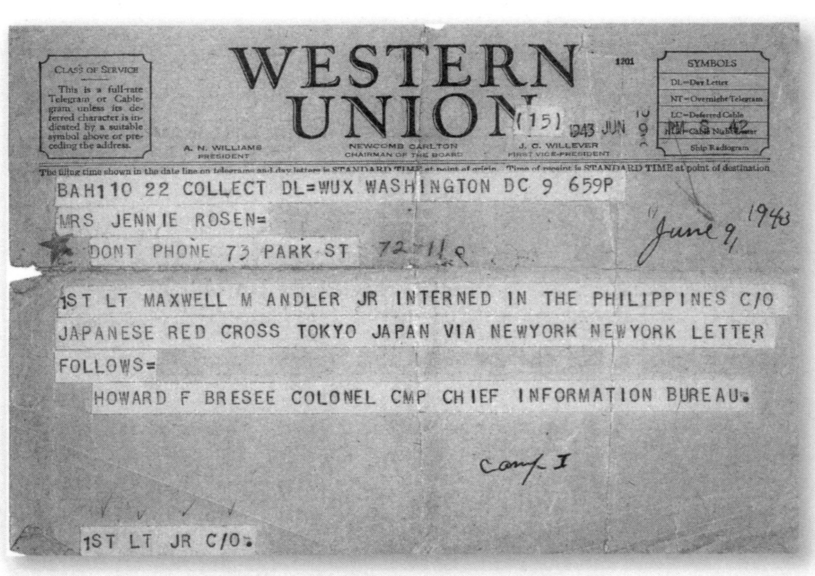

WESTERN UNION

CLASS OF SERVICE
This is a full-rate Telegram or Cablegram unless its deferred character is indicated by a suitable symbol above or preceding the address.

A. N. WILLIAMS, PRESIDENT — NEWCOMB CARLTON, CHAIRMAN OF THE BOARD — J. C. WILLEVER, FIRST VICE-PRESIDENT

1201

SYMBOLS
DL=Day Letter
NT=Overnight Telegram
LC=Deferred Cable
NLT=Cable Night Letter
Ship Radiogram

(15) 1943 JUN 9 PM 6 42

The filing time shown in the date line on telegrams and day letters is STANDARD TIME at point of origin. Time of receipt is STANDARD TIME at point of destination

BAH110 22 COLLECT DL=WUX WASHINGTON DC 9 659P

MRS JENNIE ROSEN=

DONT PHONE 73 PARK ST 72-11

June 9, 1943

1ST LT MAXWELL M ANDLER JR INTERNED IN THE PHILIPPINES C/O JAPANESE RED CROSS TOKYO JAPAN VIA NEWYORK NEWYORK LETTER FOLLOWS=

HOWARD F BRESEE COLONEL CMP CHIEF INFORMATION BUREAU.

Camp I

1ST LT JR C/O.

Outside Camp Nisi Asibetsu. British troops after end of war.

RAMP (Recovered Army Military Personnel) chosen to represent all recovered POW. Left end, back row: Max.

Group 6, Island of Hokkaido—Muroran.